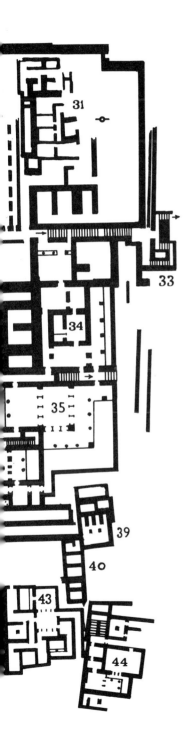

The Minoan Temp[le] [rec]onstruction of the 'ground-fl[oor]'

1 – Theatral Are[a]
2 – North-West [...]
3 – Initiation A[...]
4 – Induction [...]
5 – North-Wes[t]
6 – Lotus Lamp [San...]
7 – West Store-Rooms.
8 – Lower West Wing Corridor.
9 – Throne Sanctuary.
10 – Snake Goddess Sanctuary.
11 – West Pillar Crypt.
12 – East Pillar Crypt.
13 – Tripartite Shrine.
14 – Colonnade of the Priestesses.
15 – Destroyed Sanctuary.
16 – Columnar Shrines (South-West Pillar Crypts below).
17 – Cupbearer Sanctuary.
18 – West Porch/Entrance.
19 – West Porch Shrine.
20 – Procession Corridor.
21 – South Terrace.
22 – South-West Porch/Entrance (at lower level).
23 – Stepped Portico or paved ramp.
24 – South Corridor (at lower level).
25 – South (or Silver Vessels) Sanctuary.
26 – South Porch/Entrance.
27 – North Entrance.
28 – South Pillar Hall.
29 – North Entrance Passage.
30 – Service Quarter: North-East Store-Rooms and Kitchens.
31 – North-East Kamares Pottery Store.
32 – North-East Sanctuary.
33 – East Entrance.
34 – Temple Workshops.
35 – Double-Axe Sanctuary.
36 – Dolphin Sanctuary.
37 – Triton Shell Sanctuary.
38 – Late Dove Goddess Sanctuary.
39 – Monolithic Pillar Crypt.
40 – Pre-Temple buildings.
41 – House or Shrine of the Sacrificed Oxen.
42 – House or Shrine of the Fallen Blocks.
43 – Chancel Screen Sanctuary.
44 – South-East Sanctuary.
45 – Grand Staircase.

Arrows on staircase indicate 'down' direction, asterisks indicate temple respositories (stone-lined strongrooms for religious cult objects), and stippling indicates tell material not quarried away at this level. The winged circle indicates that the site was too badly damaged at the time of excavation for reconstruction to be more than tentative.

THE KNOSSOS LABYRINTH

THE KNOSSOS LABYRINTH

A new view of the 'Palace of Minos' at Knossos

RODNEY CASTLEDEN

Illustrated by the author

R

ROUTLEDGE

London and New York

First published 1990 by Routledge
11 New Fetter Lane, London EC4P 4EE
29 West 35th Street, New York NY 10001

© 1990 Rodney Castleden

Printed in Great Britain by
Richard Clay Ltd, Bungay, Suffolk

British Library Cataloguing in Publication Data
Castleden, Rodney
The Knossos Labyrinth.
1. Places ancient Crete. Knossos. Palace of Minos
I. Title
939'.18

Library of Congress Cataloging in Publication Data
Castleden, Rodney.
The Knossos Labyrinth/ by Rodney Castleden.
p. cm.
Bibliography: p.
Includes index.
1. Palace of Knossos (Knossos) 2. Knossos (Ancient city)
3. Crete (Greece) — Antiquities. 4. Greece — Antiquities. I. Title.
DF221.C8C37 1990
938 — dc20 89-6234

ISBN 0-415-03315-2

For Kit

You know, Sosius Senecio, how geographers, when they come to deal with those parts of the earth which they know nothing about, crowd them into the margins of their maps with the explanation, 'Beyond this lie sandy, waterless deserts full of wild beasts', or 'trackless swamps'. I might very well follow their example and say, 'All that lies beyond are prodigies and fables, the province of poets and romancers, where nothing is certain ...' [but] let us hope I shall succeed in purifying fable, and make her submit to reason and take on the appearance of history.

Plutarch, *Life of Theseus*, c. AD 100.

Contents

List of illustrations

CHAPTER TITLE ILLUSTRATIONS

Acknowledgements

I should like to thank the Greek Archaeological Service and Dr Tzedakis, the Director of Heraklion Museum, for arranging for me to see the locked Minoan sites at Knossos, and Karambinis Emanolis, Custodian of Knossos, for his endless patience while I explored the Palace Dependencies. Exchanges of ideas, discussions and arguments with both friends and strangers on Crete often stimulated new lines of thought. I value the conversations I had with my travelling companions in 1985, John and Trudy Urmson, and with Angelika Schönborn, an archaeology student from Duisburg whom I met at the Temple Tomb in 1988; there was also an unknown German woman with whom I had a candlelit disagreement about Schliemann in the birth-cave of Zeus on Mount Dikte. Above all, I have to thank Kit, who visited Crete with me in 1988 and 1989 and was eager to see all the Minoan sites in central Crete – however inaccessible.

In England, Peter Warren, Professor of Ancient History and Classical Archaeology at the University of Bristol, was kind enough to answer my queries and give me some useful pointers. I should also like to thank Mrs Ann Brown of the Department of Antiquities at the Ashmolean Museum in Oxford for guiding me carefully through the Evans and Mackenzie archives. The excellent prints in the Evans Photographic Archive were particularly useful to me in revealing in fine detail the state of the Knossos Labyrinth when it was first excavated and at various stages in Evans' reconstruction work – an invaluable resource for this book; four of the archive prints are reproduced here by permission of the Ashmolean Museum. I am grateful to Mr Brian MacGregor, the Librarian, for allowing me unrestricted access to books and journals in the Ashmolean Library.

Tony Lemon and John and Celia Clarke were generous in their hospitality, which made the spells of library research in Oxford all the more congenial.

In addition, I have to thank Keith Drury of John Proctor Travel for efficiently tailoring transport and accommodation arrangements to some fairly exacting specifications, Diana Cooke for providing me with an eyewitness account of a French vâche-fight, Joan Newey for supplying translations from the Greek, and Countess Anne Romanov for her uncanny skill as a research assistant, nosing out books and articles I had given up all hope of finding.

Extracts from Sir Arthur Evans' diaries are reprinted here by permission of Mark Paterson and Associates for the Sir Arthur Evans Trust.

R.C.
Brighton, 1989

Introduction

Knossos is a symbol. Part of the appeal of Knossos, the principal city of bronze age Crete, lies in that symbolic nature. Like the Acropolis, Stonehenge, or the Pyramids, it stands powerfully for an entire ancient culture. Older by far than Athens, the Knossos Labyrinth was first built in the reign of Sesostris II, a Middle Kingdom Egyptian pharaoh; it is sobering to reflect that the sarsen monument at the heart of Stonehenge was little more than a century old when the first Labyrinth was raised at Knossos in 1930 BC. It was from the start the focus of a strange, glittering, artistic and exotic culture, its people honouring lithe and virile boxers, athletes and bull-leapers, revering mysterious snake goddesses and other animal deities, earnestly worshipping their gods and goddesses on mountain tops and in caves, delighting in every aspect of nature.

Homer has left elusive clues about the court at Knossos. Odysseus claimed to have visited it and some scholars have wondered whether Homer's description of King Alcinous and his people, the civilized and pleasure-loving Phaeacians, is really a description of the bronze age Knossians and their benign ruler. There was a persistent classical Greek tradition of a great and ancient sea-empire stretching across the Aegean Sea and ruled from Knossos by King Minos. In the nineteenth century AD, as the lost site of Knossos gradually re-emerged from obscurity, it was inevitable that the first three people to take an active interest in excavating it – Minos Kalokairinos, Heinrich Schliemann and Arthur Evans – should be predisposed to seek archaeological evidence of Homer, or at any rate evidence of the past as presented in classical Greek literature.

One theme of this book is that this line of thought was actually a false trail, and one that has obscured the true nature of the Labyrinth. Arthur Evans' Palace of Minos, 'this dwelling of prehistoric kings' as he called it, has gripped the imaginations of scholars and tourists alike for nearly a century. The reasons why Evans followed this interpretation of the building and the reasons why he may well have been mistaken will be explored. Alternative explanations are available. The Labyrinth may have been a necropolis or a temple, and we will need to examine these alternative hypotheses with considerable care; if the Labyrinth is central to the Minoan culture, or at least to our perception of the culture, then changing our view of the Labyrinth significantly changes our view of the culture.

Both Evans and his lieutenant at Knossos, Duncan Mackenzie, recognized that the Labyrinth had some sort of religious function. Mackenzie's Daybook for 18 April 1905, for instance, reads:

> Up to the time of the destruction of the Palace of Knossos that Palace itself was at once a residence of the King and chief sanctuary of the city ... the Minoan Polity had no temples as separate buildings set apart entirely for religious usage.

As we shall see in Chapter 5, Evans struggled to reconcile the widespread evidence of a religious function with his expectation that the Labyrinth would prove to be a royal residence.

Visiting Knossos in 1985 and 1988, I was impressed by the overall form of the Labyrinth and by the sprawling ruins, though not by their state of preservation. In some places the walls have been eroded away to their foundations, making them impossible to trace with any confidence; in some places the walls survive to a height of 2 or 3 metres but in such a restored and repaired state that they seem to be virtually new walls; in some places Evans has built massively on to what were originally only stumps of degraded walling, as his own excavation photographs show. It is nevertheless just possible to visualize the site as it might once have been, *without* Evans' reconstitutions, and *with* the frescoes and cult objects that are now housed in Heraklion Museum returned to their proper places. It is possible to reconstruct imaginatively what must originally have been a very remarkable piece of architecture, opulently equipped and brilliantly coloured, with many of the now-bare surfaces of walls, ceilings, and even floors decorated with friezes, frescoes, painted panels, or painted plaster mouldings.

The site as we now see it has suffered a great deal. At the time of its abandonment, in 1380 BC (see Appendix A for chronology), a fire swept through the building and the mud-brick walls of the upper floor crumbled and fell in fairly soon afterwards, sending a rain of artefacts down one, two or more storeys into the ground floor and cellarage as the building collapsed. The destruction began anew with the archaeological excavations 3,250 years later, thanks to exposure to attack by the weather, damage done by the excavators and the well-intentioned work of the restorers. At least the pines planted round the site soften the effects of the archaeological trauma.

On my initial visit to Knossos I was dissatisfied with the Evans explanations for the various rooms and their functions. I sensed that the building was not a palace but a temple and the more I learnt about Knossos and the Minoan culture that produced it the more likely it seemed that my initial reaction had been right. I knew that many distinguished archaeologists with excavation experience at Knossos went along with the Evans hypothesis to some extent and felt uneasy about developing a rival explanation which contradicted their views. I came upon Paul Faure's *La Vie quotidienne en Crète au temps de Minos* late in my researches, when my interpretation of the Knossos Labyrinth was already developed; it gave me the reassurance I needed to find that someone else, and an experienced Minoan archaeologist at that, had followed a similar line of thought and reached a similar conclusion. Athough Faure follows the same general line of reasoning, here I develop the argument more fully and base it on far more detailed evidence from the Labyrinth; I trust that this more detailed approach to the one building may convince readers that the temple hypothesis fits the evidence best.

My hope is that the reader will gain an alternative insight into the Labyrinth which is every bit as exciting in itself and in its implications as the traditional explanation, and one that is also much closer to the truth. 'Tourist Knossos', the Palace of Minos with its new cement, reinforced concrete and blandly labelled royal rooms, is a place and an experience of its own. This book attempts a different approach, an approach that will enable the reader to see the original bronze age building for what it was before it was burnt and ruined, before it was overwhelmed by the accretions of classical legend, before it was interpreted and reconstructed by Sir Arthur Evans.

Somewhere along the way the real nature of the Labyrinth at Knossos was lost, and the opening chapters of the book show how this happened. As men of the late nineteenth century, the first excavators and publicists of the rediscovered bronze age site were predisposed to see it through the eyes of classical authors. Just as Schliemann saw Troy, and indeed identified it, through the writings of Homer, Evans saw Knossos through Homer, Plutarch, Diodorus, Thucydides and Herodotus. We need to explore that classical view of Minoan Crete in order to understand Evans' dogged search for evidence of King Minos and his insistence that the building he was uncovering was a royal palace.

Evans' excavation of the Minoan 'Palace of Minos' at Knossos has rightly established itself as one of the great excavations, a major landmark in the history of archaeology. The site, quite apart from its inferred importance in the bronze age, has become a classic reference point in archaeological literature. In order to understand how it acquired this monumental status, we need to look back to the peculiar circumstances of its discovery and excavation. We may wonder, for instance, to what extent Schliemann's interest in buying and excavating the site after his (superficially, at any rate) highly successful excavations of Homeric sites at Troy and Mycenae influenced Evans' approach to Knossos. Evans was profoundly impressed by Schliemann's example, but it is very difficult to assess how far his interpretation of Knossos was coloured by it.

Evans made the Knossos excavations a resounding success, by his tenacity as a negotiator and organizer, by his scholarship, by his patience and persever-

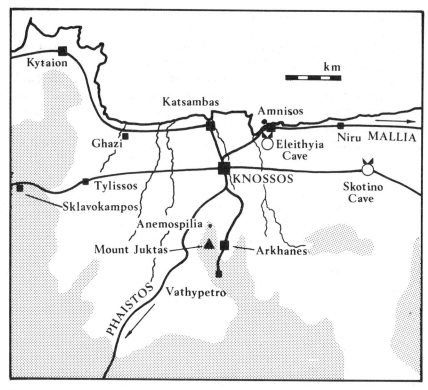

Figure 1 Map of the Knossos area. The stippled area is land above 400 metres

ance, by his extraordinary grasp of an enormous amount of archaeological detail. We may have reservations about some of his interpretations and reconstructions, but we can still retain our admiration for the undertaking as a whole. Evans would in any case not mind our disagreement: he thrived on dissension and controversy.

Evans was, of course, ably supported by Duncan Mackenzie, the assistant who closely supervised the excavation team and observed and noted finds as they were made. It is in Mackenzie's Daybooks that we find most of the raw data of the Knossos digs. They show an eye for accurate detail and also, now and then, a grasp of the overall significance of accumulations of finds. The carefully pencilled notes occasionally take off in a flood of imaginative prose in which the bronze age palace comes back to life; Evans drew on some of these passages for *The Palace of Minos at Knossos*. There were sometimes differences of view between the two men and one cannot help thinking that Mackenzie, who went on working at Knossos when Evans was in England or at conferences elsewhere, may often have been the better judge; unfortunately we also know that Mackenzie's judgement became less reliable until he was finally overtaken by mental illness, so it is difficult to evaluate the conflicts of opinion.

It will become clear that the history of the idea of Knossos and the history of its excavation are crucial background elements, which will need to be explored before the bronze age architecture and archaeology of the site can be unravelled and reassessed. The reassessment takes an appropriately tridental form. Three major hypotheses exist for the Labyrinth's original function – palace, necropolis, temple – and they are discussed and evaluated against the archaeological evidence from the Labyrinth itself and the growing amount of evidence about the nature of bronze age Cretan culture in general.

Apart from establishing what will be for many readers a new perspective on the Labyrinth's original purpose, the book functions as a guide to the site, including descriptions and explanations for many of the surviving chambers, corridors, and other structures, as well as suggesting what may have been lost by fire, collapse, or erosion. Readers will, I feel sure, be helped by the new plans of the ground floor (Figure 31) and reconstructed first floor (Figure 48), which make significant departures from previously published plans. There are also detailed plans of several of the sanctuary suites (e.g. Figure 14). I hope that these will help to make a visit to Knossos a more meaningful and intelligible experience. In order to avoid unduly lengthy captions to illustrations, there are 'Notes on the illustrations' at the end of the book.

Place-names on Crete are often a source of confusion. Spellings vary, both on maps and in books. There may, for instance, be all sorts of arguments for preferring Candia, Heracleion, Iraklion or Iraklio at different points in the narrative, but it seems altogether simpler and more comprehensible to stick to one spelling; I have arbitrarily used 'Heraklion'. At Knossos itself, I have been faced with a dilemma which is central to the book's purpose. To use Evans' names for the various part of the building is, in a very real sense, to imply that we go along with his interpretation; to call the building as a whole the 'Palace of Minos' or even a 'palace' at all is to imply that we agree with the palatial interpretation. I tend to use Evans' names initially, when discussing the Labyrinth as Evans saw it, but to replace them with my own names as I replace his interpretation with my own. I apologize if the reader should find this disorienting, but there seems to be no alternative when the overall conception of the building is radically different. To clarify the situation, two maps of the Labyrinth are included, one using Evans' room names (Figure 7), one my own (Figure 31): reference to these two maps should reduce the problem.

Exploring the Labyrinth is a difficult undertaking, fraught with problems. The building itself, as it stands, misleads and deceives us; it is, as Erik Hallager says, an extremely unreliable and dangerous source of information. The casual visitor will find it hard to tell which walls are original and which reconstructed, and even experienced scholars have come to accept as reconstructions some of the insertions that have little or no archaeological foundation. Evans bought the site for 122,000 piastres at the end of the nineteenth century. When he acquired this extraordinary property, he surely did not intend to uncover an ancient masonry labyrinth and convert it into an even more bewildering modern thought-maze – but that is what it has become. Lavishly reconstructed and monumentally published, Evans' Palace of Minos dominates our thinking about the Cretan bronze age, now as in the early 1900s. It is vital that we understand the building's original layout and function correctly if we are to understand the rest of the culture correctly. The Knossos Labyrinth is both the key and the stumbling-block to our understanding of Minoan civilization.

1
The legendary Knossos

Out in the middle of the wine-dark sea there is a land called Crete, a
rich and lovely land, washed by the sea on every side; and in it are
many peoples and ninety cities. There, one language mingles with
another. In it are Achaeans, great-hearted native Cretans, Kydonians
and Dorians in three tribes and noble Pelasgians. Among these
[ninety Cretan] cities is Knossos, a great city; and there Minos was
nine years king, the boon companion of mighty Zeus.

Homer, *Odyssey* (Book 19)

Any search for the real bronze age Knossos will inevitably be diverted and
distracted to some extent by archaic images rising up from the mythic
Knossos, the exotic city round which the ancient Greeks wove fantastic
legends. Images of Ariadne and Theseus, of Daidalos and King Minos, of the
Minotaur in the Labyrinth, are hard to shake off. It is best to confront these
images at the very beginning and so be aware of the possibility of bias in our
thinking, before we look at the archaeological evidence and infer a history
from it. It is all the more important to do so since the interpretations of Evans
and his contemporaries were strongly influenced by them.

A significant proportion of the Greek myths use Crete as their setting,
implying that a Minoan substratum may underlie the cultures of archaic and
classical Greece. Some of the myths use the wild scenery of the mountains;
others are set in and round an extraordinary building raised at the command
of Minos the king, a maze-like palace of unparalleled splendour. Knossos is
one of the few places on Crete whose prehistoic name we know. Remarkably,
the original denizens of the Labyrinth called it by the same name. Both
'Knossos' and 'Labyrinthos' are to be found on clay tablets that were
excavated from the ruins of Knossos. The peculiar syllabic script of the
Minoan period gives them as ko-no-so and da-pu-ri-to-jo. Only a handful of
Minoan sites have retained their Minoan identity in this way. The clay tablets
mention a-mi-ni-so, pa-i-to, tu-ri-so, ku-do-ni-ja: Amnisos, one of the ports
of Knossos, Phaistos, the great 'palace' centre on the southern side of the
island, Tylissos, a farming estate not far to the west of Knossos, and Kydonia
or Khania at the western end of Crete.

That the names have survived almost unscathed from a proto-literate era is remarkable. It is even more remarkable that the walls, staircases, drainage systems, frescoes, archives, and treasures of the Knossos Labyrinth have survived well enough for us to be able to reconstruct both the architecture of the building and some of the events that took place there. Girdled by a swathe of cypress and pine trees to shield them from the scouring wind, the pale gold stones of Knossos lie exposed to the sky, revealing to the modern visitor a bewilderingly complicated plan (Figure 31).

The building is roughly square, about 150 metres across, and covers an area of some 20,000 square metres; it consists of the foundations at least of around 300 chambers on the ground floor and, with its original upper floors, may well originally have consisted of a thousand chambers altogether. There were other labyrinths on Crete, notably at Zakro, Mallia, and Phaistos, but this one was easily the largest and the most complicated to be built, the one that was to be remembered in succeeding centuries as the legendary Labyrinth.

The Homeric sagas are thought to have been written down in the eighth century BC after they had been transmitted orally for several centuries. In Book 19 of the Odyssey, Homer tells of Knossos. By 700 BC, it was already a fabulous city, lost in legend, '...and there Minos was nine years king'. The 'nine years' is ambiguous. It may mean that Minos ruled for nine years altogether or for nine-year periods; it may mean that Minos was only nine years old, although that seems less likely.

Minos had an extraordinary pedigree. His mother was Europa, the daughter of Agenor, king of the city of Sidon in Phoenicia. One day while collecting wild flowers by the sea shore she rashly climbed onto the back of a particularly fine bull that she saw grazing majestically with her father's herd. It had a silver circle on its brow and horns like a crescent moon. Without warning, the bull, none other than Zeus himself, leapt into the waves and carried her off to Crete. There the bull-god made love to her beneath a plane tree, which was still pointed out as a landmark at Gortyn in the days of Theophrastus, in about 300 BC.

Europa conceived three sons, Minos, Rhadamanthys, and Sarpedon. All three were adopted by Asterios, the king of Crete, who subsequently became Europa's husband. When Asterios died, Minos succeeded him and reigned in accordance with laws given him every nine years by his father Zeus. He divided Crete into three kingdoms, each with its own capital; one he took for himself, another he gave to his brother Rhadamanthys. The third he had intended for this brother Sarpedon, but after a disagreement Sarpedon left Crete for Asia Minor. Minos married Pasiphae, the daughter of Helios and the nymph Crete, and she bore him four sons and four daughters in the palace at Knossos.

Minos was just and wise and yet his reign was not untroubled. When he was claiming Asterios' throne, he boasted that the gods would answer whatever prayer he offered them. He dedicated an altar to the sea-god

Poseidon and prayed that a bull might emerge from the waves. Poseidon gave Minos a magnificent white bull, which swam towards the shore and ambled up out of the sea; Poseidon believed that in gratitude Minos would offer it directly back to him in sacrifice, but he did not. Minos kept the bull, a particularly fine specimen, and sacrificed another instead. Poseidon drove the bull mad so that it terrorized the island. According to one version of the myth, it happened that Heracles was on Crete at the time, so Minos summoned the hero to Knossos and appealed to him to do something about the rampaging beast. Heracles agreed, captured it and carried it on his back across the Aegean to Argolis.

Here we can see a reflection of the Minoans' obsession with bulls, an obsession which the Labyrinth's archaeology has proved again and again to be a prehistoric fact. The rhytons, the ceremonial vessels made for pouring libations to the gods, were sometimes designed to look like bulls' heads. Frescoes decorating the Labyrinth walls showed bulls charging and athletes leaping over them or grappling with their horns. Stylized clay and plaster bull horns were used to decorate the cornices and embellish at least two of the Labyrinth's shrines. Many a modern tourist has been photographed against the l-metre-high Horns of Consecration which now overlook the South Terrace and which probably once stood out of reach on a high cornice. Everywhere at Knossos there are references to the bull. This bull cult was apparently carried across to Argolis, as the myth suggests; at Mycenae a very similar bull's head rhyton to the one at Knossos was found, but with a gold disc on its forehead.

Poseidon was angered by Minos' arrogance and may have resented the Cretan king's unrivalled command of the seas: Minos was credited later with founding the first naval fleet. In another version of the story, Poseidon inspired Minos' wife Pasiphae with a perverted and uncontrollable desire to have sex with the white bull. Pasiphae confided her lust in Daidalos, a gifted Athenian engineer who was living in exile at Knossos. In obedience to his queen, Daidalos built a wooden facsimile of a cow, hollow so that Pasiphae could secrete herself inside it. The cow was then taken to the bull, who promptly mounted it.

From this bizarre union terrible consequences were to spring. Pasiphae gave birth to a hideous monster, a creature that was half-man, half-bull and would feed only on human flesh. It was Asterion, the Minotaur. Minos was horrified and caused Daidalos to build a huge and complex maze to house the monster, the Labyrinth. According to other versions of the myth, Minos consulted an oracle for advice, as a result of which he spent the rest of his life hiding in Daidalos' Labyrinth, out of shame; at its heart he concealed both the Minotaur and its mother, the disgraced Pasiphae.

The upper, mud-brick walls of the Labyrinth must have crumbled away fairly rapidly when it fell into disuse, but the lower walls were made of strong masonry and substantial remains, perhaps two storeys or more high, endured into the post-Minoan period. As the classical city of Knossos grew up adjacent to it, the ruined sprawl of the Labyrinth evoked all kinds of exotic possibilities about the past. The classical Knossians used both the Labyrinth and the Minotaur on their coins: a simple, stylized plan of the building became almost a civic badge, a logo for the classical city. Interestingly, according to Plutarch, the Knossians had their own version of the Labyrinth's story; in it the Labyrinth was no more than an elaborate prison from which no escape was possible. Minos, they said, instituted games in honour of his son Androgeus and the prize for the victors was those youths who were currently imprisoned in the Labyrinth. So one local tradition at least had it that the tribute-children were not put to death in the Labyrinth. They may have suffered any kind of degradation or abuse at the hands of the victors, but they did not die in the Labyrinth. Plutarch mentions Aristotle's view, which was similar: the youths lived on as servants and slaves, sometimes to old age.

But this is to speed ahead of the story. Following his humiliation over the birth of Asterion, Minos was struck by a new misfortune when the Athenians killed one of his sons. Prince Androgeus had gone to Athens to participate in the games. He had won all the prizes and the Athenians had become so incensed by his success that they murdered him. In revenge, Minos mounted a punitive expedition against the mainland, besieging and conquering Megara, Athens' neighbouring city, and then laying siege to Athens itself. The siege dragged on until Minos implored his father Zeus to intervene. Zeus brought a plague down on the Athenians and this finally made their king Aigeus submit. He had to consent to send Minos an annual tribute of seven youths and seven maidens to be fed to the Minotaur in the Labyrinth. The Athenians had no choice. Year after year, a ship was sent to Crete with a consignment of fourteen tribute-children.

In the darker recesses of Evans' reconstructed Labyrinth it is still possible to feel that it is a place where some rapacious, child-devouring monster might lurk. In shadowy passages like those at the foot of the Grand Staircase in the East Wing, or the narrow claustrophobic corridor leading from the Lobby of the Stone Seat towards the West Pillar Crypt and the West Magazines, it is still possible to imagine that something unpleasant lies in wait. In spite of the large numbers of people and in spite of summer sunshine, it can still seem a haunted place. A correspondent told me of a visit to Knossos some decades ago when he and his party were virtually the only people in the Labyrinth. They reached the empty, featureless rectangle of the Central Court and became aware of a very strong smell of bull, although there was no bull in the vicinity. Evans too found Knossos a haunted place. There is a well-known passage in *The Palace of Minos* where he describes a solitary visit to the Grand Staircase at night when he was feverish and unable to sleep. Looking down into the dark stairwell he saw the ghosts of Minoan lords and ladies passing elegantly to and fro on the landings below him. At Knossos, mystery, the occult, tragedy and the smell of sacrifice still hang on the air.

Minos' tragic destiny caused him to lose two of his daughters to the gods. He sent his daughter Deione to Libya, where she was seduced by Apollo. She bore him two sons, Amphithemis and Miletus, the latter eventually founding the town named after him, a Minoan colony on the coast of Anatolia. Another of the king's daughters, Akakallis, fell in love with Hermes and bore him a son called Kydon, who later founded Kydonia in the north-west of Crete. She had a daughter by Hermes, Chione, who in her turn was seduced by Hermes; the result of this incestuous union was Autolycus, who inherited from his father the gift of making the objects he touched invisible.

Minos had a son called Glaukos who, as a small boy, went exploring the palace cellars and was curious to see inside the huge storage jars. He climbed up one them and fell in, drowning in the honey it contained. It was some time before the boy's body was discovered and then only thanks to the clairvoyance of the seer Polyeidos. Minos knew that Polyeidos had supernatural powers and ordered him to bring his son back to life, locking him in the cellar until the task was done. After a time Polyeidos saw a snake wriggling across the stone floor and killed it. Then he saw another snake come to the side of the first one, go away and return with a plant in its mouth. It rubbed the body of its dead companion with the herb and immediately revived it. Polyeidos used the same technique on the boy's body and brought him back to life.

New troubles were brewing for Minos in Athens. King Aigeus had a son called Theseus. At least, the king was one of Theseus' fathers: Theseus' mother Aethra shared her affections between Aigeus and Poseidon, and Theseus was conceived as a result of this double union. Like Heracles, Theseus lived an heroic life of combat and challenge. From the beginning his life was filled with dangerous adventures. When he was 16 and in Troizen, his mother told him the secret of his birth and that he was to go to Athens to join his father. After an eventful and dangerous journey, Theseus arrived at his father's court where Medea, Aigeus' new wife, tried to poison him. Feeling the menace of hostility about him the boy drew his sword, which Aigeus at once recognized as his own. Realizing from this that Theseus was his son, Aigeus drove Medea and her offspring from his court, thenceforth sharing his throne with Theseus.

Then came the punitive expedition from Crete and the exaction of a terrible annual sacrifice. The third time the Cretan envoys arrived to collect the tribute, Theseus himself volunteered to go as one of the fourteen victims and Minos agreed that if Theseus should succeed in overcoming the Minotaur with his bare hands the tribute would be forever ended. When the ship arrived in Crete, it was greeted at the quayside by King Minos. Knossos was 5 kilometres inland and served by two ports. One was Katsambas, now a nondescript suburb between Heraklion and its airport; the other was Amnisos, which is now silted up but still recognizable as a harbour, with the submerged foundations of a handful of Minoan houses still visible at the water's edge. The Athenian ship bearing Theseus and the other tribute children may have sailed into either of these harbours.

Stepping ashore, Theseus proudly told Minos that he was the son of the god Poseidon. Thinking this an idle boast, and perhaps remembering his own hubris, Minos threw his gold ring into the harbour and told Theseus that if he was Poseidon's son he would be able to retrieve it for him. Theseus dived into the sea, surfacing again with the ring and also, to the amazement of all, a crown which Amphitrite had given him under the water.

Theseus was nevertheless taken away with the other Athenian youths and maidens to the palace of Knossos where they were led into the Minotaur's Labyrinth. Ariadne, one of the king's daughters, fell in love with Theseus the moment she saw him and resolved to save him somehow from the clutches of the Minotaur. Secretly she gave him a ball of thread which he could unravel as he went into the Labyrinth and use to find his way out again after slaying the monster.

Theseus fastened the thread to the stone door lintel at the entrance to the Labyrinth and unreeled it as he went in. When we look at the ruins on the low Kefala hill today, it is not easy to find the entrance to the Labyrinth even from the outside. It is a pre-classical, inward-looking building with none of the later architectural concerns for symmetry or impressive façades. The edges of the building are severely damaged in some places, so it is not easy to be sure, but it looks as if there were seven or eight entrances, all different in design. From the terminus of the 'Royal Road' in the Theatral Area, an area possibly set aside for ceremonial greeting, visitors or victims might be led along paved paths to the North Entrance or the West Porch at ground level, or up steps to the North-West Entrance which may have provided direct access to the first floor of the West Wing; Evans never reconstructed the North-West Entrance staircase which he proposed and Graham, writing in the 1960s, does not think that the evidence would sustain it (1969, p. 118). Visitors arriving from the south might enter by the South Porch or, if they came across the bridge over the Vlychia ravine, the Stepped Portico at the building's south-west corner. On the Labyrinth's east front there was a formal entrance by way of an elaborate winding stair, the East Entrance (Evans' 'East Bastion') (Plate 16), or another staircase 30 metres to the south, although this last may only have connected the palace with a terrace garden area above the revetment walls.

Even when newly built, the entrances may have been difficult to identify, and once the visitor/victim was safely through one of them the way in from there would have been far from obvious. It is worth emphasizing, for reasons that will become clear later in the book, that this is a building conceived within a tradition that was very different from the classical one. To the legend-weavers of the classical age, the Labyrinth was a synonym for 'puzzle building', a by-word for geographical enigma and for barbarously illogical, irrational architecture: it was to become a metaphor for mental confusion. It was, in other words, an ideal setting for an heroic quest, an ideal problem

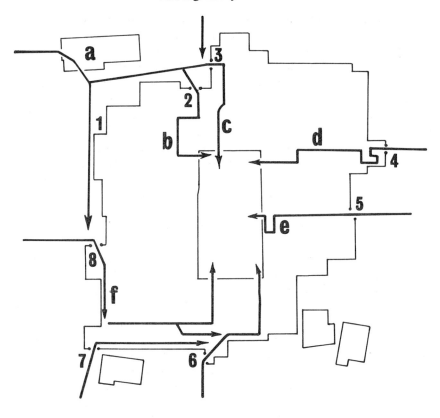

Figure 2 The Labyrinth: a plan of the entrances and access routes. a – Theatral Area, b – North-West Entrance Passage, c – North Entrance Passage, d – East Staircase, e – Grand Staircase, f – Procession Corridor. Entrances: 1 – North-West Entrance, 2 – North-West Portico, 3 – North Entrance, 4 – East Entrance, 5 – Garden Entrance, 6 – South Entrance, 7 – Stepped Portico

situation for a classical hero of the stature of a Heracles or a Theseus.

Into the Labyrinth Theseus walked, threading his way along the winding corridors in search of the Minotaur that lurked at the centre, but the centre is even harder to identify than the entrances, even on the excellent modern plans of the building that are now available, unless we assume that the large blank space of the central Court is what was intended. When we come to consider the possibility that the Minoan bull games were held in this paved arena (see Chapter 10), the idea of a central confrontation between a hero and a bull-monster of supernatural strength takes on a new dimension. The myth meanwhile has it that Theseus encountered the hideous bull-man at the centre of the Labyrinth, killed him in unarmed combat and found his way back out of the maze by following Ariadne's thread. He took Ariadne, her sister

Figure 3 The struggle in the Labyrinth: Theseus
slays the Minotaur

Phaedra, and the rest of the tribute-children to one of the harbour towns and
they made their escape to the island of Naxos, eluding Minos' ships under
cover of darkness.

The king was angry when he discovered that the Minotaur had been killed
and angrier still when he discovered Theseus had escaped and abducted two
of his daughters. To cap it all, his servant Daidalos had given Ariadne the ball
of thread so that Theseus could find his way out of the Labyrinth. The king
punished this act of treachery by imprisoning both Daidalos and his son
Icarus in the Labyrinth. Fearing that worse punishment might follow,
Daidalos set to work to devise a means of escape. He designed and made two
pairs of wings and with these the father and son flew from the Labyrinth to
their freedom. Exhilarated by the sensation of flying, Icarus flew too high, too
close to the sun; the glue holding the wing feathers together melted, the wings
disintegrated and Icarus plummeted to his death in the Aegean.

Daidalos flew safely on to land in Cumae and from there he travelled to
Sicily, where he gained the patronage of King Cocalus. The great engineer's
talents were well known throughout the Mediterranean and any king would
have been glad to have Daidalos at his court. Daidalos was credited with
inventing the axe, the saw, and even the modern form of statues of the gods.
Until his day, the gods were represented by *xoana*, shapeless and primitive
wooden icons; Daidalos was the first to attach arms and legs to make them
look more realistic. In this we can perhaps detect a folk memory of the
marvellous icons that were made in and for the Knossos Labyrinth, such as
the snake goddess figurines found secreted in the Temple Repositories.

Minos eventually heard that Daidalos had sought refuge in Sicily and led
an expedition in pursuit. Minos carried with him a spiral shell, a kind of
portable labyrinth, and promised a great reward to whoever should succeed in
passing a thread right through the shell. He believed that in this way he would
discover Daidalos, and he was right. When he arrived at the court of King
Cocalus at Kamikos in Sicily, Minos announced his reward. Cocalus took the
shell, saying that he could thread it and passed it secretly to Daidalos whose

pride spurred him to solve the puzzle. He tied a thread to an ant, bored a small hole in the centre of the shell and allowed the ant to draw the thread round the spiral maze. Cocalus presented the threaded shell to Minos, who at once knew that the craft of Daidalos had been at work and demanded that Daidalos be returned to him. Cocalus refused to comply. In the atmosphere of mutual suspicion which quickly developed, Cocalus caused his daughters to drown Minos in a bathtub. Minos was buried in Sicily and his tomb was often pointed out in classical times at the town named after him, Minoa.

So ended the long and unhappy chain of events set in motion by King Minos' failure to offer the appropriate sacrifice to the gods. It is a classic case of an ignominious and tragic downfall resulting from heroic hubris, over-confidence or arrogance in the face of the gods.

Minos had none the less been a just and wise king with a flair for law-making and he had his reward for these qualities in the afterlife. In the Underworld, most mortals became diaphanous and insubstantial, losing their individual personalities. It was only the privileged few who were allowed to continue much as they had been on the Earth above. Orion was able to go on hunting, Heracles to go on overthrowing monsters, Minos to go on sitting in judgement. Gradually, the underworld came to be more a place of judgement and posthumous justice, less a shadowy limbo.

Minos finally became an immortal. In origins he was divine; in his judgement seat in the underworld he also had a divine role to play. He is a truly mythic figure. But stories about his earthly career were often told in the ancient world as a matter of history. The Athenian historian Thucydides wrote of King Minos as the first known ruler to build up a powerful navy and, in so doing, gain control of most of the Aegean Sea; he expelled the Carians from the Cyclades, installed his sons as governors there and reduced the level of piracy on the high seas. The mythic elements and the fragments of what we today might regard as genuine history were impossible to distinguish.

Minos and the story of ancient Knossos are mentioned by Homer, Hesiod, Thucydides, Herodotus, Apollodorus, Bachylides, Plutarch, Pindar, and Diodorus Siculus, often with different slants, different motives, and endless small variations. Homer, for instance, gives us an interesting insight into Cretan history in the period immediately after Minos' murder in Sicily, although it is hard to know what value to give his account. The *Iliad* contains the celebrated list of ships which took part in the expedition against Troy. Crete sent a large number, indicating the continuing power of post-Minoan Crete, eighty ships under the command of King Idomeneus of Knossos, the grandson of Minos.

Later on, in the fifth century BC, the historians Herodotus and Thucydides wrote confidently that once King Minos of Crete had controlled the Aegean. Herodotus wrote, 'Of old [the Carians] were subjects of Minos and were called Leleges. They inhabited the islands [Cyclades], paying no tribute as far as I can determine in all my enquiries. Instead, whenever Minos required it, they manned his ships.' Herodotus tells us of another Cretan expedition, sent to avenge Minos' death. All the cities of Crete participated in this except Polichne and Praisos. The Cretans disembarked at Minoa and laid siege to Kamikos but to no avail. When they raised the siege and tried to return home, they were prevented by a great storm; they were obliged to resettle in southern Italy, founding the colony of Hyria and leaving Crete itself virtually unpopulated. It was, Herodotus says, because of this that Crete was recolonized by people from the Greek mainland.

Diodorus Siculus, writing as an historian in the first century BC mentions Minos' death in Sicily, describes the tomb at Minoa and adds a new detail, that Theron, tyrant of Akragas in Sicily in the fifth century, unearthed Minos' bones and caused them to be sent back to Crete for re-burial at Knossos. From the description of the Sicilian tomb of Minos, it would seem to have been uncannily like the Temple Tomb at Knossos, not far south of the Labyrinth: both have twin-storied arrangements of sanctuary and burial vault. Perhaps one of the kings of Knossos really was killed on an expedition and brought back to be buried in the Temple Tomb. When it was excavated, it was found that there was a late, intrusive burial of a man in the north-east corner of the burial chamber: the burial pit can still be seen there.

Whatever their truth in points of detail, these various writings tell us that there was a strong Greek tradition going back to about 750 BC when the Homeric sagas were written, and probably further back in oral tradition, that ancient Crete had played a crucial role in shaping the destiny of the Aegean world. Zeus himself had been born in a Cretan cave; some said, though they were liars, that Zeus was dead and that his tomb could be seen not far to the south of Knossos on Mount Juktas. Later chapters will show how the religion of Minoan Crete left an important legacy to the belief-system of 'Mycenean' and classical Greece. The memory of the Labyrinth, where many legendary events were centred, itself became a symbol in the ancient world, its winding passages and many dead ends turning into an archetypal metaphor for dangerous journeying and confrontation with dark forces. The classical city of Knossos, growing up right beside the deserted, collapsing ruins of the Labyrinth, used a simplified version of the monument's plan as its cipher; the design became a templet for later mazes.

The political and military might of their Cretan forebears was often food for thought to the mainland Greeks. On the Athenian stage, Minos was often satirized as implacably bloodthirsty and violent, and yet Hesiod called him 'supreme among kings': it was a powerfully ambivalent memory. From the documentary evidence we can see the Minoans, the inhabitants of bronze age Crete, through the minds of the ancient Greeks. In outline, their view of the historic Crete, in so far as we can disentangle it from the mythic Crete, was as follows.

The native population of Crete was made up of Kydonians and Eteo-cretans. One of their kings was called Asterios, who married an oriental princess called Europa and so founded the dynasty which produced Minos and boasted descent from Zeus. The Cretans were master-mariners, lords of the seas, founding port-colonies in the islands of the Aegean and travelling long distances through the Mediterranean to east and west. The ascendancy of the Cretan sea-empire came to an end when 'storms' came and destroyed the Cretan navy off the Italian coast; Crete itself was emptied. The remaining Kydonians withdrew to the western part of the island and the surviving Eteocretans to the eastern part.

By the time of Minos' grandson Idomeneus the Cretans had recovered themselves sufficiently to send eighty ships to Troy, a massive force even when compared with the hundred ships sent by Agamemnon, king of Mycenae, and the ninety sent by Nestor, king of Pylos.

There are all kinds of resonances in the ancient Greek view of Crete: overtones of bardic story-telling, undertones of political point-scoring, echoes of real historical events, reverberations of myth-making. It is tempting to try to match up fragments of the documented Greek view with the archaeology – tempting but fraught with danger. The great king we are trying, as Arthur Evans also tried, to track down in his mazy palace lived on Crete some time before 1380 BC. The first written accounts that we know of were not committed to paper until about 750 BC, and far away on the mainland at that.

Even on the mythic level there are variations and inconsistencies which speak of endless compressions, reassessments and transformations of the various passages of the myths. What is it that the differences in Ariadne's fate conceal? In one version she is abandoned by Theseus on the island of Naxos after their escape from Knossos and she hangs herself. In another she is abandoned by Theseus and immediately courted by Dionysos. In yet another she is killed on the island of Dia by Artemis – and so on. There is a solution to this particular problem, which I hope will become clear in Chapters 9 and 13 as we reconstruct the pantheon and religious beliefs and practices of ancient Crete. Even so, an important inherent point is that we should not accept any of the Greek stories about Minos, his fabulous palace, his sea-empire, his Labyrinth, or his exotic court simply at their face value. We should bear them all in mind – they are evidence of a sort for what might once have been at bronze age Knossos – but not allow them to colour or distort our interpretation of the solid archaeological evidence.

2
The discovery of the Labyrinth

I am persuaded that I could ... comfortably excavate it in a week
with a hundred workmen.

Heinrich Schliemann, March 1889

IDENTIFYING THE SITE

In the ancient Greek imagination, Crete, the island at the threshold of the
world, was the perfect setting for the epic events of mythology. When we look
with a cold and rational eye at the stories about Daidalos, Theseus, Ariadne,
Minos, Pasiphae and the Minotaur, we can see that not all of them can be
literally true. The whole fabric of Cretan legend is sewn through with
supernatural threads. We might even be tempted into thinking that they
cannot be worth giving any serious consideration. Yet in the eighth century
BC, when the Homeric epics evolved into their present form, the ancient
Greeks were convinced of the historical reality of bronze age Knossos.

Minos' descendant, Idomeneus, was credited with sending ships to Troy.
Real though the 'history' of Crete may have seemed to the ancient Greeks, we
know that, whatever precise form the Trojan War took, it happened in about
1250 BC, some 500 years before the *Iliad* was written down. It is difficult to be
sure in this situation which elements in the Knossos story represent historic
reality, in the sense of objectively verifiable events, and which elements
represent a mythic or poetic world that existed only in the imagination.

Homer lays traps for the unwary. Scholars, fools, and fantasists have been
lured into endless speculation, partly because there are many real place-names
in the epics. Pylos, Mycenae, Troy and Knossos were real cities of the ancient
world, but we cannot be sure what really happened in those cities. When
Homer has Odysseus tell Penelope one of his 'lying yarns' in Book 19 of the
Odyssey, he puts us into a curious position. We know that Odysseus is lying to
his wife. We know he is not Prince Aethon, the brother of King Idomeneus,
so he cannot have entertained Odysseus (himself) as he describes. Yet at the
same time we are told circumstantial details about the port of Knossos –
Amnisus, 'a difficult harbour to make' – and about the Cretan royal family, so

that we feel the background to be accurate. Odysseus had visited Crete, and Homer or his informant had too. The description, though brief and sketchy, recognizably depicts the Knossos area.

Amnisos, one of the ancient but now silted and abandoned ports of Knossos is close enough to Knossos for a visitor to go there quickly and on impulse, a mere 5 kilometres. The sacred cave of Eileithyia is indeed very close to the site of Amnisos, on a hillside overlooking the harbour. In ancient times, the port must have been closed for weeks at a time as a result of strong and persistent north winds. Odysseus' account rings true even though it is a lie.

> He [King Minos] was the father of my father, the great Deucalion, who had two sons, myself and King Idomeneus. At the time I have in mind, Idomeneus had gone off in his beaked ships to Ilium with the sons of Atreus; so it fell to me, the younger son, Aethon by name and not so good a man as my elder brother, to meet Odysseus and welcome him to Crete, where he was brought by a gale which had driven him off his course at Cape Malea when bound for Troy. He put in at Amnisus, where the Cave of Eileithyia is – a difficult harbour to make. The storm nearly wrecked him. The first thing he did was to go up to the town [Knossos] and ask for Idomeneus, whom he described as a dear and honoured friend. But nine or ten days had already gone by since Idomeneus had sailed for Ilium in his beaked ships. So I took Odysseus to my house and made him thoroughly welcome .... The good fellows stayed with me for twelve days, pent up by that northerly gale.

Odysseus made all these lying yarns of his so convincing, says Homer, that as she listened the tears poured from Penelope's eyes.

This one anecdote from Homer sums up the problems we face when we sift through the legends that surround Knossos, and yet there are clues that seem to make sense of a tangle of confusing stories.

There is, for example, the pre-Hellenic word *labyrinthos*, from which the word labyrinth is derived. *Labyrinthos* is very close in form to the word *labrys*, which means 'double-axe'. So there is a close linguistic connection between the idea of a maze and the idea of a double-axe. The Labyrinth of the Minotaur in the Theseus legend was also the House of the Double-Axe.

On its own, that connection of ideas means little. But it suddenly assumed focal importance during an excavation in the year 1878. For many years before that there had been speculation about the location of King Minos' Labyrinth; some thought they had found its sinister ruins at a site near Gortyn, about 35 kilometres south-west of Knossos, and wrote evocative descriptions of the remains.

The first modern survey of Crete, by Cristoforo Buondelmonti, was based on an 11-week tour in 1415. Buondelmonti saw the ancient mine workings in the hills behind Gortyn and identified them as the site of the Labyrinth. The story was repeated at intervals right up to the nineteenth century. In 1632,

William Lithgow wrote that he had seen the entrance to Daidalos' Labyrinth:

> I saw the entry into the Laborinth of Dedalus, which I would gladly have better viewed, but because we had no Candle-light, we durst not enter: for there are many hollow places within it; so that if a man stumble, or fall, he can hardly be rescued. It is cut forth with many intricating wayes, on the face of a little hill, ioyning with Mount Ida, having many doors and pillars. Here it was where Theseus by the helpe of Ariadne the daughter of King Minos, taking a bottome of thread, and tying the one end at the first doore, did enter and slay the Minotaurus, who was included there by Dedalus.

This description of Lithgow's shows how easy it is to be carried along by the atmosphere of a place, especially when the mind has been conditioned to discover locations for the great events of the mythic past. Lithgow's account is as salutary as it is vivid. The place he was looking at was not at Knossos but near Gortyn: a place that had been known since the mid-sixteenth century to be the quarry which supplied the builders of the Roman town of Gortyn with their stone. Lithgow imagined a Roman stone quarry into a bronze age Labyrinth to house a Minotaur.

The misidentification of the Gortyn quarries as the Labyrinth persisted, but there were always dissenting voices, even in the middle ages. In 1435 a keen-eyed and astute Spanish traveller called Pero Tafur produced a short description of Crete in which he put the Labyrinth at Knossos, 'with many other antiquities'. There were other travellers who agreed. Richard Pococke in 1745 favoured 'an eminence to the south' of the Roman ruins at Knossos – the Kefala hill.

In the 1830s, the traveller and antiquarian Robert Pashley visited and described the site that he believed was Knossos, with masses of Roman brickwork as the only surviving surface remains; the palace of Knossos, or whatever was left of it, was invisible, buried underneath these later ruins. Close by there was a village, Makrytichos, a detail which confirms that Pashley really was inspecting the site now recognized as Minoan Knossos. Curiously, though, Pashley rejected with a sneer the heavy hint offered to him by a local place-name. He wrote, 'Savary and Sonnini both assert that the hamlet where these ruins are situated is called Gnossu', but he doubted Savary's suggestion that the hamlet's name preserved the name of the ancient city: he thought it a mere coincidence.

> According to an ancient tradition [Diodorus], Idomeneus and Meriones were buried at Cnossos, and a Christian legend has long pointed out, near this site, the tomb of Caiaphas. But, since I write as a traveller, and nothing more remains to be examined at Makro-tekho, I shall at once bid farewell to this capital of ancient Crete, which ... has dwindled down into this miserable hamlet, and the few shapeless heaps of masonry, which alone recal to the remembrance of the passing traveller its ancient and bygone splendour.

Whether Robert Pashley was correct in his identification of the tomb of Caiaphas or not is open to question (it has since been demolished), but he was very close indeed to the twentieth-century view of Knossos as a buried bronze age city camouflaged and overlapped by much later Roman ruins. In 1865 Thomas Spratt, in his *Travels in Crete*, also argued that King Minos' palace had once stood on the Kefala hill. It is important to remember these earlier identifications when we come to assess the sometimes exaggerated reports that the site of Knossos was 'discovered' in the 1870s, 1880s or early 1900s.

Probably, from time to time during the long centuries that have elapsed since the fall of bronze age Knossos, other travellers stumbled on fragments of its ruined walls. Perhaps even in the classical period a few adventurous spirits found narrow crevices through which they were able to scramble down into dark chambers not yet filled with rubble. Certainly, the idea that the city of Knossos and the Labyrinth of King Minos might be an historical reality with tangible surviving remains has intrigued people ever since stories were first told in ancient Greece. The search for them has gone on intermittently ever since.

There is a story that in the reign of Nero an earthquake brought to light some tombs at Knossos. In one of them, a shepherd found a tin box containing pieces of bark with writing of some unknown kind on them. The emperor sent scholars off to Crete to decipher the writing. They recognized it as Phoenician and translated it. Unfortunately, these 'Chronicles of Dictys' were faked in the third century AD. Even so the story demonstrates that, at the mid-point between the heyday of the Minoan culture and our own times, people were fascinated by the mystery of Knossos. Ironically, when Sir Arthur Evans eventually launched systematic excavations at Knossos, he did indeed find inscriptions; they were not Phoenician and he could not interpret them, even though he spent the rest of his long life trying.

But this is to leap ahead to the early years of the twentieth century, and it was towards the end of 1878 that a Cretan merchant with an interest in antiquities, Minos Kalokairinos, struck the first pick into the hill of Kefala at Knossos. It was a time when there was a great public awakening to the excitement of archaeological discovery. Throughout 1877 there was a constant stream of publicity from Schliemann about his finds at Mycenae on the Greek mainland. His lectures and reports developed the theme that excavation could demonstrate that Homer was historically accurate: 'not describing myths but real events and tangible realities' (Lecture at the Society of Antiquaries, March 1877). In 1877 and 1878, the treasures that Schliemann had found at Troy were exhibited and his ideas concerning Troy were widely discussed in the press.

Kalokairinos was just one antiquarian among the many who became fired with the same enthusiasm as Schliemann for rediscovering the Homeric past. He claimed that he had wanted to open up the site as early as 1864 but had been prevented by circumstances, mainly civil unrest. It seems likely that he was spurred into action by Schliemann's exciting discoveries at Mycenae, though it is still not known how he came to choose exactly the right spot for his dig: perhaps it was the scatter of 'Mycenean' potsherds across the site that attracted him, perhaps it was local tradition, or perhaps it was the 'well-wrought blocks of limestone' visible at the surface, mentioned by Schliemann.

MINOS KALOKAIRINOS AND HEINRICH SCHLIEMANN

Whatever the impulse, Minos Kalokairinos dug twelve trial trenches into the centre of the broad earth mound of Kefala and was immediately rewarded by becoming, it is generally believed, the first person in modern times to see into the dark underworld of the great building's cellars. Everywhere in his trenches, opened between December 1878 and the following February, Kalokairinos came upon the massive walls of an extensive building. He realized at once that he had found a palatial complex measuring at least 55 metres by 40, according to the account published by Fabricius. There was a curving corner to an outer wall (the north-east corner of the Throne Room's antechamber), some red-painted walls, part of the imposing masonry of the west front and – above all – row upon row of storerooms.

Minos Kalokairinos knew straight away, from the simple, angular double-axe carvings on the stonework, that he had found the lost palace of King Minos. The area that he had broken into was the extensive area, mainly of narrow storerooms and corridors, that has become known as the West Wing. In its dark and cramped alleys, Kalokairinos found serried rows of colossal storage jars (*pithoi*), some of them still containing remains of peas, barley, and broad beans from the last weeks of the building's use – whatever that might have been. Perhaps more importantly, though, Kalokairinos saw the double-axes carved into the stone. This was the House of the Double-Axe, the palace of the kings of ancient Crete (Plate 1).

News of Kalokairinos' discovery and the fine collection of Cretan bronze age artefacts spread quickly. In February 1879 the native Cretan parliament intervened to stop Kalokairinos unearthing any more of Knossos; the fear was that his finds might be removed from the island to be housed by the Turks in the Imperial Museum in Istanbul. News of the pilot dig nevertheless spread far and wide, and Kalokairinos did everything he could to promote worldwide interest in Knossos. He sent specimens of the giant storage jars he had found to London, Paris and Rome as part of his publicity campaign: three more went to the Archaeological Collection in Heraklion. His large private collection from that first dig was unfortunately destroyed during the fighting against the Turks in 1898, when his house near Heraklion harbour was burnt down. His excavation notes were also lost. There are only meagre records of that historic dig, such as diary extracts, the accounts of visitors to the site and letters, but they are useful in helping us to recover the state of the building as it was when Evans first saw it and before he, Evans, started altering it.

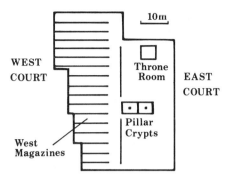

Figure 4 The extent of the 'Mycenean palace of Knossos', as interpreted by Kalokairinos, Schliemann, and Evans (until 1900)

An American journalist who had formerly been American Consul in Crete, W. J. Stillman, had the idea that the maze-like building Kalokairinos was opening up on the Kefala hill might be the Labyrinth of Greek mythology. Stillman was frustrated when the excavations were stopped and hoped to be allowed to re-start them himself if necessary: but he too was prevented by the authorities. Stillman reported on Kalokairinos' discovery to the newly formed Archaeological Institute of America. He produced drawings of some strange signs, later to become known as 'mason's marks', carved on the stones and recorded their positions. Stillman's role at this time was a crucial one, alerting the international community to the possibilities that an excavation at Knossos might offer. The publicity that Kalokairinos and Stillman generated led indirectly to the eventual excavation of the entire palatial complex. It was as a result of their publicity that Schliemann's attention was drawn to Knossos.

Heinrich Schliemann was born in Germany in 1822. By the 1860s he was an exceptionally wealthy self-made businessman, and after a series of profitable tea and cotton deals he liquidated his companies in order to devote his time to what he claimed was his boyhood dream – the discovery and excavation of ancient Troy. Egocentric and boastful, he was not above falsifying both the events of his early life and his site evidence to make a better story. He seems to have been too preoccupied with finding treasure and with owning it once he had found it: in these respects, his approach perhaps belongs more with the early than with the late nineteenth century.

Given Schliemann's attitudes and the alarming impatience and single-mindedness with which he worked, it is surprising that so much of value has come out of his excavations. His highly trained and competent assistant, Wilhelm Dörpfeld, contributed incalculably to their success. For their time, they were surprisingly thorough and productive, and they were always written up afterwards in lengthy, detailed reports. Since Schliemann began his career in archaeology at the age of 46, with an antiquarian tour of the island of Ithaca, he had excavated Troy, Mycenae, and Tiryns. Now he was actively looking for a new site to conquer. He read about the discovery on the Kefala hill just outside Heraklion and in the early summer of 1866, when he was 63, went to Crete to see for himself.

Schliemann's arrival on Crete was perhaps the greatest single threat to Knossos since the catastrophic destructions of 1700 and 1470 BC. Although Schliemann had rediscovered the site of ancient Troy and excavated Mycenae, he had also inflicted extensive damage, especially on Troy: he had actually dug away and destroyed, unexamined, virtually all of 'King Priam's Troy', the level known as Troy VI. If he had been permitted to excavate Knossos, we can be sure that we would not have the magnificent edifice that now stands on the Kefala hill, nor would we have learnt so much about so many aspects of the culture of the people who raised the original building.

Kalokairinos invited Schliemann into his house to show him his finds and then took him out to Knossos, where the bronze age walls stood exposed, in some places, to a height of 2 metres. Schliemann was overwhelmed. He was so excited by what he saw that he wrote, allegedly from Knossos itself, to his friend Max Müller. The letter, written in English, is dated 22 May 1886:

> Dr. Dörpfeld and I have examined most carefully the site of Knossos .... Nothing is visible above ground, which might be referred to the so-called heroic age – not even a fragment of terracotta – except on a hillock, almost the size of the Pergamos of Troy, which is situated in the middle of the town and appears to be altogether artificial. Two large well-wrought blocks of hard limestone, which were peeping out from the ground induced Mr. Minos Kalokairinos of Heracleion to dig here five holes in which came to light an outer wall and parts of walls with antae of a vast edifice *similar* to the prehistoric palace of Tiryns, and apparently of the same age, for the pottery in it is perfectly identical with that found in Tiryns.

Max Müller's reply to Schliemann, written from Oxford in 5 June, contains a curiously prophetic comment: 'Crete is a perfect rookery of nations, and there, if anywhere, you ought to find the first attempts at writing, as adapted to western needs.' It was to be at Knossos that Arthur Evans would later discover two previously unknown ancient scripts, Linear A and Linear B.

In another letter, written just over a year after his visit to Crete, Schliemann wrote,

> I should like to complete my life's labours with a great work, the excavation of the age-old, prehistoric palace of the kings of Knossos in Crete, which I believe I discovered three [sic] years ago. Unfortunately, however, for this purpose I must buy a whole estate which includes the site of Knossos, for I cannot reach my goal in any other way.

Schliemann characteristically exaggerated the importance of his visit to Knossos. He could not have believed that he had discovered the site when he knew that Kalokairinos and Stillman had been there before him. There were

variablegation.

Stillman's articles to prove the falsehood, and the publications of Schliemann's correspondent Fabricius, but in many untruths Schliemann was not found out. During his lifetime, it was alleged that he had 'fixed' his evidence and many who met him were profoundly suspicious. Matthew Arnold found him 'devious'; Ernest Curtius, who excavated Olympia, called him 'a swindler'.

In 1888 Schliemann went to the island of Kythera, where he excavated in the hope of finding the Temple of Aphrodite, but he had not forgotten about his dream of rounding off his career as an archaeologist by opening up the palace of Knossos. In March 1889, he wrote in a letter,

> The palace [i.e. the great building at Knossos which Evans, too, was to think of as a palace] is 55 metres long, 43.30 metres wide, and I am persuaded that I could ... comfortably excavate it in a week with a hundred workmen. But ... 32,000 marks are too much for me to throw away on labours completed in a week whose results – down to the very last potsherd ... would benefit the museum in Heraklion.

Nevertheless, Schliemann seriously contemplated buying Knossos and began to negotiate with the Turkish owners of the site. It was perhaps fortunate for Knossos that Schliemann was still very much the hard-headed businessman. The negotiation broke down when he counted the olive trees on the plot he had agreed to buy and, instead of the 2,500 he had been told were there, found only 889. Furious at what he saw as an attempt at fraudulent deception, he withdrew from the deal at once, irrevocably sacrificing all possibility of excavating Knossos. It seems an extraordinary piece of self-destructive pride, to call off the deal for the sake of some olive trees that he did not want anyway, but Schliemann was an extraordinary man.

In 1894, less than four years after Schliemann's sudden death on Christmas Day in Naples, Arthur Evans made his first visit to Crete. He had seen and been impressed by the exhibition of Schliemann's treasures in 1883, but his visit to Crete was, it seems, entirely unconnected with any vision of un-earthing bronze age Knossos. He had an idea that sounds almost pedestrian by comparison with Schliemann's ambition – to discover the ancient system of picture-writing that must once, he thought, have been used in Europe. He had, earlier on, been very interested in collecting coins, but he was becoming increasingly interested in carved sealstones.

Evans saw the bronze age sealstones found at Mycenae by Schliemann, whom he greatly admired, and was convinced that a civilization as advanced as the Mycenean must have developed some system of writing. The sealstones had designs on them which looked as if they might belong to a hieroglyphic script comparable with the hieroglyphs of ancient Egypt. Evans wanted to extend his knowledge of the unknown script of the sealstones, and to do this he needed as many examples as possible. He found some, just like the Mycenean stones unearthed by Schliemann, in an antique shop in Athens.

The proprietor told him they had come from Crete. It was a collection of sealstones that took Arthur Evans to Crete in 1894 – that, and not Knossos at all.

3
Arthur Evans and
the 1900 dig at Knossos

'Could you come superintend under my direction important excavation Knossos. Personal not School affair terms four months 60 pounds and all expenses paid to begin at once.'

'Agreed coming next boat.'
Exchange of telegrams between Evans and Mackenzie, 1900.

PRELUDE TO EXCAVATION

The stepping-stones which led Arthur Evans to Knossos are important in explaining his interpretation of the site. The twentieth-century view of Knossos has been conditioned very largely by Evans' interpretation, and that interpretation was conditioned by his background, experience, and expectations. Evans was born in 1851, when Schliemann was 29 and already well on the way towards making his first fortune. Schliemann worked his way up through the world of commerce towards great wealth: Evans was to inherit it. Schliemann was a self-educated, self-made man: Evans was educated at Harrow, Oxford and Göttingen. The two men had totally different backgrounds and their approach to antiquity, as to life in general, was also very different. Evans' father, John, was an antiquarian and collector: he was one of an influential group of people, including Sir John Lubbock, who established the studies of anthropology and prehistory on more scientific lines. Evans was brought up in a home where antiquity, properly and scientifically studied, mattered greatly.

Physically a small man, Evans often concerned himself with small objects. He had a penetrating eye for tiny detail, which he was able to apply to great effect both in his studies of coins and sealstones and also in the excavations at Knossos; his extreme shortness of sight is thought to have contributed to this ability. But Evans' abilities did not end at the keen observation of small artefacts: he was also an excellent field researcher, tough, persistent, patient and determined. He had the temperament to see a major dig like Knossos through – however long it might take.

He had an explorer's instinct in relation to both things and places. From his late teens until he was middle-aged, he loved making long expeditions on foot or horseback across rough and difficult terrain. Evans' initial interest, on reaching manhood, was anthropology. At the age of 22, he travelled north to Lapland and south-east to the Balkans. While he was in the Balkans he developed a particular interest in Bosnia; its coins and antiquities interested the academic in him, its social and political problems stirred his emotions. Bosnia is now part of Yugoslavia. Then, like Crete, it was under Turkish rule. Evans was in Sarajevo during the 1875 rising and afterwards wrote a book about the atrocities committed by the Turks.

In 1877 Evans became a special correspondent to the *Manchester Guardian*, reporting on the poverty and misery of the Bosnians and Herzogovinians, and also covertly distributing relief supplies among those who had suffered in the Austro-Hungarian and Turkish conflict. He had by this time become a passionate supporter of independence for the Balkan peoples. The Austrians became aware of his activities on behalf of the Slav nationalists and imprisoned him for a while at Ragusa (Dubrovnik) before deporting him in 1881.

Alongside these political adventures, Evans went on developing his interest in antiquities. He managed to be in England to see the Kensington exhibition of Schliemann's Trojan finds in 1878 and was deeply stirred and excited by what he saw. It was in this same year that he married Margaret Freeman.

Then, in 1883, Evans and his wife made a momentous journey to Greece, to see Mycenae and Tiryns and also to meet Schliemann in Athens. Unfortunately, there seems to be no record of the conversation between Evans and Schliemann, but we do know that Schliemann showed him the treasures he had unearthed at Mycenae at his house and that Evans spent some hours looking at them. It seems unlikely that at this stage Evans had begun to think about Knossos or Crete, but Crete may well have been discussed. Schliemann would visit Knossos in the near future and his correspondents would shortly be suggesting that he should look to Crete as the origin of the culture that produced the Mycenean shaft graves. It may have been discussed. We cannot be sure, but Evans must have asked himself, if not Schliemann, while he was examining the treasures from Mycenae, *where* the culture had sprung from that had produced such distinctive artefacts. They seemed not to be native to Greece: they seemed not to belong to the Middle East either. Whatever the specifics of Evans' conversation with the older archaeologist, it must have launched triremes of surmise and speculation about the Aegean.

During the years that followed, Evans gradually expanded his knowledge of Mediterranean prehistory. In 1892 he visited the Sicilian tombs then being excavated by Orsi: one of the tombs, it turned out, contained a vase from Mycenae. Just before this visit, he had met Federico Halbherr in Rome. Halbherr had a considerable reputation as a scholar and had travelled all over

Crete, recording the antiquities and inscriptions he found. The conversation between Halbherr and Evans may well have suggested to Evans that he might develop a special interest in Cretan prehistory, especially since Halbherr must have drawn attention to the fact that Crete was still completely unexplored and unprospected as far as prehistoric remains were concerned. The ground was prepared.

The year 1893 was a turning-point for Evans. A new book, Reinach's *The Oriental Mirage*, supplied him with an important idea that he would shortly be able to use to great effect: the idea that *ex oriente lux*, for so long the guiding principle of European thought, was a fallacy. *The Oriental Mirage* developed the idea that not everything had come from the east. Where had the Mycenean civilization come from, if not from the east? From the south perhaps?

It was also in 1893 that Evans' wife Margaret died, a personal tragedy which may have jarred him into taking a new direction. It was while he searched among the antique dealers' trays in Athens that year that he came across the tiny three- and four-sided stones that were to take him to Crete. The stones carried engraved symbols from some unknown system of writing. He had seen sealstones similar to them in Oxford; now he saw them in Athens and was told that they had come from Crete. Evans decided to go to Crete.

On 15 March 1894, Arthur Evans sailed into the little harbour at Heraklion and started searching for inscribed sealstones straight away. His diary entry was as follows.

Arrived considerably the worse for voyage. Juno, Austrian Lloyd, bad. 24 hours voyage from Peiraeus .... Able to visit bazar: found Chrysochoi and a man from whom I bought 22 early Cretan stones at about 1½ piastres apiece .... Joubin [an archaeologist of the French School in Athens trying to buy the site of Knossos for excavation] had 'prospected' Knossos for the French and come to an agreement with one proprietor, but the pretensions of the other were too exorbitant.

Evans met Minos Kalokairinos, who showed him a single clay tablet he had found in the cellars during his 1878–9 excavation: it was inscribed with symbols that Evans had not seen before – the script that later became known as Linear B. He also went out to Knossos and recorded the first, momentous visit in his diary.

Mar. 19 ... The site of Knossos is most extensive and occupies several hills. The Mykenaean akropolis however seems not to be the highest but that to the south-west, nearest to the gorge, which on this side divides the rich undulating site of the chief Cretan city from the limestone steeps beyond. Here at a place called ta pitharia are the remains of Mykenaean walls and passages noted by Stillman and others. They are very complex as far as one can judge from what is visible to the eye, but were hardly as Stillman supposes the Labyrinth itself (Later: No, on further examination I think it

must be so). I copied the marks on the stones, some of which recall my
'hieroglyphics'.... From a school-master at Makro-teichos I obtained two
Mykenaean stones .... The site of Knossos brilliant with purple, white and
pinkish anemones and blue iris.

The diary entry epitomizes Arthur Evans' wide-ranging approach to the site.
His sure and sensitive awareness of the topography, his eye for detail, his
interest in the remains of the great building itself, his willingness to consider
the ideas of others and reconsider some of his own assumptions, his
possessiveness about the inscriptions ('*my* hieroglyphics' is a revealing aside in
view of later events) and his love of Cretan flowers. It is all there, in his
reaction to that historic first day at Knossos.

Evans revisited Knossos in the company of Kalokairinos and Halbherr,
with the particular object of seeing the strange marks, later to be called
'mason's marks', that Stillman had drawn. Even when he was on the threshold
of excavating Knossos, Evans was still very much concerned with his
hieroglyphics, still pursuing the idea of an early European form of writing.
But the idea of opening up the rest of the 'Mykenaean palace', which is how
Evans then thought of it, had taken root, and he began the long and tedious
negotiations for the purchase of the Kefala hill from its Turkish owners.

Fortunately, Evans was helped in these by Joseph Hazzidakis, the
President of the Society for the Promotion of Education and founder and
president of Heraklion's Collection of Antiquities. Without the help of
Hazzidakis, later to make his mark as an archaeologist in his own right,
Evans would never have completed the purchase. As it was, it took over five
years.

THE EXCAVATION BEGINS

It was on 23 March 1900, six years almost to the day after Evans' first visit,
that the excavation started. Assisted by Duncan Mackenzie, and with some
initial guidance from D. G. Hogarth, the Director of the British School of
Archaeology at Athens, Evans chose to open up more continuously the part
of the hill that Kalokairinos had trenched in the winter of 1878–9. If that now
seems odd, we must remember that at this stage everyone believed that the
palace, labyrinth, or whatever else the building might turn out to be, was a
modest 55 metres from north to south by 43 metres from east to west – a large
building by prehistoric standards, certainly, but not the sprawling giant that
eventually emerged. Evans thus sought only to expose more completely the
roughly rectangular cellarage area that we now call the West Wing, starting in
its south-east corner and working his way north towards the (totally
unexpected) Throne Room. (Figures 4, 7.)

The area to the north of Kefala had been damaged by later buildings of the
classical period, but the building Evans was uncovering had miraculously
survived virtually unscathed. Just a few centimetres below the modern land

surface lay the eroded tops of the walls, some still plastered, some with coloured frescoes still adhering to them. Little by little, the detail – so telling to Evans' imagination – began to emerge. The well-preserved walls had in places been blackened and damaged by a catastrophic fire, a fire which had ruined the palace three thousand years before. The rims of more of the huge storage jars began to appear. On 30 March, Evans found a 'kind of baked clay bar, rather like a stone chisel in shape though broken at one end with script on it and what appear to be numerals'. It was the ancient script he had hoped to find, and in a prehistoric context.

But then, on 13 April, just three weeks into the excavation, came the most spectacular discovery of the year – the Throne Room. It was a modest chamber with frescoed walls that still stood 2 metres high. On the south side there were steps down into a recessed area which Evans excavated first and interpreted as a tank or bath chamber. The north wall was lined with stone benches flanking a gypsum throne with a high back and standing on a square base. Scattered across the floor in front of this (clearly royal) throne were beautiful alabaster ritual vessels: Evans thought the last king of Knossos must have been engaged in some desperate ritual of propitiation just before the palace was engulfed in its final catastrophe.

The discoveries Evans made during the first month of his 1900 dig were sensational, however they are interpreted. The thing that startled Evans most was their great antiquity. What he was finding semed to go back in time beyond anything he had seen on the mainland of Greece, beyond the treasures of Mycenae that he had gazed at in Schliemann's house in Athens. Even before the Throne Room was discovered, Evans was writing excitedly in his diary,

> The extraordinary phenomenon – nothing Greek – nothing Roman – perhaps one single fragment of late black varnished ware among tens of thousands. Even Geometrical pottery fails us – though as tholoi found near central road show a flourishing Knossos existed lower down ... nay, its great period goes well back to the pre-Mycenaean period.

Evans realized, just five days into his excavation, that he was uncovering a major building that dated back to before Mycenae.

The 1900 dig lasted nine weeks: it used up to 180 men to clear a two-acre site. In just two months, Evans established his reputation as an archaeologist and established Knossos itself as one of the most significant digs in the history of archaeology. The excavation, conservation, and reconstruction of Knossos were to occupy Evans for another thirty years and become his life's work. Initially, the work was largely funded by handsome donations from his father, Sir John Evans, as Evans found it very difficult to get sponsors for it; most of his countrymen were preoccupied with supporting the Boer War. Sir John responded generously to his son's telegrams telling of some spectacular new find by sending him money. I would not suggest that Evans consciously exaggerated or romanticized his discoveries in a way that would appeal to his father, but he certainly had an incentive to present his discoveries in a dramatic and powerful way. Evans' description of the throne produced a predictable response from his generous father – £500. When Sir John died and his son inherited his fortune, the financial constraints were removed and much of the later work was done thanks to Evans' own generosity.

'RECONSTITUTION': PERSUADING WITH CONCRETE?

The main work of excavation really focused on the first four years of the century. Much that followed was what Evans himself liked to call 'reconstitution', rebuilding, reconstructing and even redecorating whole rooms. Evans has been widely criticized for these reconstitutions, but it is important to understand why he thought the procedure necessary in the first place. He was faced with a serious conservation problem, as the excavated state of the Throne Room shows. The frescoes were obviously fragile and very vulnerable to weathering, in particular the loosened fragments of fresco that had slipped down onto the benches and floor. The throne was made of gypsum and would not stand up to exposure to the sky for long. In fact, the Throne Room *was* left open to the sky that first winter and it suffered some rain damage. The walls were intact to within half a metre of ceiling height and it was a fairly easy task to put a roof on top in 1901. Evans had some wooden columns made to fit into the original sockets in the balustrade separating the bath chamber from the main part of the Throne Room; some brick piers were added at one or two points to bear the load, then a timber frame and a flat roof.

It was an act of expediency and the exterior was jarring on the eye, but Evans liked the interior. A stouter, pitched tile roof was put on the Throne Room three years later, but it still did not look at all prehistoric, or even remotely sympathetic to the original architecture of the place. It was not until 1930 that Evans completed the reconstitution of the Throne Room by rebuilding, in masonry and reinforced concrete, the ceiling of the Throne Room and its antechamber, the light-well and chamber Evans presumed had been situated above the bath chamber and Throne Room. The final effect, with the stone staircase beside it that had been rebuilt in 1923, was aesthetically much more pleasing, as well as fulfilling the initial purpose of keeping the weather out of the Throne Room complex.

Over on the other side of the Central Court, in 1901, Evans found the partially collapsed remains of the Grand Staircase. The upper storeys had not been supported by solid masonry, brickwork, or stone columns; in the main they had been held up by horizontal baulks of timber braced by huge wooden posts. As the building collapsed, rubble falling from the upper storeys had filled the stairwell up, holding much of the masonry in position while the wooden columns and beams burned or rotted away. As Evans' men tunnelled into this extraordinary and completely unexpected feature, he was obliged to add beams and consolidate the walls with reinforced concrete, simply to make the structure safe. If he had not reconstructed the staircase, there would have been a real danger that the whole structure would collapse on the excavators. If we tend to underestimate how dangerous an archaeological dig can be, we should remember the tragic and untimely death of Professor Spyridon Marinatos, caused by a collapse accident on Thera in 1974. If Evans had not cautiously consolidated the structure of the many-storeyed Grand Staircase, the walls might well have collapsed and killed a dozen excavators. Clearly Evans was right to reconstruct it.

There are several such instances on the site, where safety and conservation demanded some restoration of the fabric. It also seems worth emphasizing that in many places the restoration was fundamentally correct. The Grand Staircase was definitely there in the bronze age and it took the general form which Evans constructed for us to see. The Throne Room, its bath chamber and antechamber must also have had something very close to the form that Evans has reconstructed. Similarly, we can be fairly sure that the outline of the Hall of the Double Axes was restored in a fairly authentic way; Evans' photographs show that the floor plan was very well preserved and one wall was preserved to a height of 4 metres. But a great deal of what we see in the Hall of the Double Axes was, even so, simply not there when Evans excavated it.

A more serious problem has been created by Evans' addition of elements which he thought were originally present, or at any rate felt were conformable with the function of the rooms: and this is where we may be led astray. In the Throne Room, for instance, fragments of fresco were found still attached to the walls and others were found slumped onto the benches. The photographs taken immediately after excavation in 1900 show just how incomplete those fragments were (e.g. Plate 4). The largest piece, which had slipped from the west wall, was a piece of red dado with white stripes: this ran along the top of a pictorial fresco as a kind of frieze. A recumbent griffin was depicted below it, facing north, now on display in Heraklion Museum.

There was very little evidence for believing that there were griffins on the north wall. To the right of the throne, as we look at it, there was a landscape with a luxuriant palm tree reaching to the top of the throne and more vegetation lower down, which might be undergrowth. There is a vigour and breadth to the brushwork on the original fresco fragments which are entirely missing in Gilliéron's etiolated 'reconstruction'. The feature which Gilliéron or Evans took to be the griffin's front paws could as easily be some more of the boldly brushed-in foliage which seems to have predominated in this fresco. Initially, Evans thought of the fresco as a riverbank scene and tentatively identified the 'griffin paws' as part of an eel: it was in February 1902 that the curving, frond-like brush strokes were first seen as griffin paws, and that very doubtful interpretation has stuck. One griffin, on the west wall, is certain, although Gilliéron's 1913 reconstruction shows it facing the wrong way. The remaining frescoes of griffins, added in 1930, may be striking and memorable but they were never part of the original design. This becomes crucially important when we realize that the wall paintings at Knossos were not mere decoration but were integral with the chamber's function (see Chapter 7, pp. 77–9, 'The Throne Sanctuary').

The fresco on the north wall was originally reported, by Evans himself, to show a landscape with a stream. On its banks were rushes and sedge-like plants with red flowers; in the background there were hills. The pleasant riverside scene was, Evans thought in 1900, 'suggested by the recurring Nile pieces of contemporary Egyptian art'. In fact the wavy lines were intended to suggest hills and mountains, but that detail of interpretation did not affect the reconstruction. How different the atmosphere of the Throne Room would be with the scene Evans initially described, as compared with the severe and formal griffin composition he asked Gilliéron to paint, is hard to visualize. Tourists and scholars alike seem to have accepted the griffins as part of the Throne Room's original décor.

Out in the antechamber, Evans found two short stone benches built against the north wall, just as in the Throne Room. Once again there was a gap between them. On the strength of these parallels, Evans had a wooden facsimile of the gypsum throne made and placed it in the gap between the benches, where it still stands today. In front of the wooden throne there is a large, beautifully made porphyry basin. It stands right in the middle of the antechamber as its focal point, and the throne seems to preside purposefully over it. But it was Evans who placed the bowl in its present position. He found it a few metres away in the passage to the north of the antechamber, and thought it would add interest to the chamber. Photographs of the antechamber taken immediately after the excavation in 1900 show it completely empty. A photograph taken a few weeks later, when the broken pottery on the floor of the Throne Room had been removed and the floors of both chambers swept clean, shows the stone basin introduced into the antechamber, albeit 1 metre south of its present, central position (Plate 4).

The furnishings of the antechamber may strike the tourist as evocative of ancient and royal ceremonial, but – apart from the stone benches – they are the fruit of Sir Arthur Evans' imagination. The gap between the stone benches may have housed a wooden table, cupboard or effigy rather than a seat, and the centre of the paved floor may have been completely empty. Evans has made suggestions in his reconstruction that in effect narrow off our responses to the chamber and our speculations about its possible original use.

It would be possible to go on listing examples of similarly picturesque but misleading additions, and give the impression that Evans went out of his way to mislead us. That was certainly not the case. It was rather that Evans developed a very sure sense of what Knossos was and what the cultural traits of its builders were; as a result, he literally built his interpretation of both the building and the culture into his reconstruction and restoration work.

If we want to make our own interpretation of the huge complex on the Kefala hill, Sir Arthur Evans has made it very difficult for us. He consolidated and extended the fabric of the building, added furnishings, added frescoes and in one extraordinary foray even added a large new staircase – all to persuade the visitor of his vision of the site's original royal splendour. In order to make our own interpretation, we need to be very aware which elements belong to the bronze age of the prehistoric Cretans, and which belong to the art nouveau and reinforced concrete age of Arthur Evans. We have to look beyond the persuasive alterations to the building's original outlines. Only then will we be able to explore afresh what its original purpose might have been.

PERSUADING WITH WORDS

Evans has created an additional problem for us in the way that he has given many of the chambers names that carry us along with his interpretation. Evans saw the building as a royal palace right from the start and seems never to have swerved from that overall interpretation. At first he thought it was a Mycenean palace, but later revised his view as he realized its great age: it was *pre*-Mycenean, he thought, and belonged to a highly original culture which he called 'Minoan' after King Minos. But there was still no doubt that the building was a royal palace: it simply became a Minoan palace in Evans' imagination.

Evans saw the East Wing as the 'Domestic Quarter' of the palace, the sector of the building where the Knossian royal family had their apartments. He decided, on the evidence of the miniature frescoes found in the Northern Sector, just west of the North Entrance Passage, that the sexes were segregated in the palace, and this was in line with what archaeologists on mainland Greece believed. He therefore assumed that the spacious 'Hall of the Double Axes' must have been the King's Hall. There was a connecting passage to a suite of smaller rooms to the south and Evans decided that these were the women's quarters. The principal of these rooms he called the Queen's Hall. Opening out of it was the Queen's Bathroom. In the same suite were carefully engineered lavatories, which suggested an air of refinement about this area. The area also had restricted access to provide seclusion.

Above all, the names he gave to the different elements of the suite are persuasive. The 'Court of the Distaffs' implies an association with feminine domesticity: it suggests women, or indeed high-born ladies, quietly spinning in a broad and sunlit courtyard. Yet the 'Court of the Distaffs' is nothing more than a dank light-well measuring 3.5 by 4 metres, scarcely a resort for queens and princesses.

The 'Room of the Plaster Couch', suggests a bedroom or withdrawing room where the ladies might recline elegantly on a chaise longue. In fact this room is a mere antechamber to the lavatory which opens out of it to the east. The 'couch' is only 1.3 metres long and 1.5 metres from the lavatory door: it was probably a stand for ewers of water used to flush the toilet. There is actually a hole in the floor that would have been in the antechamber, just outside the lavatory door, and we can imagine either the user of the lavatory or a servant pouring water into this hole to flush the toilet through the duct that passes under the floor: a distinctly less romantic image than Evans'. The Court of the Distaffs, the Room of the Plaster Couch, the Queen's Hall, the Queen's Bathroom – the names are beguilingly persuasive.

The persuasion was completed by Piet de Jong, who was first Evans' architect and then Curator of the Palace of Minos at Knossos. De Jong was a gifted draughtsman and he produced a series of artist's impressions of Evans' palace, showing how Evans visualized the different parts of the building when new. More persuasively than any archaeologically based discussion, the pictures evoke a highly cultured and refined civilization. His painting of the Queen's Hall or Megaron shows us elegant, aristocratic women sitting about in idle conversation in a bright hall decorated with frescoed rosettes and dolphins; sunlight floods in from the light-wells. Now it is difficult to see the chamber in any other way.

Whatever flights of imagination and whatever intellectual insights Arthur Evans had, he was fundamentally a man of his time. What he pieced together in his mind as Minoan Knossos was to a significant extent an idealization of late Victorian or Edwardian London. 'Broad Knossos' was a teeming metropolis of, according to Evans' estimate, some 80,000 people: 100,000 if the harbour town was included as well. This flourishing capital was the dynamo behind the Golden Age of Minoan Crete. From it a great king ruled not only a prosperous island but a whole empire of overseas colonies, with the aid of a powerful navy. The 'Pax Minoica' visualized was not unlike the 'Pax Britannica' of the late Victorian period.

The city contained the king's palace, a fairly dense aggregation of houses clustered round it and then, further out, less densely populated suburbs. Here and there were to be seen the great houses of princes, for so, presumably, we must interpret buildings such as the 'Royal Villa' and the 'Little Palace'. Beyond the suburbs was the open countryside, the fertile farmland that produced the food supply for palace and city: dotted about in it were the villas of the landed gentry.

It is not clear to what extent Evans was conscious of the parallels between his Minoan civilization and Edwardian England, but part of the excitement of his discoveries lay in the surprising familiarity of many of the things he was unearthing. A large part of the appeal of the Minoan civilization was, in the early years of this century, and is still today, rooted in its apparent modernity. Here was a powerful, well-organized state benevolently ordering the lives of a refined, artistic, pleasure-loving and peace-loving people. It chimed in harmoniously with the idea that while Britannia ruled the waves civilization would develop in a secure peace. It also chimed in well with the naughty nineties and the cult of 'art for art's sake'. And it was no accident that some of the fresco reconstructions have a hint of art nouveau about them. There were intensely exotic elements, it is true – Edwardian ladies did not go about with their breasts exposed, as bronze age Knossian women did – but there is a very real sense in which Sir Arthur Evans' Knossos was a mirror held up to Edwardian London.

But Edward VII was a far cry from the Minos of ancient Greek legend, and Evans was as keen to link his finds to legend as Schliemann had been when excavating Troy and Mycenae. How then do we view Knossos? Do we begin with Arthur Evans' England and look back over three thousand years; or do we begin with the garbled legends of the ancient Greeks and look back at Minoan Knossos from a distance of perhaps six hundred years? Perhaps it is wiser to approach the Knossos of the bronze age more cautiously, from the far side, and ask how it was that such a capacity for building 'palaces' and such a range of accomplishments in technology and the arts came about.

4

The neolithic and pre-palace periods at Knossos

Suppose one stood in the middle of a field and said 'I have an open sesame', the ground will open, a Palace will appear.

Arthur Evans, Wootton Lecture, 1906

DEVELOPMENT OF THE NEOLITHIC SETTLEMENT

Neither the Labyrinth nor the Minoan civilization discovered by Sir Arthur Evans at Knossos sprang into being fully formed, but developed over a long period. The highest point of the civilization seems to have been reached around the year 1500 BC, shortly before its spectacular collapse. The first 'palaces', as far as we can tell, were built around 1900 BC. But what led up to the building of the 'palaces'? Where did the idea for them come from? Were they perhaps an exotic implant from Anatolia or the Near East? These are questions that need to be answered if we are to arrive at an understanding of their function.

Unfortunately, much of the evidence for what happened immediately before the 'palaces' were built was destroyed as their foundations were laid. At Knossos, the site was cleared and levelled ready for the first 'palace', and this process removed the early bronze age levels. Even so, it is still possible to piece together in general terms how the civilization may have evolved. Its gestation seems to have been a long and generally gradual one.

The Kefala hill where Evans' reconstituted Palace of Minos now stands was inhabited continuously for over four thousand years before the bronze age building was raised. It was a favoured site; standing beside the confluence of the Vlychia stream and the Kairatos river, it was one of the best-watered spots on Crete – and that counted for a great deal in the prehistoric period. The mean annual rainfall in the area is only 475 millimetres and of that about 80 per cent falls in the winter half of the year, October to March. Problems arose in the summer, when only 20 per cent of the rain falls and much of that is lost by evaporation. The Kairatos river, under the original, natural conditions, did not dry up in summer.

When people first settled on the hill, the landscape was covered with an open woodland of scattered pistachio, juniper, oak, and wild olive trees. Little by little the woodland was cleared round the settlement until, by the time of the first 'palace', the nearest patches of forest would have been some distance away on the higher ground, but timber was still more plentiful and accessible than it is today.

The first settlement, a simple, quarter-hectare (half-acre) encampment of mud-brick dwellings housing perhaps a hundred people, was built in 6100 BC. It stood on a low natural rise just to the north-west of the point where the two streams join (Figure 26). Curiously, no other village is known to have existed on Crete at this early date. The people of this first village seem to have had no knowledge of pottery, but they grew a variety of crops such as bread-wheat and six-row barley, and raised cattle, pigs, sheep, and goats, so they represent the very beginning of the neolithic period on Crete. The pottery, a dark burnished ware, appeared around 5600 BC. Over the thousand-year period that followed, the rectangular houses deteriorated, fell down and were replaced: the settlement gradually expanded. By the end of the early neolithic, it already covered the whole site of the palace, but it does not appear to have spread much further. There were a few scattered, outlying houses.

The site on the Kefala hill must have been thought a good one, since it was used over and over again. By 4500 BC, the new stone age village had expanded to ten times its original area: it now covered about 2 hectares (5 acres) and close to a thousand people lived there.

In 1900 Evans uncovered the West Wing of the 'Palace of Minos'. On each side of it, to east and west, he identified large courtyards. When he, or rather his assistant Duncan Mackenzie, excavated the West Court, he found under the pavement the remains of still older floor levels of the bronze age building: they formed a layer 5 metres thick. Below that debris, there were a further 6 metres of neolithic remains before the solid bedrock was reached. The modern land surface that Evans and Kalokairinos dug into was actually 11 metres higher than the natural land surface on the Kefala hill. The original site was a low mound and it had been raised and accentuated by the added debris of one building level after another. Knossos is really very like the *tells* of the Near East or the *hüyüks* of Anatolia. The neolithic layers at Knossos are among the deepest in Europe, with evidence of as many as ten distinct successive settlements within that period.

By the fourth millennium BC, Knossos was outgrowing village status, and we might almost begin to think of it as a town, except that we have very little evidence for its function: normally we would expect town-dwellers to go in for specialized activities. There is a hint of the beginnings of a textile industry in the sudden increase in the numbers of spindle whorls and loom weights and so, possibly, professional spinners and weavers. But, whatever went on there, Knossos had become, by the late neolithic, one of the largest and most important settlements in the Eastern Mediterranean region.

In 3000 BC, major economic changes were under way that would change the face of the Aegean in many unforeseen ways, changes that would set off chain reactions with major social, political, and religious side effects. Three major trade goods made their appearance around 3000 BC. They were not the first by any means; the first settlers at Knossos three thousand years before were using sharp, black obsidian blades imported from the island of Melos. But the trade in grapes, olives and metals developing in 3000 BC had more profound repercussions.

We can visualize some of the effects that the introduction of the grape might have had. The discovery of fermentation quickly led to the deliberate and large-scale manufacture of wine. Grapevines were planted on previously unused steep slopes and this would have made necessary the establishment of market centres for the grape growers to exchange their produce with that of the traditional farmers on the lower ground. The market centres would have developed a social function too, becoming places where people might sit around chatting and eating together, exchanging news, singing and dancing. We can be sure that quantities of wine were drunk on these occasions; goblets were manufactured for the purpose. Drinking led to intoxication and this was given a religious or mystical dimension because of the surreal and often extraordinary new images and perceptions that it permitted. The religious life became richer and assumed a higher profile.

One stimulus – the introduction of the grape – could thus have many results. Not least, the demand for the new product created new webs of economic and political relationships across the Aegean Sea. From about 3000 BC there was an onrush of developing trade, exchanges of ideas, and increasing wealth. Societies throughout the Aegean became more elaborate, more subtly stratified, more organized. Civilization developed apace, culminating in the Minoan and Mycenean 'palace' societies, which peaked in about 1500 BC.

Some of the rapid changes occurred because there was pressure for change from population growth. Just as Knossos itself grew from a mere 100 people in 6000 BC to 1,000 in 4500 BC, and then went on growing to an estimated 40,000 in 1500 BC, so too did the rest of the Aegean region, albeit on a more modest scale. In the neolithic period, the islands of the Cyclades were conspicuous in taking the cultural lead, but they were small islands that did not offer the same scope for development that Crete offered.

THE 'PRE-PALACE' BRONZE AGE

Homer saw ancient Crete as an island favoured like no other, and so it must have seemed a thousand years before Homer, as the Minoan culture evolved in all its exotic splendour among the cypress and olive groves. Crete was far and away the largest island in the Aegean region, 250 kilometres long from east to west, and because of its size and diverse topography it offered a rich

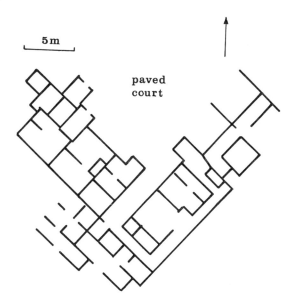

paved
court

Figure 5 The House on the
Hill, Vasiliki

variety of environments and resources. With its range of sharply contrasting
habitats, it is not surprising that cultural developments on Crete overtook
those on the much smaller islands of the Cyclades. More resources were
available for manufacturing, consumption, and trade, and more people were
available for work of every kind, from agricultural work to administration,
from crafts to military service.

Nevertheless, the development of the spectacular 'palace culture' on Crete
was not a sudden eruption. The stratigraphy Evans and Mackenzie uncovered
at Knossos may have implied that it was, with the neolithic layers giving way
abruptly to ruins of the final version of the bronze age 'palace', but we know
that the layers representing the transitional phases were cleared away before
the first palace was built, in about 1900 BC. During the thousand years leading
up to this, the culture emanating from the Cyclades dominated the Aegean
Sea, but on Crete a gradual evolution towards the 'palace culture' was under
way.

The evidence for this is missing on the Kefala hill, but we can find it
elsewhere. In eastern Crete there is a narrow neck of land, the Isthmus of
Ierapetra: just 13 kilometres wide, it was a natural focus for a prehistoric trade
route connecting the south and north coasts of Crete. The main valley route
across it is dominated by a small, ship-like hill – Vasiliki. The House on the
Hill at Vasiliki perfectly represents the culture of 'pre-palace' Crete and shows
us where the very large buildings of the later bronze age came from, in
architectural terms at least. The House on the Hill consisted of a large paved
court with suites of rectangular rooms fronting it on two sides. It was
basically L-shaped and seems to have been designed from the courtyard

outwards; in this respect it is very similar to the plans of the later labyrinths, but only half-finished. The Vasiliki building was oriented with its corners pointing north, south, east and west; the later labyrinths were oriented with their sides facing the cardinal compass points. The Vasiliki building was built mainly of mud-brick, with ceilings of clay-plastered reeds; the later 'palaces' had upper storeys of mud-brick, but their ground floors at least were built of stone.

There are differences, certainly, but it is possible to see in Vasiliki a forerunner of the 'palaces' or labyrinths. This important building was occupied between 2600 and 2200 BC; it was burnt and abandoned about 300 years before the first 'palace' was built at Knossos. The date when Vasiliki was built may be significant, since it was from 2600 BC onwards that the evolution of Cretan culture was more rapid. It may be that new ideas for structuring the economy filtered in from abroad or that foreign migrants, perhaps from Anatolia, came to Crete at this time and precipitated sudden changes. But we do not need to suppose that there were any colonists or invaders; the idea of 'new people' to explain new ideas is itself old and suspect. A newer view is that a society may evolve gradually for a certain period, but when any one of its sub-systems is taken across a threshold, stresses are created, sending a whole sequence of changes rapidly through the whole society, like a chain reaction. Sudden changes can thus be produced from within. If this sounds abstract and theoretical, we have only to think of the radical and far-reaching changes that spread through Russian society in 1917 and the decade following.

Given the evidence of the building at Vasiliki as a missing link between the native neolithic culture and the Minoan 'palace culture', there seems to be no reason to suppose that the labyrinths, the Knossos Labyrinth included, were anything but the result of native cultural development. I shall show later (Chapter 8) that the architecture of the Labyrinths does in fact borrow some significant features from buildings overseas, but that does not in any way damage the assertion that the 'palaces' or labyrinths were native Cretan buildings. The prehistoric Cretans were travellers, seafarers and traders; from the earliest layers at Knossos, there is evidence of contact with other parts of the Aegean region. It would have been remarkable if the Cretans had travelled and traded without gathering some ideas from abroad.

From 2600 BC, when the House on the Hill was built, a tentative half-palace, the preparations were under way. The Cretans moved with increasing momentum from a sub-neolithic culture into the bronze age. They began to manufacture coloured pottery, engraved seals, metal objects and magnificent stone vases. At they reached the end of the pre-palace phase, around 2000 BC, the Cretans had highly developed skills in a wide range of craft industries. They were engraving on ivory and steatite seals, making carved and inlaid stone vases and perfecting granulation and filigree techniques in gold. More significantly, towards the year 2000 BC, the Cretans of the pre-palace bronze age raised substantial buildings with many rooms on the sites of the labyrinths that were to come.

5
The bronze age palace:
Sir Arthur Evans' interpretation

We know now that the old traditions were true. We have before our eyes a wondrous spectacle – the resurgence, namely, of a civilization twice as old as that of Hellas. It is true that on the old Palace site what we see are only the ruins of ruins, but the whole is still inspired with Minos's spirit of order and organization, and the free and natural art of the great architect Daedalos.

Evans, speech on receiving honorary citizenship of
Heraklion, 1935.

THE WEST WING

We left the story of Sir Arthur Evans' 1900 excavation at one of its climactic moments, the discovery of the Throne Room and its antechamber. It was an important moment because it came towards the end of the first phase of the dig, when virtually the whole of the West Wing was open to the sky, and because it gave Evans a peg on which to hang his interpretation of the building as a whole, an interpretation which has prevailed right down to the present day.

During the years leading up to the Knossos excavation, a general assumption had developed that the Kefala hill site would yield the remains of a bronze age palace. Minos Kalokairinos in 1878–9 thought he had uncovered parts of a palace complex; Schliemann believed so too, expecting (in 1886) that the excavated building would turn out to be 'a vast edifice similar to the prehistoric palace of Tiryns and apparently of the same age'. So, as Evans opened the site and followed the outline of the maze of chambers in the West Wing, he was predisposed to find evidence of palatial accommodation. It was on 13 April 1900 that Evans' workmen started uncovering the north wall of the Throne Room with its palm fresco fragments and the throne itself.

Harriet Boyd, the American pioneer archaeologist who would later excavate the Minoan town of Gournia, was at Knossos when the Throne Room was opened up. She described in her diary how Evans straight away

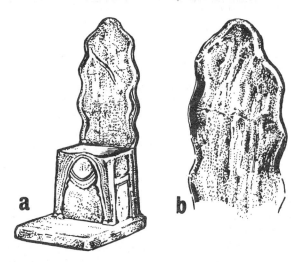

Figure 6 Symbolism in the gypsum throne. a – the gypsum throne in the Throne
Sanctuary, b – the mountain summit in the picture of a peak sanctuary shown on the
Zakro rhyton (see Figure 37 for the larger design)

named the stone seat 'the Throne of Ariadne'. The throne's broad moulded
seat, Evans explained, was more likely designed for a woman's hips than a
man's. But the association of the throne with Ariadne did not lead Evans
anywhere, evocative though it was. If the building was to be a bronze age
palace and the palace of King Minos at that, there had to be an audience
chamber for the king. Evans sometimes referred to the Throne Room as 'King
Minos' Council Chamber' to get round this problem. Even so, that initial
inspiration witnessed by Miss Boyd, that the throne was Ariadne's, persisted.
In 1906 Evans gave a talk about the Knossos excavations. He called it 'Magic
of the Spade' and his notes for it include the telling passage, 'The old tales
have come true – Minos – Ariadne – Theseus – The Tribute Children – the
Minotaur itself'; he also referred to the stone seat as 'Ariadne's throne' and
the sunken area opposite as 'Ariadne's bath'. Evans gave different impressions
about the throne on different occasions. In 1922 he sailed to Crete with some
neighbours from Oxford, the ffennells of Wytham Abbey, and gave them a
guided tour of Knossos. Hazel ffennell, then aged 17, was unimpressed but
one or two of her diary comments, unhindered by excessive reverence for
tradition or scholarship, are significant. 'Knossos, not quite a heap of stones
as usual, but on the verge thereof . . . . There are many stone staircases leading
into different chambers, none of which can really be called palatial . . . and a
small throne of King Minos.'

Hazel ffennell may have been bored by Knossos or by Evans, who was
suffering badly from seasickness and certainly not at his most inspiring on
this visit, but she does seem to have been told that the seat was the throne of

King Minos. The accuracy of the name was perhaps unimportant to Evans. What seems to have mattered most to Evans was that the names evoked the right response in the visitor, that he or she should feel the place to be a great palace and connected with glittering and exotic names from Greek myth.

Most of the West Wing must in reality have been a disappointment to Evans, just as it was to Hazel ffennell. None of the chambers in the West Wing impresses us as palatial in scale. Most make more sense as passages and storage or service rooms of some kind. Those who subscribe to the interpretation of Knossos as a palace see the surviving remains to the West Wing as an understorey. The truly palatial apartments, Evans and his supporters argue, were up on the first floor. Certainly the sort of palace high life Evans envisaged, the court life surrounding the great king of a powerful sea-empire, would have needed supporting with provisions on a very large scale. The so-called West Magazines, the corridor-like store-rooms that fill the western half of the West Wing , make a lot of sense interpreted as larders for a great palace. They nevertheless gave only below-stairs evidence of palatial culture.

The Throne Room was a welcome discovery in that it supplied a direct and positive proof of kingship, a perfectly preserved royal throne. Yet Evans nursed nagging doubts about the function of this chamber. He had particular problems with the interpretation of the rectangular sunken area approached by six steps (Figure 14). First he thought it was a fish tank, and his second idea, that it was a bathroom, was equally incongruous. Evans came to regard the sunken area as a lustral basin, an area specifically reserved for ritual cleansing: after purification in the half-enclosed chamber, the king (or princess?) emerged to perform whatever ceremonies took place in the Throne Room proper. The ritual use of the bathroom for ceremonial purification was a way out, but it still left Evans with a very peculiar Throne Room.

Approached by way of a deep antechamber depressed slightly below the level of the Central Court, windowless and fairly low-ceilinged, the Throne Room has a dismal, cheerless, and claustrophobic atmosphere. It seems scarcely large enough to have been a throne room in any recognizable sense. If we exclude the sunken lustral area and its steps, it measures only 6 by 4 metres, the size of an average European living room. It is difficult to visualize the great king of a city-state, let along the high king who wielded power over much of the Aegean, being content with a throne room of that size. The benches along the walls may betoken a gathering presided over by a principal figure who sat on the throne, but it would have been a small cabal only who gathered in that small chamber. Allowing a half-metre of bench space to each person, there would have been seating for only eighteen people.

Evans was worried by the Throne Room and in particular by its *en suite* bathroom. In later years, he came to think of them as ritual and religious in function rather than secular, although he would not let go of the royal association. The lack of truly palatial rooms in the West Wing as a whole was

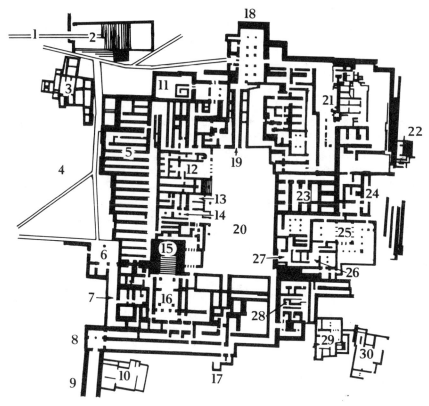

Figure 7 Evans' Palace of Minos: ground plan. 1 – Royal Road, 2 – Theatral Area,
3 – North-West Treasure House, 4 – West Court, 5 – West Magazines, 6 – West
Porch, 7 – Corridor of the Procession, 8 – South-West Porch, 9 – Stepped Portico,
10 – South House, 11 – Initiatory Area and lustral basin, 12 – Room of the Throne,
13 – Temple Repositories, 14 – East and West Pillar Crypts, 15 – Staircase to Piano
Nobile, 16 – South Propylaeum, 17 – South Porch, 18 – North Pillar Hall, or
Custom House, 19 – North Entrance Passage, 20 – Central Court, 21 – North-East
Magazines, 22 – East Bastion, 23 – Royal Magazines, 24 – Workshops, 25 – Hall of
the Double-Axes, 26 – Queen's Megaron, 27 – Queen's Toilet, 28 – Shrine of the
Double-Axes, 29 – House of the Chancel Screen, 30 – South-East House

a problem to Evans. Immediately to the south of the Throne Room's
antechamber he found the remains of the lowest four steps of a 5 metre wide
stone staircase leading westwards out of the Central Court. By 1923 this
Royal Staircase had been inflated to thirty steps, twelve leading up to the first
floor, where there was a porticoed landing, and then a further eighteen steps
leading up to a supposed second floor. Evans had eagerly built it up into a
major feature connecting the Central Court with the missing upper floors.

Since the first floor was missing, Evans was able to say what he liked about it. It is likely that there were further floors above and that in the final destruction of the building, around the year 1380 BC or thereafter, they disintegrated and fell in. Evans visualized, from the rain of fragments that had cascaded down from the upper floors, that the first floor had consisted of spacious royal apartments. A palace on the scale of Knossos must have had halls and reception rooms where ambassadors and distinguished foreign visitors might be received in an appropriately formal and impressive way. Among other chambers, there were a Sanctuary Hall, a Tricolumnar Hall, a Loggia and a Great Hall. The Great Hall, which stood above store-rooms 6, 7, 8, 9, and 10, would have been some 15 by 13 metres, altogether more palatial in scale than the claustrophobic Throne Room. It may even have had windows.

In the southern part of the West Wing, Evans found a poorly preserved area about 14 metres square, where the Minoan building had been wrecked by the insertion of a later Greek temple. Evans seized his opportunity. He dismantled the remains of the temple, which he thought was a Temple of Rhea, and used the stone to construct an impressive staircase from south to north up to the first floor. The twelve steps, 6.5 metres wide, make an impressive and suggestive prelude to the ceremonial apartments which we are to imagine occupied the first and second floors. South of this new staircase was a rectangular hall with projecting piers and columns. This was probably an important chamber in its own right in the bronze age (see Chapter 7, pp. 83–5, 'The Cupbearer Sanctuary'), but Evans made it into a majestic foyer to his new staircase.

This 'South Propylaeum' is one of the most unfortunate of Evans' reconstitutions. What he created is entirely different in orientation and intention from the original Minoan architecture. The excavation photographs show very clearly that there were no stairs whatsoever on the site of the present staircase, so no stairs should have been built. The demolition of what is now considered to have been a megaron-type hall of the late, possibly Mycenean, stage of the building's use was in itself an unnecessary piece of destruction. Perhaps the worst aspect of the remodelling, though, is the entirely misleading suggestion that is made to the mind of the visitor: the suggestion that here was a grand ceremonial entrance to an upper floor of the palace where, if only time and destiny had preserved them, magnificent and spacious state apartments would await us.

Evans tried hard to show that above the unpromising ground floor cellarage of the West Wing there might have been whole suites of chambers that were truly palatial in scale. Significantly, he was relieved to discover that there was more to the palace than just the West Wing. When the excavation of the West Wing was completed, it was clear that the building extended along the north side of the Central Court. Evans was delighted when he found the building continuing along the eastern side as well and that the East Wing contained some chambers that he could interpret as royal apartments.

THE EAST WING ROYAL APARTMENTS

The Grand Staircase, opening from the Central Court and connecting the several storeys of the East Wing, was just the sort of architectural evidence Evans was looking for to confirm his palace interpretation. It was in May 1901 that a team of workmen under Duncan Mackenzie's supervision tunnelled into the Grand Staircase rubble. It was full of debris that had fallen from upper floors. Here, as we saw in Chapter 3, Evans' reconstruction was fully justified. The architecture, in outline and in detail, was carefully reconstructed to give a good impression of the original; the work was in any case essential to prevent the whole structure collapsing. The situation was very different from that in the South Propylaeum area, where the staircase was conjured out of nothing.

Leading away from the landings of the Grand Staircase were the crumbled remains of suites of chambers on several floors. Half-way down the stairwell from the level of the Central Court, Evans found the remains of a suite which he called the Upper Hall of the Double Axes: at the bottom he found the remains of the Hall of the Double Axes itself. This is a good example of Evans' ear for a good, memorable name. It evokes an atmosphere of martial power wielded by a great king, of sinister symbols, of the power of life and death over subjects, of capricious and tyrannical sentences, of executions. But where did the phrase, with all its resonances, come from? Evans noticed during the excavation of the light-well at the western end of the suite that many of the blocks of stone carried masons' marks: the sign of the double-axe. In fact there are double-axe marks incised on the west wall of the light-well and trident marks on the south wall. They may have been put on in the stone-mason's yard simply to indicate to the builders where the blocks were to go. There is no more to the name than that.

Evans was quick to identify these rooms as palatial in scale; he had, after all, found large numbers of small rooms on the site but had not until now found one room that could be convincingly described as palatial. Here in the East Wing were chambers 'evidently designed for receptions'. The Hall of the Double Axes is in fact about twice the size of the Throne Room, rather small by comparison with Mycenean megarons on the Greek mainland, even though the mainland palaces were themselves smaller than the Palace of Minos at Knossos. So, although we may find the Hall of the Double Axes refreshingly spacious after the confined service passages and storage rooms of the West Wing, it is a smaller room than the main room of a much smaller mainland palace. The Hall appears larger because of the rows of doorways, reconstructed by Evans without their doors, bounding it – or rather failing to bound it – on three sides. The room opens out westwards into an inner room of equal size and to the south and east onto a broad L-shaped colonnade; there is an illusion of space (Figure 23).

In the inner hall, which he called the Audience Chamber, Evans found a cast of another throne. This time it had evidently been enclosed under a wooden canopy supported by wooden pillars. In the final disaster, fire reduced the gypsum coating on the wall above the throne to a calcined rubble which fell onto the canopy and solidified there: it preserved the shape of the feature long after the wood itself had disintegrated. The throne was, of course, exactly what Evans must have hoped for: it confirmed the royal function of the building. He reasoned that there must have been a similar throne in the similar-sized hall through the row of double doors to the east, and had another wooden facsimile of the gypsum throne made to furnish the room and give it a focus (Plate 10).

But was the Hall of the Double Axes a throne room in the generally accepted sense? Was it a *double* throne room, as Evans suggested? Although the Hall is significantly larger than the Throne Room he found in the West Wing, it seems very oddly located. We come upon it at the foot of the Grand Staircase, but it does not form the climax of a suite of reception rooms. To the east and south-east there is a small L-shaped courtyard: to the south lies a suite of small rooms which Evans identified as the Queen's apartments; to the north was a sequence of workshops and storage rooms. So, even though Evans now proposed *three* throne rooms instead of one, the problem was still not resolved.

There is also the Hall of the Double Axes' puzzling location, buried over 8 metres below the level of the Central Court. The Kefala hill slopes away sharply to the east of the Central Court, so that we walk from the court into the Grand Staircase a metre or so above the East Wing's second floor level. No windows can admit light into the ground floor or first floor rooms from the west, because those walls abut onto the core of the hill. Chambers and corridors stretch away 50 metres or more to north and south of the Hall of the Double Axes, so no daylight can ever have penetrated from those directions either. Evans proposed that the Hall was lit by borrowed light from the small rectangular light-well to the west and the larger L-shaped courtyard to the east. On the face of it, there is no reason why the eastern courtyard should not have been open on its eastern and southern sides to admit direct sunlight, but it seems that it was not. The courtyard was bounded both to south and east by a substantial wall. The foundations and lower courses of masonry were excavated and the 1-metre thickness of the wall implies that it may have risen in stone courses to a height of 4 metres or more; it may in addition have carried a lighter mud-brick wall to a greater height still.

This wall (Plates 12, 15) seems to have formed part of the eastern boundary wall of the palace; the four strongly buttressed walls to the east were designed to revet the steeply sloped hillside and make the palace wall foundations secure. This being so, security would have demanded that the light-well wall should be high enough to exclude intruders, thieves, and assassins. It would also have been desirable to build the wall high enough to give the rooms shelter from the force of the *Notia*, the strong south-easterly that would otherwise have sent wind and dust into the chambers. On the West Front of the palace it seems there were no windows at all on the ground floor, apparently for security reasons. Given the ceiling height of about 3 metres in the West Wing, it seems unlikely that the lowest window sill at first-floor level would have been less than 4 metres above the level of the West Court. If that was the height of wall that the Knossian rulers required to make their building safe, we can reasonably assume that the boundary wall on the East Front would also have been at least 4 metres high. It may, of course, have risen much higher.

Relatively little light would have found its way into the Hall of the Double Axes. The remains of the Grand Staircase prove that there were at least two storeys above the Hall; the building was perhaps as many as five storeys high. The smaller light-well would originally have been as much as 20 metres deep, if the upper floors were all as lofty (4 metres) as the Hall of the Double Axes. Less than 3 metres wide from east to west, the rectangular light-well would have admitted only the smallest amount of light. If the Hall of the Double Axes seems a rather gloomy place today, it would have been gloomier still with the rest of the East Wing towering round and over it, sealing out the daylight. It would have been a dismal, twilit place, buried away deep in the basement of the Labyrinth (Figure 8).

Another peculiarity of the Hall of the Double Axes, and one that makes it seem less suitable as an audience chamber for a powerful high king, is its location next to four workshops. Only a narrow corridor separates the Hall from a lapidary's or sculptor's workshop and the so-called School Room, whose benches may have been designed for the preparation of clay tablets, amulets, pottery or some other craft work. It may have been in these

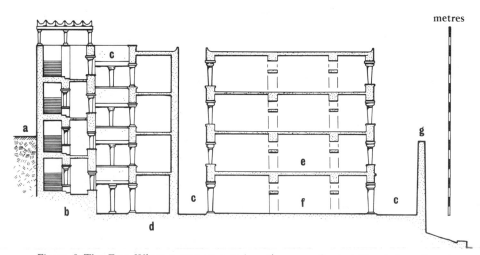

Figure 8 The East Wing: a reconstructed section. a – Central Court, b – Grand Staircase, c – light-well, d – staircase landings, e – Upper Double-Axe Sanctuary, f – Lower Double-Axe Sanctuary, g – high boundary wall

workshops that some of the large range of religious votive gifts were manufactured. Noise from the workshops would have been audible in the Hall of the Double Axes, hardly conducive to the sort of ceremonial receptions Evans had in mind. For visiting strangers passing down flight after flight of steps into this subterranean world, it must have been something like Wagner's Descent into Nibelheim.

As we pass south, by way of a little dog-leg passage, into the Queen's Hall, we encounter even more problems. Evans liked to see this area as a suite reserved for the Queen: set apart from the King's Apartments, more secluded and smaller in scale, it seemed to him quite natural to interpret the rooms in this way. But as we saw in Chapter 3 the darkness and extreme seclusion of this area made it more prison-like that palatial. It is hard to visualize any queen willingly submitting, let alone choosing, to live in apartments as oppressive as these.

The principal room is not large, only 4.5 by 6 metres. To the south is a well $1\frac{1}{2}$ metres wide. To the east, beyond a sheltering colonnade, is a larger well, but still enclosed by high walls. Many of the so-called light-wells and courts are really little more than chimneys, and when the building was its full, original height they must have functioned as ventilation shafts rather than light-wells; very little light indeed would have penetrated to the bottom of the Queen's south light-well.

The east wall of the eastern light-well was apparently added later. So the Queen's Hall began with relatively poor lighting from the east, and then it was sealed off: whether deliberately to make it darker, or more private, or more secure, or for some obscure ritual reason, it is impossible to tell. Interestingly, the Hall of the Double Axes was also made less accessible later on; the west-east corridor that provided access originally led to a door in the East Front, but this was sealed off when a staircase was added to provide access from the east directly up to the first floor. What was going on in this part of the Labyrinth is hard to imagine, but we have to visualize these suites of rooms becoming progressively more cut off from the outside world. We might speculate that, as the political power of Minos or one of his successors was challenged by rival kings, the palace had to be made more secure. Perhaps the dynastic rulers became obsessed with the prospect of assassination and their lives turned inward into the palace interior. And then again the whole set of assumptions based on the precept that the building was a royal palace may be wrong.

ARCHITECTURE, FRESCO AND THE STATUS OF WOMEN

Whatever reservations we may be developing, Sir Arthur Evans' interpretation of the Labyrinth as a palace has held the day for almost a century. It must be expected that an alternative view, such as the one that this book develops, will meet a large measure of resistance from such a well-entrenched tradition. The official guide of 1981 calls itself *A Complete Guide to the Palace of Minos*: *The Palace of Minos at Knossos* is the title Evans chose for the four-volume account of his excavations. The recent plan of the building undertaken by Sinclair Hood and William Taylor (1981) carries the same title. Many have followed Evans' interpretations or implicit interpretations of the various sectors of the building. Professor James Walter Graham's interpretation, first expressed in the 1960s and subsequently revised, agrees closely with Evans' in broad principle and often in detail. He refers to the central zone of the East Wing as the 'residence of the royal family'. Like Evans, Graham believes that the main state reception rooms lay on the first floor of the West Wing; he therefore emphasizes that the rooms buried away in the centre of the East Wing are likely to have been private apartments.

Here and there, Professor Graham's cautious and scholarly eye spots inconsistencies in Evans' view of the building and he tries to bring his interpretation into line with what was later learned about the other palaces, at Phaistos and Mallia. He shrinks from the picturesqueness of some of Evans' names and substitutes more neutral names. He prefers to call the Hall of the Double Axes 'The Men's Hall'. It is clear, in spite of such changes, that Graham believes implicitly in the functions attributed to the chambers by Evans.

There are two particular contributions which Professor Graham has made to our understanding of the Knossos Labyrinth; one relates to the bull games (see Chapter 10) and the other is the very useful comparisons he draws between Knossos and the other Cretan 'palaces'. We can take the King's and Queen's Apartments in the East Wing as an instructive example. These suites were built in a deep cutting sliced almost 9 metres down into the eastern side of the Knossos tell, with the result that people entered the East Wing, by way of the Grand Staircase, about half-way up it; when you stand in the Central Court, two storeys of the so-called royal apartments are below you and originally two storeys or maybe three were above you. The *descent* into the Hall of the Double Axes turns out not to be an accident of the building's evolution or a quirk of the site's topography. It was created.

At Phaistos, the comparable suite of rooms is similarly located well away from the more public areas and on a terrace excavated out of the northern slope of the hill. As at Knossos, the approach to it was by way of a long staircase descending from a court: in this case not from the Central Court but from a smaller courtyard called the Peristyle Court. At the foot of the stairs, a door opens into a large room similar in concept to the Hall of the Double Axes: there is a light-well, a colonnaded outer hall and then a more enclosed inner hall with two pier-and-door partitions.

From the inner hall (not the outer, as at Knossos), a dog-leg passage leads to a suite of smaller chambers which includes a sunken lustral basin. As in the original design at Knossos, both the 'Women's Hall' and the 'Men's Hall' seem to have had access to a verandah and a shared terrace. There are some differences – the north aspect, the access from a minor courtyard, an L-shaped staircase, and an additional room with a central light-well beyond the access corridor – but the conceptual parallels are very striking. The design of the East Wing at Knossos should certainly be seen as purposeful and deliberate, in view of the similarities with Phaistos.

The suite in the East Wing at Phaistos opens out onto a natural rock terrace, which Graham believes was for picturesque effect, a piece of prehistoric landscape gardening. He visualizes an attractive flower garden along the top of the steep slope, with a superb view across the valley. But there is a problem. This second royal suite exhibits the same sort of combinations of large and small chambers, pier-and-door partitions, steps and colonnades, though on a smaller scale. The explanation floated at Knossos by Evans sinks at Phaistos, because there can have been no need for two suites of royal apartments, close together in the same palace.

There is an additional problem with the distinction, made by both Evans and Graham, between the accommodation for men and women in these alleged royal apartments. The relatively small rooms allocated by both men to Cretan princesses implies that women were regarded as less important than men in Minoan society. The privacy and seclusion of the rooms implies that Minoan ladies were retiring and self-effacing. The arrangement and design of the rooms – and the function attributed by Evans and Graham – seem to show, in Graham's words, 'a nice respect for the privacy of the fair sex'.

The problem here is that both men were mistakenly assuming that modern sexual stereotypes prevailed in the Cretan bronze age. They assumed that, given a parallel situation, the ladies of Cretan high society would have withdrawn discreetly at the end of dinner, leaving the gentlemen to their port. In fact, the archaeological evidence indicates the contrary. Women are shown dressed with spectacular boldness, exposing their breasts. Some of the Miniature Frescoes do show, as Evans pointed out, some segregation of the sexes, but that may have been only an artistic convention, an easy way of conveying that both men and women were present at a ceremony. Given the artistic convention of painting men and women in different colours – the men are Indian red and the women white – it would certainly have been much easier to indicate men and women in separate groups or blocks rather than to have them all mixed together.

In a small room to the north-west of the Central Court, where Evans found this collection of fresco fragments, he unearthed over a score of pieces that belong to what he called the Grandstand Fresco. This has been tentatively reconstructed and it tells us some very important things about Minoan attitudes towards the sexes. The restored fresco shows a crowd of people in the usual stylized way. There are large continuous areas of red to indicate men, with the faces in profile sketched on in black. There are also elongated patches of white with identical facial profiles that are intended to represent women. They are all looking to left or right as if watching tennis.

In the middle of the large mixed crowd is a representation of a Triple Shrine surmounted by horns of consecration, a favoured symbol in Minoan religious ritual (Figure 18). On each side of the shrine sit five ladies and they are painted in far greater detail; they lounge in their opulent dresses and seem to be sunk in relaxed and animated conversation, heedless of whatever spectacle is before them (Figure 9). Beyond these groups are porticoed staircases leading up through the crowd, each one empty of people except for a small group of women standing about like officials or usherettes. Further off to each side there are more groups of standing or seated women, again shown in front of a crowd of male spectators.

The Grandstand Fresco shows a large crowd of spectators watching a formal event, a spectacle of some kind. They are arranged on stepped terraces with staircases passing through. The spectacle is taking place in front of the plane of the fresco, so that we cannot see what it might be, but the location seems to be the western side of the Central Court in the Labyrinth. The Triple Shrine was located just south of the Porticoed Staircase, and it may well be that this staircase served as the architectural model for the four stylized stairways that are shown in the fresco. The Grandstand Fresco carries important resonances in our study of the Labyrinth's original function: others will be touched on in Chapter 9 (pp. 115–18, 'The Priestess of Knossos') and Chapter 10 (pp. 135–6, 'The Bull Court'). If we are being shown the spectators at one of the events that took place in the Central Court at Knossos, the fresco could answer many questions. For the moment, we will focus on the way in which women are portrayed in the fresco.

The women in the crowd are painted with exactly the same degree of care and attention as the men. In fact, apart from the white background colour, the women are indistinguishable from the men. The special groups of women, for example those on each side of the central shrine, are given a great deal of attention. They are painted slightly larger, which suggests that they are to be regarded as important, and their elaborate dresses are drawn in some detail. They also emerge as individuals. One raises her left hand to emphasize a conversational point, while the woman next to her rests her hand on her lap and relaxes attentively. The fresco painter obviously held this group of women in high regard.

Figure 9 Priestesses from the
Grandstand Fresco

There is no sign in the Grandstand Fresco of a princely figure of any kind, no sign of King Minos. Just who the high-status women are is clearly a matter of great importance and one that we will return to later (Chapter 9). The main lesson to be learnt from the fresco in relation to the East Wing problem is that women were not regarded as inferior to men and actually seem to have enjoyed a dominant role on major ceremonial occasions. The idea that these great ladies would have tolerated being incarcerated in the cramped chambers that Evans called the Queen's Apartments is absurd. These ladies would, if anything, have taken the larger suite next door. They were important and, to judge from the way in which the artist has portrayed them, they were well aware of it. They are relaxed and entirely lack the sort of shy, self-effacing traits that would lead them to shut themselves away out of a sense of propriety. Their posture and easy, uninhibited gestures show them to be outgoing and sociable by inclination.

If this seems to be arguing too much from one fresco, a very similar prominence is given to women in the Sacred Grove Fresco, another of the Miniature Frescoes found in pieces by Evans in a room just to the west of the North Entrance Passage. The heavily restored Sacred Grove shows a large crowd of over a thousand people. Once again women are emphasized, whether seated under the olive trees or dancing in the foreground. The bias is in favour of women. Once again the setting seems to have been the Labyrinth itself: the open space with olive trees and pathways marked out on the ground strongly suggests the West Court. Once again the focus of the ceremony cannot be seen; both the crowd and the dancers, who appear to be possessed by narcotic or religious ecstasy, are oriented towards an object of veneration in the bottom left-hand corner of the fresco, which unfortunately is missing. Representational frescoes like these and others at Knossos are very rare at the other Cretan palaces. Phaistos had simpler mural decoration and that seems to have been part and parcel of a simpler and more austere approach to architecture generally at Phaistos.

Evans himself drew from the two Miniature Frescoes the key idea that women were more important than men in Minoan society. He noted that the women were shown occupying the front seats of the 'grandstands' and inferred that this proved their higher rank. He also, but separately, proposed that the women retreated into semi-purdah in the Queen's megaron. The two ideas of retreat and pre-eminence are inconsistent, but Evans seems not to have noticed.

ROOM FOR DOUBT

Another minor inconsistency can be found in Evans' interpretation of the 'bathrooms'. As we saw earlier, he quickly rejected his initial interpretation of the Throne Room bathroom as a fish tank. He also found it difficult to reconcile the use of the sunken area as a bathroom for mundane ablution with

the use of the stone seat only 4 metres away as a royal throne. In the end he
decided on a ritual use for the sunken area in the Throne Room; it was a
lustral area in which the king purified himself before performing ceremonies
in the Throne Room proper. Yet, in the East Wing, Evans was apparently
content to interpret the bathroom opening out of the Queen's megaron as a
conventional bathroom. The painted terracotta bath that he found near by
(not actually in the sunken area) was perhaps too reminiscent of the short,
deep baths to be found in many an English home for Evans to question its
secular use. He observed that there was no sink-hole in the sunken area or the
bath and drew from this the inference that the bath must have been emptied
by hand.

Even so, the situation is unsatisfactory. There are comparable sunken
lustral areas at several points in the Labyrinth (see Figure 13) and we ought to
assume that they were used in a similar way for a similar purpose. A structure
used for ritual in the West Wing is not likely to have had a secular use in the
East Wing. The lustral areas in the Throne Room, Queen's megaron and the
North and South-East Lustral Basins must all have been used for the same
purpose. If Evans felt that the Throne Room tank must have had a ritual
function, and we agree with him, then the other sunken basins of similar
design will also have had a ritual purpose. The only reason this did not strike
Evans is that he was so relieved and pleased to have stumbled on palatial
apartments in the centre of the East Wing that he fell on them like a starving
man on a crust. Having failed to find rooms that he could convincingly
interpret as state apartments for King Minos, Queen Pasiphae and their
dynasty in the West Wing, Northern Sector and the northern half of the East
Wing, Evans really had to make these chambers the dwelling-place of the
royal family.

He had to do so if, indeed, his interpretation of the whole building as a
royal palace was going to be credible. We have now reached a critical point in
our review of the building on the Kefala hill, a point where we may begin to
feel that Sir Arthur's initial assumptions – admittedly received from his
predecessors on the site, Kalokairinos and Schliemann – led him to bend the
evidence of his excavations to fit in with his explanation. The over-emphatic
interpretation of the ground-floor rooms at the foot of the Grand Staircase as
a royal residence does not really convince; the fact that there were two such
suites fairly close together in the palace at Phaistos argues against it. The
optimistic 'reconstitution' of two majestic staircases in the West Wing, one
beside the Throne Room and the other leading up from the South
Propylaeum, does not convince either. Clearly there were upper storeys in
the West Wing and there were stairs up to them, but Evans went out of his
way to imply, with concrete and stone nudges, that there were royal
processions up to the first floor and royal apartments there too.

Occasionally Evans' gift for evocative room-names failed him. At the North
Entrance are the substantial ruins of what must once have been a very large

chamber. Today it is often known as the Hall of the Eleven Pillars, or the North Pillar Hall; its 10-metre-wide ceiling was held up by large pillars, the bases of which can still be seen. The hall lay just inside the North Entrance and Evans thought that because this was the palace gate closest to the sea, goods would have been inspected here by customs officials. It is very unlikely that this was the case, in that controls of this kind would have been the function of the harbour town. Evans speculated that the Pillar Hall functioned as an entrance loggia and drew comparisons between it and the South Propylaeum. He even went so far as to claim that the pillar layout 'exactly matches', but it is significantly different as his own plans show and the South Propylaeum was never an entrance anyway.

His misleading name for the North Pillar Hall, the Custom House, has had a significant damping effect on the imagination. It has none of the romance of the 'Throne Room' or the 'Hall of the Double Axes' and as a result it has not attracted much attention or interest. The chamber must originally have measured some 22 by 10 metres. It is, in other words, the largest surviving room in the palace, as big as the entire Hall of the Double Axes suite (light-well, outer hall, inner hall, colonnaded verandah, with the adjacent passage and staircase thrown in for good measure). The Throne Room would fit into it three times over. Yet, curiously, the power of Sir Arthur's pen has been such that he has been able, sometimes intentionally and sometimes unintention-ally, to interest us in some parts of the building and uninterest us in others. It seems odd that Evans was not concerned to make more of the Custom House, but perhaps he was put off by his own rather pedestrian name for the room. Now, there is a trend towards interpreting this substantial chamber as an undercroft for a major room on the first floor (e.g. Graham, 1969, p. 127). It is likely, given the large number of utensils found in the ruined store-rooms to the east, an area known as the North-East Magazines, that the North Pillar Hall supported a refectory or dining hall. The adjacent service rooms may have functioned as larders and kitchens, but they are too poorly preserved to interpret with any confidence.

Throughout his writings, from the first reports of 1900 right through to the completion of the final volume of *The Palace of Minos* in 1936, Evans emphasized the royal associations of the building he excavated at Knossos. When his workmen found fragments of the famous Prince of the Lilies Fresco, Evans unhesitatingly identified the figure as the king of Knossos and called it the 'Priest-King Relief'. A man's head on a seal was identified as a portrait of Minos. The minor male figures that often appear in religious art were identified as deified or heroized members of the dynasty of priest-kings. The elaborately decorated gaming-board found in the northern part of the East Wing was named the Royal Draught Board. A separate building a short distance to the north-east of the main building was named the Royal Villa; a more extensive building further off to the north-west became the Little Palace; the road connecting the two palaces was named the Royal Road. The lodge in the West Porch, at the start of the Corridor of the Processions, was the place where the priest-king sat, on yet another of Evans' thrones, ready to acknowledge the salutes of the streams of visiting subjects.

It would not be appropriate or useful to digress into an exhaustive discussion of these identifications, many of which are in any case mere assertions that do not stand up to scrutiny. Page by page, Evans established a connection between the ruin on the Kefala hill and the legendary royal dynasty of King Minos. He established it by repetition – the royal this, the king's that – persuading himself and his readers that the building really was a bronze age palace.

Evans' palace interpretation has had many strong supporters. Professor Graham's detailed review of the architecture of the Cretan 'palaces' implicitly follows Evans' lead. He is nevertheless prepared to dispute with Evans on points of detail. In the north-west corner of the West Wing, Evans reconstructed, on paper but not in stone, a third major staircase leading up to the first floor. In Evans' imagination this was a spectacularly elaborate entrance to the palace for visitors arriving along the Royal Road. It ascended by three flights of steps 5 metres wide and two broad landings to a pillared loggia decorated with horns of consecration, and opened by way of two pairs of double doors into the Sanctuary Hall. Graham disputes the existence of a North-West Entrance staircase and has his own interpretation of the first floor plan as a whole (Graham, 1969, pp. 118–19 and Figure 85). The main feature according to Graham was an enlarged stateroom called the North-West Hall, an impressive and spacious chamber measuring 18 by 16 metres, almost twice the area of the largest surviving room on the ground floor, the North Pillar Hall. So although Graham disagrees with the Evans interpretation in detail, he gives generous support to the palace concept by providing more luxurious apartments on the West Wing first floor than Evans himself imagined. Graham is so persuaded of the fundamental correctness of Evans' view that he can write of Evans' term 'Little Palace' as 'suitably non-committal' (Graham, 1987, Addendum 3).

Nicolas Platon (1968, p. 162) follows the palatial interpretation, believing that it is possible to identify within the bronze age palaces the apartments of kings, queens, princes, and courtiers. The Throne Room he sees as a kind of senate house where the king, a high-priest as well as a monarch, conferred with his advisers. Platon applied the same concepts to the 'palace' he found and excavated at Zakro (1971), identifying suites of rooms as King's and Queen's Apartments on the grounds that they appeared majestic and were similar to suites identified as royal apartments at Knossos. Sinclair Hood too follows the Evans model, seeing state apartments on the missing first floor of the West Wing and the royal living quarters across in the East Wing at Knossos (Hood 1971, pp. 68–70). Palaces, as Hood says, imply kings and queens. But the underlying assumption that the building on Kefala hill was a royal palace may be incorrect. There is plenty of room for doubt.

6

Wunderlich's 'Palace of the Dead'

The souls, the images of dead men, hold me at a distance and will not let me cross the river and mingle among them, but I wander as I am by Hades' house of the wide gate. And I call upon you in sorrow to give me your hand; no longer shall I come back from death, once you give me my rite of burning.

The ghost of Patroclus speaks to Achilles: Homer, *Iliad* (Book 23)

In the 1970s, Hans Wunderlich put forward an alternative interpretation, born of an understandable dissatisfaction with Evans' explanation of the building as a royal palace. Wunderlich pointed out peculiarities such as the sheer inefficiency of the layout of rooms and corridors. Visitors entering the palace from the west had to make a long detour to the south and east in order to get to the Central Court. Curiously, the design of the first palace, as detected by Evans, included a more direct west-east entrance passage, through what were later to become store-rooms: the delayed and labyrinthine entrance corridor of the second palace was deliberately contrived, according to Wunderlich, as a directional lock to prevent evil forces reaching the inner sanctum.

Wunderlich also argued that the building's orientation is at variance with the ancient, by which he meant classical, tradition. It has north, south, east and west entrances, just like a Roman city, but they were apparently used differently. The Romans associated the east gate, the *porta praetoria* with arrival, good news, and good fortune, yet the eastern entrance at Knossos appears to have been little more than a back stair. The Romans associated the west gate, the *porta decumana*, with departure, misfortune, and even death; the cohorts traditionally marched out to battle through this gate of the Roman city. That the western entrance at Knossos seems to have been the more important emphasizes an association with departure and death. From this, Wunderlich tenuously argued that Knossos was in some sense a palace dedicated to the dead.

The building was unsuitable to be used as a royal dwelling. Windowless, dark and cramped for the most part, its overall large scale belied the nature of the individual rooms. The West Wing, as we have seen, was incompatible with Evans' theory, with its windowless cellarage; the Northern and Southern Sectors turned out to be equally unsuitable, although they at least incorporated some structures apparently designed for ostentatious public access; the East Wing rooms which Evans settled on as his royal apartments were buried away in the darkest basement.

Wunderlich's alternative interpretation – a palace of the dead – was not entirely original. It had been foreshadowed by Oswald Spengler in his *Decline of the West*, written just before the First World War. Spengler was sceptical of Evans' interpretation of the Knossos excavations and he saw the 'Throne of Ariadne' as a stand for a religious image of some kind or for a priest's mummy.

The specific extra dimension that Wunderlich brought to the Knossos problem was his geological expertise. He had gone to Crete to investigate the process of mountain building but when he saw Knossos, like Evans eighty years before him, he found a new objective entirely. It was the peculiar choice of building materials that particularly mystified him. The guidebook described the natural beauty of the crystalline alabaster sheathing the walls and floors of Knossos, its white surfaces reflecting light from the light-wells and diffusing a subtle radiance into the gloomy lower floors of the palace.

But when Wunderlich looked closely at the surviving casings of the white stone he saw that the alabaster was nothing more than soft gypsum. It was an odd choice, given that a more serviceable limestone could have been obtained from quarries just a few miles away. The main problem with gypsum is that it will not withstand heavy wear; although it might serve as a wall-sheathing it is unsuitable for flooring, wearing down quickly under the tread of well-shod feet. The thousands of tourists were having a visible effect on stair treads that were restored as late as the 1930s. The softness of the gypsum floors means that they were not designed for normal foot-traffic.

Another problem with gypsum is that it is easily eroded by rainwater, although Wunderlich admits that almost everywhere it was used it was roofed over, so that it would have been protected from the weather. More difficult to explain is its use on the floors and walls of the lustral areas; water spilling from the baths would quickly have eroded away the gypsum floors. The lustral areas could therefore not have been used for washing. The 'baths' were not used as baths in the modern sense at all, but must have had some other function.

If the fabric of the building was impractical in its design and in the materials used, so too were the majority of the small artefacts found in it. Much of the pottery was of the Kamares type. Often called 'eggshell' pottery, it was made with very thin walls to look like bronze: some of it had appliqué bands and rosettes and some even had pottery chain links hanging from the rim, to complete the illusion of metalwork. This pottery was so fragile that it would have been difficult to use. Its function, Wunderlich argues, was purely ritual; the objects were ghost vessels for the spirits of the dead to carry with them to the otherworld. Most of the other artefacts found at Knossos can also be seen as votives or grave-goods.

Wunderlich makes much of the paintings on the sides of the celebrated sarcophagus found at Agia Triadha near Phaistos. These paintings show, among other things, an elaborate ceremony in which offerings are being made to the deceased who, significantly, is depicted either standing up or propped up. It seems possible, then, that the embalmed and mummified bodies of distinguished Knossians were propped up on benches or thrones for reverence. The Throne Room takes on a very different atmosphere if we picture its stone benches as shelves for mummified corpses. The throne itself has notches in its back which may have been used to hold in place the straps that would have been needed to stop the mummy falling forward. One problem with this ingenious idea is that the one surviving throne was built right back against the wall with plaster lapped up to its edges, so that no straps could possibly have passed behind it.

Wunderlich visualized tens of thousands of corpses being washed, embalmed, and revered in the Knossos Labyrinth. The large numbers of mysterious 'female bath attendants' mentioned in the Linear B tablets were there to wash the bodies and embalm them. Euphemisms of this kind still prevail among funeral directors of our own day. Sacrifices were also offered to the dead in the Labyrinth.

The frescoes that misled Evans into thinking of the Minoans as given over to lives of graceful self-indulgence and endless pleasure and sport were a piece of wishful fantasy. They represented an ideal afterlife, the sort of life the bronze age Cretans wanted to lead and hoped to project, by magic if necessary, after death. The world they painted on the walls at Knossos was not the world they actually lived in but the world they hoped to inhabit when they died.

The whole building was given over to various aspects of the funerary rite. The baths that caused such problems in interpretation were in reality coffins. There are examples of several baths used as coffins, although not at Knossos, so where we find baths we should interpret them as sarcophagi. The Minoan dead were also buried in clay chests of about the same size as the baths and sometimes in the large storage jars. Larnax burials, pithos burials, and bathtub burials: all three are known from Minoan Crete. Wunderlich argues that the bathtubs and storage jars in the palace at Knossos were all used for the disposal of the dead. The serried ranks of storage jars in the West Magazines were burials in a sealed vault. No wonder there were no windows.

The so-called 'flush-toilets' and drains identified by Evans were in reality plumbing arrangements connected with embalming and with the disposal of the unwanted body fluids and the blood of sacrifice. The so-called light-wells were really ventilation shafts that would have been essential to get rid of the stench of decay and offal.

THE EGYPTIAN CONNECTION

Wunderlich focuses on the Cretan connection with Egypt. The famous Keftiu tomb paintings in Egyptian tombs show either tribute or gifts being brought to Egypt, establishing beyond doubt that in the bronze age Cretans and Egyptians met and exchanged goods and ideas. The bronze age Egyptians are probably best known for their elaborate cult of the dead and in particular for their development of the art of mummification. The Cretans it may be assumed shared this knowledge and applied it in their own way at Knossos.

There is an ancient Greek legend that Daidalos modelled Knossos on an Egyptian building that was famous in classical times, but which is now crumbled to dust and all but forgotten, the Labyrinth of Amenemhet III (1839–1791 BC). Amenemhet's mortuary temple was located close to his pyramid tomb at Hawara, 8 kilometres east of Medinet el Fayum. Sir Flinders Petrie excavated the mortuary temple at Hawara in 1888–9 and found inscriptions proving a connection with the Pharaoh Amenemhet III. He did what he could to trace the outline of the wrecked structure, which he inferred was a maze of walled chambers extending across a huge area 250 by 300 metres. The building was too badly damaged for Petrie to retrieve its detailed plan, but it had certainly consisted of a large number of separate courts and chambers arranged in regimented rows.

The Hawara Labyrinth, built in about 1800 BC, could have served as a model for the rebuilding of the Knossos Labyrinth which took place in about 1700 BC, but not for the first large 'palatial' building at Knossos, which dates from about a hundred years before Hawara.

The connection between the Hawara Labyrinth and the Knossos Labyrinth, so close in date, is intriguing. Although the precise connection is as yet unclear, there is a real possibility that the two buildings were the

Figure 10 'Princes of the land of Keftiu and of the isles in the midst of the sea.' Minoan envoys to Thothmes III in the tomb of Rekhmire at Thebes

product of ideas and aspirations held in common. In the end it does not matter which of the two buildings was first, but from the dates suggested above it looks as if Knossos might have been a model for Hawara rather than vice versa.

It is a great loss that the Hawara Labyrinth, such a famous landmark in the ancient world, has crumbled away so completely. We can no longer compare the two labyrinths. But at least the Egyptian Labyrinth was celebrated enough to attract such distinguished visitors as Strabo and Herodotus: both wrote descriptions of what they saw.

Strabo travelled extensively in Egypt, and in about AD18 he compiled the seventeen books of his *Geographica*, which consisted of descriptions of the places he had seen. In some sections he leans on the writings of others, but much of the description is first-hand.

> We have here also in the labyrinth a work equal to the pyramids, and adjoining it the tomb of the king who constructed the labyrinth . . . . There is a table-shaped plain with a village and a large palace composed of as many chambers as there were formerly nomes [districts]. There is an equal number of courts surrounded by pillars, and contiguous to one another, all in a line and forming one continuous building, like a long wall with the courts in front of it . . . . There are long and numerous covered ways with winding communicating passages, so that no stranger could find his way into the courts or out of them without a guide.
>
> The surprising thing is that the roofs of these dwellings consist of a single stone each, and that the covered ways through their whole range were roofed in the same manner with single slabs of stone of extraordinary size, without the intermixture of timber or of any other material. On ascending the roof – which is not of any great height, for it consists only of a single storey – there may be seen a field of stones. Descending again and looking into the courts, these may be seen in a line supported by twenty-seven pillars, each consisting of a single stone . . . . At the end of the building is the tomb, which is a quadrangular mound . . . . They built, it is said, this number of courts because it was the custom for all the nomes to assemble there together according to their rank, with their priests and priestesses, for the purpose of performing sacrifices and making offerings to the gods, and of administering justice in matters of great importance. Each of the nomes was conducted to the court appointed for it.
>
> (*Geographica*, Book 17)

Already, by Strabo's time, many of the great Egyptian monuments were deserted and tumbling down. Already Strabo was relying on hearsay and local tradition concerning the original function of the building. Some four hundred years before, another Greek traveller saw the Labyrinth of Hawara when it was less derelict and evidently still subject to ancient taboos and still superintended by its sacred guardians.

Herodotus was born at Halicarnassus in Anatolia and died in about 425 BC in southern Italy. He travelled widely and wrote detailed accounts of the places he visited in his 'Account of Research'. In his introductory remarks about the Labyrinth of Hawara, which he saw in about 440 BC, Herodotus speaks of the Labyrinth's builders as twelve 'kings'. These were probably the district commanders of the Delta region, united by intermarriage and governing 'in mutual friendliness'.

> To strengthen the bond between them, they decided to leave a common memorial to their reigns and for this purpose constructed a labyrinth a little above Lake Moeris, near the place called the City of the Crocodiles. I have seen this building and it is beyond my power to describe; it must have cost more in labour and money than all the walls and public works of the Greeks put together, although no one would deny that the temples at Ephesus and Samos are remarkable buildings. The pyramids too, are astonishing structures, each one of them equal to many of the most ambitious works of Greece; but the labyrinth surpasses them.
>
> It has twelve covered courts – six in a row facing north, six south – the gates of one range exactly fronting the gates of the other, with a continuous wall round the outside of the whole. Inside, the building is of two storeys and contains three thousand rooms, of which half are underground and the other half directly above them. I was taken through the rooms in the upper storey, so what I shall say of them is from my own observation, but the underground ones I can speak of only from report because the Egyptians in charge refused to let me see them, as they contain the tombs of the kings who built the labyrinth and also the tombs of the sacred crocodiles. The upper rooms, on the contrary, I did actually see, and it is hard to believe that they are the work of men; the baffling and intricate passages from room to room and from court to court were an endless wonder to me as we passed from a courtyard into rooms, from rooms into galleries, from galleries into more rooms, and from those into more courtyards. The roof of every chamber, courtyard and gallery is, like the walls, made of stone. The walls are covered with carved figures, and each court is exquisitely built of white stone and surrounded by a colonnade. Near the corner where the labyrinth ends there is a pyramid, 240 feet in height, with great carved figures of animals on it and an underground passage by which it can be entered.

('Account of Research', Book 2, 148)

The descriptions of Hawara by Strabo and Herodotus are invaluable in giving us an impression of the building. Herodotus' description in particular conveys the excitement of exploring the ruin. We can only regret that the guardians of the labyrinth prevented him from descending to the lower level. Were there really kings and crocodiles buried, mummified, in those lower rooms? More exciting from our point of view is the similarity of Herodotus' impression of

Hawara to our own impression of Knossos. There are moments when we might almost feel that Herodotus was describing Knossos: the continuous outer wall, the countless hundreds of rooms, half of them below ground level, the maze of intricate passages and corridors, the decorated limestone walls.

One of the key features of Egypt as far as Wunderlich is concerned is its continuity of cultural development. Its 'iron age' culture contained inclusions from earlier ways of life, the traces of which had long since been extinguished in the Aegean. Wunderlich even goes so far as to suggest that there may be an Egyptian connection in the word 'Minos' itself. It bears a similarity with the name 'Menes', the king who unified the first empire, the Old Kingdom, in 2950 BC. King Menes was the earliest and most revered king of the ancient Mediterranean world. He was not called Pharaoh. In fact the word was not applied to Egyptian kings until the New Kingdom, after about 1300 BC. 'Pharaoh' is an anglicized form of 'Par-o', which means 'palace', 'court' and therefore only indirectly and by association 'king'.

The kings of Egypt were in any case more often known by florid circumlocutions than by short titles. The Pharaoh Thutmosis III died in 1436 BC when the Knossos Labyrinth was still in use. He was known as 'Strong Bull, Shining in Weser [Thebes], Felicity in Royalty, Re in Heaven, Mighty in Strength, Glorious in Crowns, King of Upper and Lower Egypt, Lord of the Two Lands, Son of Re'.

It is possible that, as the later Egyptian kings were known by the generic title 'Pharaoh', the earlier kings were known generically as 'Menes'. The Egyptian script does not give vowel sounds, so there is no way of telling how the word was pronounced. 'Menes' may have been pronounced 'Minos'. Wunderlich suggests that 'Minos' was actually a title borrowed from Egypt and used as a title for Minoan kings. It may have been: it may not. Certainly the idea is an interesting one, but it needs corroboration before we can go further with it.

FIRE AND FUNERARY RITUAL

The evidence of a great fire at Knossos has often been referred to and it has equally often been interpreted as evidence of the final conflagration: the disaster that brought about the abandonment of the palace. Whether the fire was a by-product of a catastrophic earthquake, which shook down the walls and floors of the upper storeys and upset lamps and portable hearths all over the building, or a deliberate piece of arson by human enemies, has been hotly disputed. But the fire itself has been generally accepted.

Nevertheless, some of the gypsum slabs that were used to face the walls and floors of the building contain veins of bitumen which somehow remained unburnt. At temperatures above 120°C, the bitumen content of gypsum escapes and is burnt off. The tell-tale grey veins in the gypsum seem to contradict the widespread evidence of fire – hardened clay tablets, blackened tiles and walls, charred timbers – so how can the contradiction be explained? The answer seems to be that there was not a single, all-consuming conflagration, but many small separate fires that did not product any great heat.

Wunderlich uses this in turn as evidence of further funerary practices in his 'Palace of the Dead', speculating that the corpses of the noble Knossians carried there for mummification may have been lightly cooked as part of the process. As corroborative evidence of this, he cites the royal corpses discovered in the shaft graves at Mycenae, corpses that had been 'singed', apparently to dry and preserve them. Although this half-way house between inhumation and cremation does not seem to have been a common practice, it nevertheless makes sense as an intermediate conservation technique when the full funerary ceremony might be delayed, especially in a warm, Mediterranean environment.

That royal funeral ceremonies were delayed for some time in the bronze age Aegean is indicated by Homer. In Book 24 of the *Iliad* we are told that the dead body of Hector was left for twenty-two days before it was burnt on a pyre. Hector's body was described as being 'as fresh as dew' at least twelve days after his death. Book 24 of the *Odyssey* tells us that Achilles' body was similarly kept for eighteen days. These bodies would have been in an advanced state of decomposition without any sort of interim treatment, and it seems reasonable to assume that embalming or some other process was used to preserve them. Since meat and fish can easily be preserved by smoking over a fire, there is no reason why this method should not have been used to preserve human corpses, at least for the short mourning period which preceded the funeral. We might see the many small fires round the palace of the dead as evidence of some sort of corpse-drying process. It seems extraordinary, though, that these corpse-fires – which Wunderlich alleges were an everyday feature of the palace's routine – were allowed to scorch and blacken walls and even burn down supporting pillars.

Wunderlich's book, *The Secret of Crete* (1975), has been a salutary reminder of many of the ways in which Sir Arthur Evans' vision of the Minoan civilization was ill-founded. At times his style is regrettably sarcastic, but he has performed an invaluable service to the development of thinking about Minoan Knossos by making us face squarely up to some of the shortcomings and inconsistencies of Evans' interpretation. The case Wunderlich makes against Evans' palace is nevertheless much more convincing than the case he advances for his own palace of the dead. *The Secret of Crete* half-persuades us of the reality of a palace of the dead at Knossos, with its sinister funerary rites and thousands of mummified corpses assiduously tended by embalmers and priests, by accumulations of suggestive details rather than with any definitive proof. He reminds us that, although we may now think of the dolphin as a symbol of gentleness, gaiety, and freedom, in the ancient world it was thought of as a symbol of death, of the spirit finally liberated from the body. He introduces the idea that the exposed breasts of the Snake Goddess statuettes may not after all have indicated female sexuality, dominance, licentiousness, or bravado, reminding us that the baring of breasts by women in the ancient world was often a gesture of grief and despair. In Book 22 of Homer's *Iliad*, Hector's mother is described as distraught at her son's death. 'His mother in tears was mourning and laid the fold of her bosom bare, and with one hand held out a breast.'

SHORTCOMINGS OF THE WUNDERLICH HYPOTHESIS

The idea that the Labyrinth was a necropolis where recently departed citizens of Knossos were mummified, honoured, and offered rituals that would ensure a happy afterlife is an ingenious hypothesis. It is not attractive in the superficial sense that Wunderlich's Knossos would have been a pleasant place to visit, like Sir Arthur Evans' Knossos, but it is attractive in the sense that it fits in with much of the architectural and archaeological evidence.

There are nevertheless problems. Although the storage jars in the West Wing may look identical to those funerary pithoi which have been found (well away from the palace) to contain human remains, the Knossos jars were found upright, whereas the funerary jars were usually laid on their sides. In addition, some of the Knossos jars still contained traces of food when they

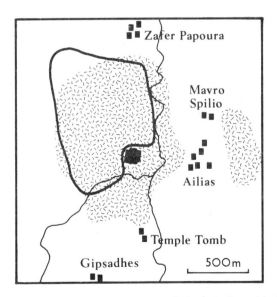

Figure 11 Minoan cemeteries near Knossos. The Labyrinth (large black square) stood near the centre of the Minoan city (intensively built-up area shown hatched). Note how the intensively occupied area of the classical city (black outline) avoided the Labyrinth

were found. There seems to be no justification at all for suggesting that the jars inside the palace at Knossos were ever used for storing human bodies. The positive archaeological evidence Wunderlich requires is simply missing.

If corpses were mummified in the palace, why is it that no mummies have been found there? It is certainly possible that the palace was robbed in antiquity but it seems odd that, of all the thousands of corpses allegedly handled there, not one has escaped the attentions of the robber. Possibly those that survived the robbing fell victim to the climate. The very dry atmospheric conditions in Egypt favoured the preservation of corpses. On Crete, the air is humid for several months in winter, and this may have accelerated the disintegration and decay of any remaining mummies. Even so, the 'palace of the dead' hypothesis is critically weakened by the lack of positive evidence of mummies. In fact, Wunderlich has been accused of inventing out of hand the technique of Minoan mummification and the funerary cult that went with it.

The idea of a palace of the dead seems redundant, except perhaps as a burial-ground, and there are plenty of easily identifiable Minoan cemeteries in the area surrounding the Minoan city, notably at Mavro Spilio and Zafer Papoura (Figure 11). There are ordinary cemeteries, presumably for the majority of the population, and also isolated individual tombs, presumably for the wealthy. Wunderlich's counter-argument is that the tombs, cemeteries, and the palace itself together made up one large 'Valley of the Dead', but there is no reason why we should think that this was the case. Major structures like the Temple Tomb clearly required no necropolis facilities for preliminary rites: they had their own ceremonial mortuary precincts.

What is left? Wunderlich argues that the Labyrinth must have been a sealed-off, taboo place, a silent sham palace that none but the dead inhabited. His argument rests finally, as it did initially, on the nature of the materials used. The softness of gypsum is a telling point, although not all the gypsum is as soft as Wunderlich says; in any case, does it really indicate that the building was not to be visited at all? Does the extreme fragility of some of the Kamares ware mean that it was never to be used? It is unwise to press these points too forcefully. The pottery is delicately made, and made to be used with great delicacy; that tells us how carefully the utensils had to be used, rather than that they were never used. Similarly, the soft material with which the floors were covered tells us that the traffic anticipated in the Labyrinth was light. The architects did not anticipate the tens of thousands of tourists who swarm over the building today, nor did they anticipate the hard-soled shoes worn by many tourists. But if we visualize perhaps two hundred people as the Labyrinth's normal household or staff, and if in addition we visualize those people shod in leather moccasins or soft-soled sandals or even padding about barefoot, we may see that the gypsum flooring was more serviceable than we at first thought. If in addition we suppose that those people were moving about the Labyrinth with care and caution, there is no reason why any undue wear should be detectable even on thresholds or stair treads.

What careful activities were conducted here in the dark Labyrinth on the Kefala hill, centuries before the Trojan War? If the Labyrinth was not the palace of royal pageant and pleasure that Sir Arthur Evans visualized and not the palace of death that Oswald Spengler and Hans Wunderlich conjured up, what was it? Was it perhaps not a palace at all, but a building raised for an entirely different purpose?

7

The temple of the goddesses

I am a mortal, a man; I cannot tread upon these tinted splendours
without fear thrown in my path.

Aeschylus, *Agamemnon*

'A VISION OF DIVINITY'

If Wunderlich's necropolis hypothesis seems unsatisfactory, it is tempting to
fall back on some sort of modification of the Evans explanation. Sinclair
Hood, Nicolas Platon and James Walter Graham have presented us with their
interpretations, which are really the palatial idea slightly modified. All three
men seem to accept the large building at Knossos as a royal residence and as a
centre of royal administration. In some instances the interpretation is more
general. Graham, for instance, has proposed calling the Hall of the Double
Axes or the King's Megaron 'the Men's Hall' and the smaller chamber to the
south 'the Women's Hall'. Other interpretations are more specific than
Evans'. Nicolas Platon (1968 and 1971) felt that at Knossos he could identify
apartments assignable to the king, others to the queen and still others to
princes; the 'vast halls with interior colonnades' were for receptions, banquets,
audiences, and council meetings. Courtiers, according to Platon, were lodged
in attractive houses adjacent to the palace.

Yet interpretations developing in this direction, however cautiously, suffer
from the same disadvantages and weaknesses detected in Evans' interpretation. We need a third alternative. If we reject the Evans hypothesis, even in the
modified forms proposed by Platon, Graham, and others, and we reject the
Wunderlich hypothesis as well, are we left with any other option?

I believe that there is a third and strong possibility and that it has been
staring us in the face from the very first days of Sir Arthur Evans'
excavations. This third alternative is that the Labyrinth at Knossos was a
temple. This chapter will attempt to show that, if we were approaching the
ruin on the Kefala hill for the first time and with no preconceptions about its
original function, and in particular no knowledge at all of the legends
surrounding the site, we would be led to the conclusion that the building had
been a bronze age temple-complex.

Figure 12 Cult objects from a first-floor shrine. These objects had fallen from a strongroom on the first floor of the West Wing into a chamber in the Snake Goddess Sanctuary

The Palace of Minos at Knossos is an extraordinary book in many ways. One of its most extraordinary aspects is Evans' preoccupation with King Minos and the site's assumed royal connections when, on page after page, he gives evidence of its religious function. Let us take the room which for Evans proved the site's quintessentially royal character, the Room of the Throne. In describing it, Evans used the following words: sacral, shrine, chapter house, ceremony of anointing, ritual, religious. He wrote that it 'teems with religious suggestion' and reminded him of initiation sanctuaries in Anatolia (Evans 1921–36, vol. 1, p. 4). And so we could continue round the Labyrinth, with one feature after another.

The double-axe symbol carved on many of the stones is held to have a 'religious significance'. The large East Hall, where 'priestesses may have woven their own sacral vestments in their special sanctuary' was a place of worship. The bronze locks of hair found in the cellars below it proved that there was a huge statue of a goddess, perhaps 2.5 metres high, at the eastern end (Figures 22 and 46): in front of her was an exceptionally large pair of sacral horns. The goddess, as Evans visualized her, 'towered above her worshippers, a radiant vision of divinity'.

Each of the pillar crypts dotted round the Labyrinth had a religious function and supported a columnar shrine on the floor above. The North-West Lustral Area was, Evans believed, for ritual washing by pilgrims or other people approaching the Palace Sanctuary for religious purposes. The walled space round this lustral area was probably also involved in some way in initiation ceremonies (Figure 21). To the south-east of this lustral area, Evans' excavators found painted plaster that had fallen from some 'highly decorated sanctuary' on the floor above.

Even the stone boxes or cists let into the floor of the West Magazines or store-rooms are given a religious overtone by Evans. The addition of doors and walling sealed off Magazines 4 to 13 and made this area in particular very secure; it became, according to Evans, a Palace Treasury 'under religious guardianship'. In a chamber which he referred to as the Central Sanctuary of the Minoan Goddess, behind the remains of the Tripartite Shrine, Evans found what he believed were temple repositories. Two stone cists had been let into the floor as containers for 'temple treasure' in the Late Minoan III period (see Appendix A). Below them were two older and much larger stone cists, each one almost 2 metres long. To Evans they were a clear indication of the continuity of the religious function of the area from the early days of the palace's history.

The clay tablets with their Linear A script were beyond Evans' power to translate, and they remain untranslated to the present day. Even so, he was confident that the script had a 'sacral use'. He found examples of libation tables and votive cups with Linear A inscriptions. One group of signs recurred so frequently in these inscriptions that Evans suggested that it might refer to the Minoan deity.

Evans saw the sunken lustral basins as possibly connected with religious ceremonies to propitiate earth deities. Like the pillar crypts, they were places where the gods controlling earthquakes might be appeased with prayers, rites, and offerings. The pillar crypts, the Tripartite Shrine and the 'Shrine of the Double Axes' were specifically identified as religious cult centres, and the Double-Axe Shrine was discovered with its sanctuary furnishings in place (Figures 25 and 49). A low shelf-altar strewn with water-worn pebbles was decorated with two double-axe stands in the form of horns of consecration; also on the altar were five statuettes including a goddess, a male worshipper offering a dove and female handmaidens or worshippers. In front of the altar, cemented onto a low step, was a plaster offering bowl or table. The rest of the shrine was filled with groups of cups, jugs, and stirrup vases, apparently placed there as offerings. The Double-Axe Shrine was small, only 1.5 metres square, but it was undoubtedly a shrine.

Several of the buildings in the surrounding area had chambers with a religious function too. The House of the Chancel Screen had a lustral basin and a pillar crypt, while the Little Palace 200 metres away to the north-west had so many religious overtones that Evans described it as a 'practically uninterrupted suite of sanctuary chambers': it had 'every appearance of a religious foundation'. In fact he saw the Little Palace as functioning as an annexe to the main palace and sharing its religious role. If the Little Palace was a religious foundation, so too was the main palace.

Evans implied that the spacious apartments that we would expect in a palace originally existed on the first floor of the West Wing; these were the audience chambers and state reception rooms. It is therefore odd to find him naming the principal room the 'Sanctuary Hall', which clearly implies a religious function.

This is but a sample of the religious interpretations and implications to be found in Evans' *The Palace of Minos*; in one part of the palace after another he found evidence or implication of a religious use. Conditioning led him to interpret the building as a royal palace at the outset and also led him to cling to it to the end of his long association with the excavations there. Yet in reality he was uncovering evidence that pointed in another direction. We can see from the evidence of *The Palace of Minos* alone that he was conscious of the religious significance of his finds and had to find ways of explaining it in terms of his initial set of assumptions. He went to Knossos fully expecting to find it a Mycenean palace. Schliemann, with whom Evans had discussed the finds from Mycenae and probably much more besides, was saying as early as 1886 that the building was 'similar to the prehistoric palace at Tiryns' and in 1887 that it was 'the age-old prehistoric palace of the kings of Knossos'. When Arthur Evans arrived in Heraklion in 1894 he already had in his mind's eye an image of the building as a Mycenean royal palace, the palace designed by Daidalos for King Minos. Somehow, the detail emerging from the archaeology of the building as it was excavated had to be fitted to this fundamental palatial preconception.

Evans' ingenious way round the problem was to assert that Minos was not just a secular monarch but a priest-king, and this neat solution has been followed by many subsequent commentators. But there is no real evidence that Knossos was ruled by such a figure. There is the classical Greek tradition that Crete was ruled by a powerful king called Minos, but there is also the tradition that his engineer built a bronze robot to defend Crete and flew to his freedom on wings made of feathers and wax; clearly we are selecting what we believe and cannot be absolutely sure which traditions are fanciful and which are based on real history. The successful man-powered flight from Crete to Santorini in April 1988 by the 31-year-old Greek athlete Kanellos Kanellopoulos, though impressive, in no way proves the traditional version of the Daidalos legend to be historically true.

There is an older Greek tradition crystallized in the Homeric epics and this indicates a pattern of fiercely territorial city-states, sometimes acting independently but also capable of confederate action, and these were ruled by kings. The pattern emerging from the bronze age archaeology of Crete would seem to conform to this mainland Greek pattern, to the extent that several 'palace' sites have been discovered and each one could have been the seat of power of a small city-state. We know that the bronze age Cretans were armed and equipped for warfare, with swords, chariots, and generals, but it is a large argumentative leap to presume kingship on the Mycenean model as presented by Homer, and a larger leap still to presume that the 'kings' lived in the 'palaces'.

For the moment it is probably better to suspend discussion of these problems while we focus on the nature and function of the 'vast edifice' at Knossos. If, again for the moment, we are considering the hypothesis that the building is a temple-complex, we do not need to look for evidence of a king at all. A temple may be organized as an entirely independent establishment from the secular authority. Often there is a relationship between the two, but the nature of that relationship varies greatly through time and space. There may be friction, distrust and hostility between the two powers, or there may be mutual reinforcement and ratification. The nature of the relationship between temple and presumed king in Minoan Crete is an issue we shall explore later. For the moment it is enough to remember that we need not expect to find any references to a king – or his equivalent – in a temple.

Evans identified a low-relief figure made of painted plaster as one of the priest-kings of Knossos. The fragments, for the figure was far from complete, were found in the passage connecting the long Corridor of the Procession with the Central Court. The whole corridor seems to have been decorated with a frieze of processing figures, so perhaps we should not draw too much interpretation out of one figure.

A facsimile of the reconstructed Priest-King Relief has been mounted close to the end of the Procession Corridor, with the implication that it was probably the leading figure. Evans suggested that the 3- or 4-metre space left probably contained the image of the goddess. In fact, Leonard Palmer points out, the fragments of the fresco were found some 7 metres further south, so there may have been several more figures ahead of the 'priest-king' (Palmer 1969). It is also not at all certain that the head-dress belongs to the reconstructed figure. It is more likely that it was originally worn by the mythical beast the attendant was leading. In the end, it looks as if the priest-king, in spite of his imperious pose, was no more than an ostler to a griffin, sphinx, or giant hound, although the papyrus lilies do tend to confirm that the attendant was in the service of the goddess; the attendant also wears a necklace made of lily-shaped beads. The East Hall frescoes include griffins tethered to columns and there are several other comparable artworks showing human attendants leading large mythical animals (Figure 54).

So, there is no representation of the presumed king of Knossos in the great building which we are now supposing to have been a temple. Nor do we need to assume that the word 'royal' (wa-na-ka-te-ro in the Linear B script) found on a few pots means that the inscribed objects were personal possessions of the king. The longer inscriptions seem to give the name of the supplier, the place of manufacture, and the name of the manufacturer; it is the name of the manufacturer which is sometimes replaced by the word 'royal'. Halford Haskell, who has made a detailed study of the stirrup jars in question, feels that kings had little or nothing to do with them, that it was scribes acting under the instructions of urban (or temple?) officials who added 'royal' merely to indicate state control or official approval of some kind. The references on the tablets to the king (wa-na-ka) imply that offerings were specifically made to him, for example on tablet LC (1) 525 and Ga (1) 675, but even these references may be open to another interpretation. Poseidon was sometimes referred to as 'King Poseidon' so the offerings may have been intended for the god rather than the earthly king.

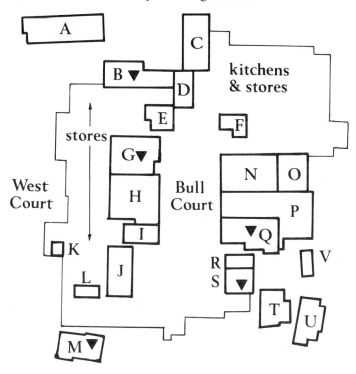

Figure 13 Functional zones of the Labyrinth. A – Theatral Area, B – Initiation Area, C – South Pillar Hall, Refectory over, D – Bull Chamber, E – Lotus Lamp Sanctuary, F – North-East Sanctuary, G – Throne Sanctuary, H – Snake Goddess Sanctuary, I – Destroyed Sanctuary, J – Cupbearer Sanctuary, K – West Porch Shrine, L – South-West Pillar Crypts, Columnar Shrines over, M – Silver Vessels Sanctuary, N – Great Goddess Sanctuary, O – Temple Workshops, P – Double-Axe Sanctuary, Q – Dolphin Sanctuary, R – Triton Shell Sanctuary, S – Late Dove Goddess Sanctuary, T – Chancel Screen Sanctuary, U – South-East Sanctuary, V – Monolithic Pillar Crypt. Black triangle = adyton

THE TEMPLE ARCHITECTURE

We turn now to the temple architecture and reflect on its suitability for a religious function. To begin with, we can accept much of Evans' reasoning concerning the religious function of many of the chambers. But it is not really sufficient to go round the building square metre by square metre inferring function without looking at the whole. Is there a whole, in fact, or is the temple-complex to be seen as a patternless patchwork?

A common underlying purpose to the whole complex of chambers is implicit in the existence of the Central and West Courts. The Central Court is an orderly rectangular space round which the suites of rooms agglomerate. Although the temples on Crete vary in points of detail, and often significantly so, they all evolved round this fundamental rectangular space. The clear implication is that some unifying, central ritual or rituals took place there. The West Court may at first sight seem to be a space left almost inadvertently to the west of the temple, but it was definitely not so, or the other temples would not possess them. Even the tiny temple in the cramped little Minoan town of Gournia has its equivalent of a West Court, a paved area significantly broader than the other alleys. From the evidence found below the West Court pavement at Knossos, it seems that the area was deliberately cleared to make a large open space for ceremonies; under the late Minoan pavement are the foundations of several earlier houses. How these courts were used we shall explore later. Architecturally, they stand in relation to the building as a whole much as the nave stands in relation to the cathedral or abbey church – focal, communal, central, public, in contrast to the multiplicity of smaller, specialized spaces round it.

Another feature common to the Cretan temples is the rows of store-rooms with large storage jars. These were particularly conspicuous behind the west front of the temple, but could be found in other sectors of the building too. At Knossos, there were two main storage blocks, along the west front and in the north-east sector. Mallia had a similar arrangement, but store-rooms extended all the way along the east front as well. At Phaistos, they were focused in the centre of the West Wing.

Obviously a temple-complex of great status and with a large household of priests or priestesses and other attendants required resources to maintain it. It needed revenue. That revenue could be gathered in either as voluntary offerings to the temple and its deities or as compulsory taxes. The produce collected could be stored for consumption in the temple or redistributed in exchange for other goods; there seems to have been no money. This role of redistribution is by no means unfamiliar in religious foundations: a very similar system operated in England in the Middle Ages when churches collected tithes and abbeys gathered enormous wealth. As we shall see, the analogy between the Minoan temple and the medieval abbey is a very useful one.

Temples in Mesopotamia in the third millennium BC operated within a similar monastic system. A substantial area of the Sumerian temple was taken up with store-rooms. Like the Labyrinth, the Sumerian temple was a major redistribution centre, amassing wealth from the land which it owned and from tribute, reworking some of the produce into manufactured goods, redistributing some as exports, diplomatic gifts, wages, or rations. It may well be, from the closeness of the parallels, that the Cretan temples were eastern in conception. The Sumerian temple functioned as the dwelling-place of deities, as a ceremonial centre and a centre for worship, as a treasury and storehouse and as a commercial and manufacturing centre. In addition it housed the priests, priestesses and temple workers. It is very recognizable as a possible paradigm for the Knossos Labyrinth.

THE THRONE SANCTUARY

As for the hundreds of rooms at Knossos that were neither workshops nor used to store produce for redistribution, it is hard to know where best to begin. Perhaps the Room of the Throne, whose discovery formed the climax of Evans' first season at Knossos, is an appropriate starting-point; it seemed to provide Evans with the solid proof of kingship that would support his palace interpretation, but it also provided him with less welcome evidence of a religious use.

The Throne Room has an oppressive, claustrophobic quality that is often missed in photographs. Windowless and low-ceilinged, approached by way of a deep anteroom that itself is depressed four steps below the level of the Central Court, the room has an almost subterranean quality. The throne does not face the doorway, but looks across the width of the room towards the half-hidden sunken adyton. Evans put in a colonnaded skylight above the adyton to let light in from the floor above, but there is no reason to believe that this was part of the original design. A doorway at the back of the Throne Room leads to a suite of nine small rooms which clearly had some support or service function in relation to the Throne Room itself. A second doorway out of the Throne Room leads to two long and narrow storage rooms and one of those opens into two small cupboard-like chambers with rectangular vaults let into the floor. We must assume that these secret vaults were repositories or safes for the precious objects used in ceremonies that took place in the Throne Room itself.

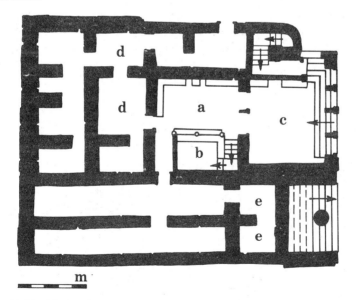

Figure 14 The Throne Sanctuary. a – Throne Room, b – adyton, c – antechapel, d – vestries, sacristies, e – temple repositories. Arrow = stairs down.

The whole complex of chambers, sixteen in all, if we include the adyton as a chamber in its own right, was evidently designed as a self-contained unit within the temple building (Figure 14). There is a public and ceremonial entrance, down steps and through a range of four double-doorways, from the Central Court; there is also a more discreet service entrance for priestesses and other attendants from the corridor to the north. In one corner there is also a service staircase down from the floor above. The overall impression is of a self-contained and sealed-off sanctuary, access to which was carefully controlled and restricted.

Evans found a strange collection of fragments scattered about the Throne Room. Overturned and lying in pieces on its side was a large plain storage jar; it looked as if it had been standing in the north-east corner of the chamber and pulled over or shaken over towards the centre of the chamber. Round it, on the paved floor, were the remains of four curiously-shaped alabaster vessels (alabastra) decorated with carved spirals. They look like large inkwells, about 30 centimetres across. Evans' manuscript plan seems to show a fifth alabastron in the north-west corner and his photograph shows a cup of some kind on the bench immediately to the left of the throne. Evans also found a trail of porcelain, crystal, and ivory fragments leading from the foot of the throne across the chamber and down into the adyton, the structure Evans called the lustral basin.

Spyridon Marinatos and his daughter Nanno have preferred to use the word 'adyton' (holy of holies) for such structures, since ritual washing may not have been the only or even the principal cult activity that was conducted there. The adyta were certainly places to descend into in ones and twos, dark and secret places for mystic rituals, places where the subterranean deities might be invoked, places for individual initiation. Platon (1971) has tried to compromise, suggesting that the 'bathroom' in the alleged 'royal apartments' at Zakro fulfilled a double function as a secular washroom and as a place for occasional ritual purifications. He felt that the secular use was indicated by the bathroom's proximity to the royal apartments but, since we now challenge the secular function of these rooms, we do not need to find a secular use for the bathroom. Platon himself recognized that the wall decoration scheme in the Zakro bathroom indicated a religious function. Two walls carried painted symbolic images of altars and horns of consecration in white on a red background, reminiscent of the sacrificial scene of a blood-spattered pair of horns in the adyton in Room 3, Xeste 3 at Akrotiri on Thera (Marinatos 1984). The accumulating evidence is that these sunken areas were isolated holy places, places of special sanctity for esoteric individual initiations.

To return to Knossos, and the Throne Sanctuary in particular: in the corner where the large jar and the collection of alabastra were found, there was a small stone-lined cupboard let into the wall just above the bench. This too was found to contain fragments of the decorative inlay work.

There seems little doubt that these curious remains are fragments of cult objects. It has often been suggested that some sort of ceremony of propitiation was in progress at the moment when the Throne Room and the Labyrinth as a whole were engulfed by the final disaster. Perhaps after days or weeks of premonitory earth tremors, the temple priestesses were trying ritual after ritual, sacrifice after sacrifice, to appease the chthonic deities and avert the full wrath of the Earth-shaker. It is an attractive idea and we know from the dramatic new evidence of the shrine at Anemospilia (see Chapter 9) that religious rites were performed right up to the moment when those offering sacrifice were overwhelmed by disaster. But which god or goddess was being worshipped or appealed to in the Throne Room is far more difficult to tell. We can only, on the evidence we have, make a general inference about its dedication. We cannot be sure whether a priest or priestess sat on the gypsum throne, but (see Chapter 9) it seems likely that it was a priestess mysteriously transformed by ritual into an epiphany of the deity. The nature of the frescoes suggests that an attempt was being made to re-create the wild landscape of the mountain tops. The peculiar wavy shape of the throne back is a representation of a mountain peak; a rhyton from the temple at Zakro shows a very similar form to indicate the summit of a mountain rising behind an elaborately designed peak sanctuary. The intention of the Throne Sanctuary, as we might call it, was to honour the same deity or deities that were honoured in the peak sanctuaries by a symbolic re-creation of the peak setting.

The rectangle of rough paving in the centre of the floor was originally smoothly finished in red-tinted plaster. The red colouring of this floor panel may also have been highly symbolic. We know that sacrificial blood offerings were poured into libation pits and may also have been splashed over altars and horns of consecration, as frescoes on Thera show. Red-painted floors and pillars would automatically have had an association with sacrificial offerings. Perhaps sacrifices were actually performed on some of the red-painted floor areas. The colour red seems also to have been associated with the underworld. The red floor panel was apparently the centre of the religious rituals in the Throne Sanctuary and the manifestation of the deity on the throne itself was their focus. The stone benches flanking the throne were probably not for sitting on but for the placing of offerings. From other shrine contexts, it is clear that this was a common practice; only the throne itself was intended unambiguously as a seat. The concept of a specific category of shrines called 'bench sanctuaries' has recently been formally recognized (e.g. Gesell 1985). The antechapel, similarly equipped with a rectangular plaster floor panel and offering benches, but without a lustral basin or adyton, may have been accessible to the uninitiated who were not admitted to the inner sanctuary.

THE SNAKE GODDESS SANCTUARY

Immediately to the south of the Throne Sanctuary, but with no inter-

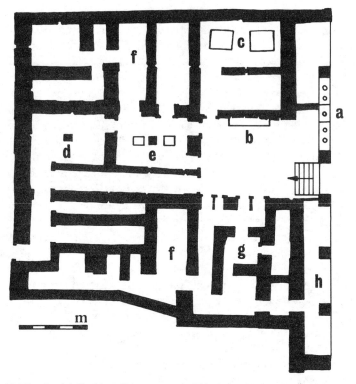

Figure 15 The Snake Goddess Sanctuary. a – Tripartite Shrine, b – bench altar, c –
Temple Repositories, d – West Pillar Crypt, e – East Pillar Crypt, libation pits in
floor, f – store-rooms, vestries, etc, g – room of the chariot tablets, h – pillared
portico

connecting door, was another self-contained suite of chambers. This slightly
larger suite of perhaps eighteen chambers had a main entrance, again down a
short flight of steps, from the Central Court. The principal ceremonial area,
marked out by a square of rough flagging, originally plastered, is what is
usually called the Lobby of the Stone Seat. As the largest chamber in the
suite, we should treat it as more than a mere lobby. Admittedly, it has eight
doorways leading out of it, but then the principal chamber in the Throne
Sanctuary had four. The seat which gives the lobby its name probably
functioned as an offering bench. There is no (surviving) throne and no adyton
here. There are several storage rooms or sacristies, one of which had two large
stone-lined cists let into its floor; this is a feature which we saw in the most
inaccessible region of the Throne Sanctuary and designed for the same
purpose. If the practice seems odd, it is one which survived into the classical
period; the Temple of Zeus built in about 330 BC at Nemea, for example, had
a similar rectangular vault or strongroom installed under its floor for the
safe-keeping of temple treasures. The 'Temple Repositories' of the Snake

Goddess Sanctuary at Knossos still had their sanctuary treasure in them when they were opened in 1903 (Figure 30).

Duncan Mackenzie found, on top, a large quantity of vases (amphorae and pitchers from the island of Melos) tightly packed together. Then, about a metre down, he found seal impressions, large quantities of painted sea shells, imitation shells, flying fish, fruit and flowers made of faience, beads, faience chalices with sacred tree motifs, decorative inlays, objects made of bone and ivory, gold leaf, a finely polished but broken marble cross, and faience figures of opulently dressed snake goddesses. There were also two beautiful faience plaques of a goat with her kids and a cow with her calf. One of the statuettes found in the East Repository had been broken before it was sealed up in the vault; a matching fragment of it was found in the West Repository. These and other pieces of cult furniture may have been deliberately, ritually, killed by breaking before being sealed up in the large repositories as a re-foundation offering. After they were filled and closed, the repositories were replaced by two new and smaller repositories.

The most significant thing about the temple treasure is that it hints at the sort of cult activities that may have been conducted in the surrounding chambers of the Snake Goddess Sanctuary. The statuettes, now reconstructed

Figure 16 The Snake Goddess

Figure 17 The Tripartite Shrine: a reconstruction

and deservedly among the most famous and memorable relics of the Minoan culture, show us how the Minoan Snake Goddess was visualized, her High Priestess ritually and ecstatically transformed into an epiphany of the goddess.

In the dark, inner region of the Snake Goddess Sanctuary are two pillar crypts, themselves evidently the focus of some chthonic or temple-foundation cult (Plate 1). Whether the rites enacted round the squared pillars, with their thirty double-axe carvings, were directed downwards into the shaking earth or upwards into the fabric of the temple building it is difficult to tell.

The feature distinguishing this sanctuary from all others at Knossos is its now-wrecked façade, positioned next to the entrance and exactly at the centre of the long western side of the Central Court (Figure 17). In fact, it is impossible not to conclude that this façade was the starting-point for the design of the Central Court: no other feature has a comparable pivotal position in the court's symmetry. Since the Central Court was the principal space from which the rest of the temple-complex developed, it may be that this central shrine was the point from which the whole temple evolved.

Figure 18 The Tripartite Shrine as shown on a miniature fresco found in the Labyrinth

The façade's footings and pillar sockets survive, but that is all. Originally it consisted of a central raised plinth with a tapering pillar mounted on it and two flanking plinths at a lower level, each surmounted by a pair of pillars. A structure very like this is shown on one of the miniature frescoes, although with one pillar on each side and two on the central raised plinth. The pillars were given small corniced roofs to bear and these in turn were surmounted by rows of horns. The 'Tripartite Shrine' was a major architectural set-piece and obviously designed to be a visual and religious focus for the Central Court and whatever rites went on there. It links together the public rites of the open court with the private, esoteric rites of the Snake Goddess Sanctuary.

THE DESTROYED SANCTUARY

The southern edge of the Snake Goddess Sanctuary has vanished as a result of Evans' building work on the staircase leading up from the South Propylaeum. This new masonry covers the western part of the sanctuary boundary. The eastern part is altered beyond recognition because the original foundations of a late megaron-type building were ripped out and some 'cosmetic' modern paving and walling put in to replace them. The southern edge of the Snake Goddess Sanctuary apparently abutted on to a large rectangular chamber about 12 by 8 metres, rather larger than the combined areas of the Throne Room and its adyton and antechapel. The Destroyed Sanctuary was large enough to have functioned as a small sanctuary in its own right and probably had its own entrance from the Central Court. More than this it is difficult to say, given the altered state of the site (Figure 19).

THE CUPBEARER SANCTUARY

Evans reconstructed the area he called the South Propylaeum in such a way that it took on the appearance of an art deco cinema foyer, preparing the way

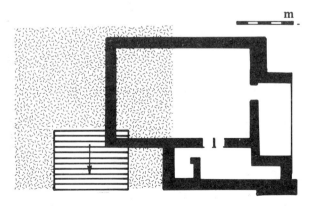

Figure 19 The Destroyed Sanctuary. The hatched area is the solid masonry platform inserted by Evans for his new staircase

for his impressive, and brand-new, staircase up to the first floor. The earliest photographs of the site, taken during the excavations, show no sign at all of a bronze age staircase and Theodore Fyfe's plan of the area, made before Evans' 'reconstitution' work began, shows no sign of it either.

On Fyfe's plan, the South Propylaeum shows as a broad hall some 9.5 metres wide, with pillars and projecting piers supporting the wide ceiling. At the southern end, outside a pier-and-door partition, there is an anteroom 4 metres deep. At the northern end, some 13 metres beyond the doorways, the walls peter out, but it is possible that the hall went on as far as the south wall of the Destroyed Sanctuary, which would have made the hall 18 metres long.

Whatever its original length – whether 13, 15 or 18 metres – the chamber as reinterpreted here becomes a functional space in its own right. It was never a foyer or an entrance hall, but a room with a specific purpose of its own. It too may have been a temple-sanctuary. Like the Throne Sanctuary and Snake Goddess Sanctuary, it had its own stone-lined treasure store in the floor. Unlike the three sanctuaries so far discussed, it did not have an entrance opening on to the Central Court; instead it seems to have been approached by way of a wide triple doorway opening out of the Procession Corridor. Another peculiarity is the double-walling, which Evans saw as evidence of two distinct building phases on the site. The outer wall he interpreted as the wall of the earlier propylaeum: the inner one replaced it later. The main reason for believing the inner wall to be a later addition is the existence of the stone cist, which passes beneath it. Why the design was changed is a matter for speculation. It may have been to provide an ambulatory along each side of the sanctuary so that processions of initiates or pilgrims might enter the

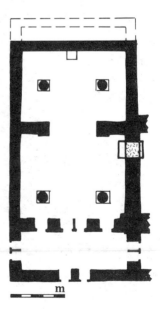

Figure 20 The Cupbearer Sanctuary

northern end of the sanctuary without intruding on whatever ceremonies were taking place in the southern end.

Given the new interpretation of the chamber's function, we can no longer call it the South Propylaeum. 'The Cupbearer Sanctuary' is a name which suggests itself, after the fresco fragments on its walls (Figure 20).

The sanctuary, along with much of the rest of the southern end of the building, was in a badly eroded state when Evans and Mackenzie excavated it. The northern end of the sanctuary had completely gone. It was there, we must assume, that the sanctuary's focus stood. That may have been an offering bench with a few goddess figurines placed on it to indicate the temple's dedication; it may have been a wooden throne of the same type that we saw in stone in the Throne Sanctuary; it may have been a large xoanon, a wooden effigy of a deity. The only clue we have is a find of four figurines of a goddess, which came from the south-east corner of the sanctuary. It is not much to go on, but it does seem to link the sanctuary with the worship of a goddess. The fresco fragments that were found fallen from its walls show temple attendants processing through mountains with conical rhytons; they represent parts of a devotional scene clearly linking up with the Corridor of the Procession fresco and the painted offerings are clearly intended for the sanctuary's deity. Although the frescoes have to be read with great care, not least because so little of the total picture survives, they nevertheless give us an indication of what happened – actually or figuratively – in the chambers where they were painted. The cupbearer in the fresco is arriving to pour a painted libation to a deity; once, real cupbearers came to the sanctuary to pour real libations.

THE LOTUS LAMP SANCTUARY

East of the Cupbearer Sanctuary the ruined 'south front' of the Labyrinth becomes very difficult to interpret. All that is left is an irregular basement area which yielded too little to give any clear idea of the function of the rooms above. The area may have been dominated by the major access corridors which crossed it on at least two levels. The Procession Corridor ran along the front of the Cupbearer Sanctuary and then turned north into the Central Court. To the south of the Procession Corridor were two more wide corridors leading into the temple from the south-west entrance: one may have risen by a flight of stairs to provide access to the Procession Corridor while the other continued along the south front, passing the South Entrance, to lead finally by way of a ramp into the south-east corner of the Central Court. These complex arrangements were apparently designed to cope with large numbers of pilgrims arriving from the south side of the temple.

To the north of the sequence of West Wing sanctuaries, we come to another self-contained suite of chambers. This is a suite of only six chambers and it appears only to have had one entrance, down a short flight of steps from the north-west corner of the Central Court. There are two principal chambers, the (outer) Room of the Lotus Lamp and the (inner) Room of the Saffron-Gatherer. The inner room is named after some fresco fragments found there by Evans. The fresco shows a blue monkey collecting crocuses and putting them into a bowl, or stealing them: the seventeenth-century BC date of the bowl indicates that the fresco is among the earliest known on Crete.

The crocus was used for making saffron, which in turn could be used as a yellow textile dye – or as a pain-killing drug. Whether it was the narcotic qualities of saffron that made it a cult substance or its use to dye the goddess's robes is impossible to tell; either way, the crocus was often painted into frescoes of a religious nature. On Thera, offering tables were found with crocuses painted on them and the Crocus Gatherers' Fresco speaks clearly of the link with the worship of the goddess, with girls who may be initiands picking crocuses and offering them to a goddess enthroned on an altar; she is attended by a monkey and a rampant griffin. Although the fresco in the Labyrinth is regrettably very fragmentary, it looks as if it belongs to a similar cult scene: a monkey in attendance on a goddess who is being offered a bowl of crocuses. It follows that the chamber which the fresco decorated was also dedicated to the cult.

The adjoining Room of the Lotus Lamp is identified as a cult room by its central square stone pillar. Evans also found beside it a decayed font-like basin made of alabaster: he felt that the basin was used for ritual sprinkling. There was a set of stone sanctuary lamps to illuminate the ceremonies that took place there but, as Evans says, it would have been 'at most a dim religious light'.

Evans also identified to the east of the Room of the Lotus Lamp a small shrine. This room too yielded fragments of miniatures, though it is not very clear whether the frescoes decorated the crypt rooms or chambers on the floor above. It was nevertheless from this area that some very important religious frescoes came, notably the Grandstand Fresco and the Sacred Grove and Dance Fresco.

Winding round three sides of the Lotus Lamp Sanctuary is the North-West Entrance Passage, which leads to the sanctuary entrance and the north-west corner of the Central Court from the North-West Adyton, an area which Evans recognized was for initiation ceremonies.

THE INITIATION AREA

The central feature of this area is a sunken rectangular adyton or lustral basin with a colonnaded staircase descending round three sides of it. There are adyta elsewhere in the temple-complex, but none as elaborate as this: the Throne Sanctuary's adyton, for example, has six steps descending into it while the North-West Adyton has fourteen. It is also distinguished by being a freestanding building within its own walled enclosure. This area was probably used, as Evans suggested, for rites of purification. Visitors or pilgrims arriving

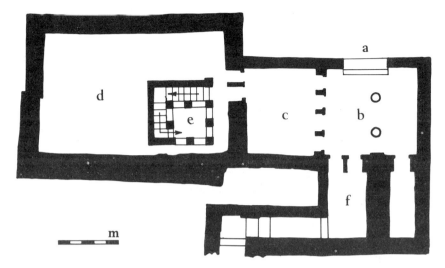

Figure 21 The Initiation Area. a – North-West Entrance, b – vestibule, c – inner chamber, d – courtyard, e – North-West Adyton, f – North-West Entrance Passage

at the North Entrance would have entered by way of the North-West Portico and its antechamber in order to undergo the ceremony of initiation, which apparently involved some kind of token ablution or anointing in the adyton and some additional rite in the enclosure.

Once ritually cleansed and 'baptized', pilgrims were allowed to enter the main temple precinct, apparently by way of the winding North-West Corridor that leads to the Central Court (Figure 21).

Ritual stone ewers found in the adyton were almost certainly used in ceremonial acts of ablution. An Egyptian pot-lid found in the enclosure suggests many possibilities; perhaps the priestesses were trading with Egypt, or perhaps an Egyptian visitor to Crete came to see the temple, which must have ranked among the wonders of the bronze age world. Either way, there was contact between the temple at Knossos and Egypt in about 1620 BC.

THE CONCOURSE AND SERVICE QUARTER

Close to the Initiation Area is the temple's North Entrance, opening into the large South Pillar Hall, a rectangular, windowless undercroft with a ceiling supported on seven pillars. It makes better sense to call this chamber the *South* Pillar Hall to distinguish it from a smaller but similar structure a short distance to the north. The North Entrance Passage leads up out of the South Pillar Hall to the northern edge of the Central Court.

Although a ritual function is possible for the South Pillar Hall (Evans' Custom House), it is more likely that it served as a gathering place for newly arrived visitors to the temple and as an undercroft for a refectory on the first floor. Graham believes that there may have been a banquet hall on the first floor. Both Graham and Platon believe that large-scale communal meals were a feature of life in the palaces, and there is every reason to suppose that communal eating and drinking were a feature of both the secular and religious life of the temples. The later, classical Cretan practice of taking communal 'brotherhood' meals, the syssitia system, may have had its roots in a Minoan practice (Willetts 1969).

To the east of the eleven-pillared undercroft and the North Entrance Passage lies the North-East Quarter of the temple-complex, a badly damaged part of the site and one where interpretation can only be tentative. There are many store-rooms in this quarter and the nature of the finds suggests that it served the domestic needs of the temple staff and perhaps those of visitors too. Evans mentions masses of plain clay cups. It is possible that this is where meals were prepared, ready for consumption in the refectory above the South Pillar Hall.

There is just one area that has a little more formality about it, Evans' North-East Hall, and we may tentatively interpret it as a small sanctuary. It stands at the top of a long staircase leading from the temple's East Entrance and may have been visited by pilgrims arriving from the east before they entered the Central Court, a few metres away to the west.

THE TEMPLE WORKSHOPS

South of the North-East Sanctuary lies the East Wing, and we need to examine its northern and southern sectors separately. The northern sector consists of yet more small store-rooms, often separated by massive walls that suggest cellarage for a major structure on the floors above, and some equally small chambers that were apparently used by craftsmen.

The chamber Evans named the School Room, because of the benches which he thought looked like school desks, may have been used for the manufacture of some of the thousands of cult objects that were used in the temple. It may have been here that the little decorative inlays were made that were found, broken and scattered across the floor, in the Throne Sanctuary. Further south, the rooms known as the Room of the Wooden Posts, Lapidary's or Sculptor's Workshop and Room of the Stone Pier seem also to have been used by temple craftsmen.

THE SANCTUARY OF THE GREAT GODDESS

The massive walls surrounding the store-rooms immediately to the west of the craft area obviously supported a substantial superstructure. Evans, true to his royal palace preoccupation, interpreted the large chamber on the floor above as 'the most important of all the reception halls in the Palace area', calling it the 'Great East Hall'. He felt that the very confusing evidence – fragments that

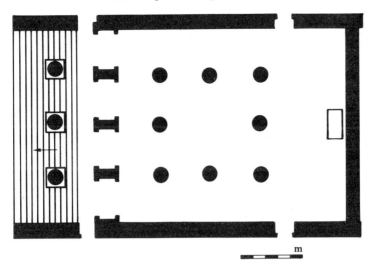

Figure 22 The Great Goddess Sanctuary

had fallen through the collapsed floor (or floors) into the cellars – pointed to two phases in the hall's development. The earlier hall had its floor level slightly below the ground level of the Central Court: the later hall had a raised floor level, twelve steps up from the Central Court (Figure 22).

The paper-reconstructed later hall is an imposing structure, with its wide ceremonial staircase up through a colonnade to a landing in front of a pier-and-door partition. Inside is a spacious room 18.5 metres long and 15 metres wide, with eight tapering Minoan pillars supporting the ceiling beams round a central square space which may have been a light-well.

The mural decoration of this hall was even more exotic than that found elsewhere in the building. In the cellars, Mackenzie found an extraordinary range of fresco fragments, suggesting all kinds of religious imagery. There were painted relief frescoes of the same type as Evans' famous 'Priest-King Fresco'. The fragments were mainly of muscular limbs and the original frescoes depicted various kinds of struggle: boxing, wrestling, and bull-grappling. In effect they showed the same sort of scene that we see on a smaller scale on the two Vaphio cups (found near Sparta but made in Minoan Crete) and on the Boxer Vase from Agia Triadha. But Mackenzie also found fragments in the same cellars of a very different kind of fresco, depicting a static mythological scene. It was a frieze of standing, winged griffins tethered to columns. Possibly the griffin frieze formed a second tier of decoration above or below the scenes of combat, and represented the patient, waiting presence of the presiding goddess.

More significantly still, bronze fittings for a large wooden statue of a goddess were found near the north wall. The pieces of moulded bronze, Evans thought, were intended to be locks of hair: given their size, about 15 centimetres long, the head must have been 40 centimetres high and the whole statue 3 metres high. Evans suggested, from the findspot of the locks, that the statue of the goddess originally stood in the north-east corner of the hall, but it is possible that it stood against the centre of the east wall and toppled northwards as a result of an earthquake or the floor giving way. A focal position like this makes more sense for what was clearly a major religious cult object.

The people of Minoan Crete were credited by the classical Greeks with inventing large wooden images of deities. The Greeks alleged that in the earliest times the gods were represented by very simplified limbless wooden idols or xoana; it was Daidalos who developed greater realism by giving them limbs. It is likely that some xoana of Minoan craftsmanship lasted many centuries, possibly even into the classical period. The statue of Hermes seen by Pausanias in Arcadia was 2 or 3 metres high and made of juniper wood. The Greek tradition was that such things came from ancient Crete and the 'Great East Hall' with its imposing wooden statue of the goddess seems to confirm that there was truth in the tradition; it is unfortunate that more fragments of the statue were not recovered.

The strong implication is that the Great East Hall was not a royal reception room at all but a Sanctuary of the Great Goddess. A self-contained unit opening on to the Central Court by way of a flight of steps, this sanctuary has some design features in common with those we saw on the western and northern sides of the Central Court. It is significantly different in being larger, in not being subdivided into small chambers, and in being much more public in feeling. It is much more recognizably a temple-sanctuary because it is architecturally closer in spirit to the later, classical idea of a temple.

Curiously, under the cellarage were found the fragmentary remains of a much earlier sanctuary that was apparently dedicated to a dove-goddess; we might refer to this Middle Minoan II shrine (see Appendix A for chronology) as the Early Dove-Goddess Sanctuary.

THE DOUBLE-AXE SANCTUARY

South of the Sanctuary of the Great Goddess lies another self-contained unit, which really consists of two interconnected sanctuary suites, one large, one small, and a stairwell. In a sense the Double-Axe Sanctuary is similar to the other sanctuaries we have looked at, in that it is approached by steps leading down from the Central Court, but it lies at a much lower level and many more steps are involved. It appears that the architect's intention was to create, and indeed repeat, the impression of descent into the earth's interior; a similar descent by staircase was engineered at Phaistos, into the chambers known as the Royal Apartments (Figures 8, 23).

The double chamber which Evans called the Hall of the Double-Axes

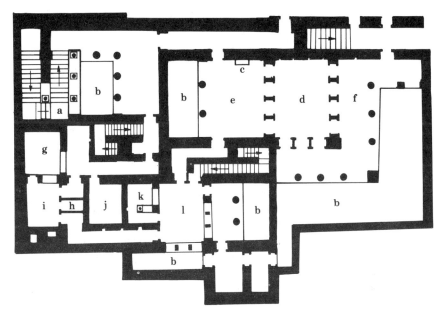

Figure 23 The Double-Axe and Dolphin Sanctuaries. a – Grand Staircase, b – light-well, c – wooden throne, d – Double-Axe Sanctuary principal chamber, e – Double-Axe Sanctuary outer chamber, f – colonnade, g – 'Court of the Distaffs' light-well, h – toilet, i – vestry?, j – respository for cult equipment?, k – adyton, l – Dolphin Sanctuary principal chamber

consisted of an outer space opening on to a light-well and an inner space which could be closed off from the outside world by eleven sets of double doors. It is an arrangement that is fairly common in places of worship, comparable with the (separable) nave and chancel of a parish church. Some rites in the Minoan religion were evidently public, others were for initiates only to witness.

Against the north wall of the outer chamber, Evans found the remains – a cast, in fact – of a canopied throne. The same problems of interpretation apply here as to the gypsum throne in the Throne Sanctuary; we cannot tell whether a life-sized statue of a deity sat there, or a priestess conducting a ritual, or a priestess as the epiphany of a deity.

Nothing remains of the focal point in the inner chamber. It may have been, as Evans guessed, a similar chair but made of wood, but it may have been something else entirely, such as a wooden statue of the goddess like the one we encountered in the Great Goddess Sanctuary.

THE DOLPHIN SANCTUARY

A short dog-leg passage connects the outer chamber of the Double-Axe Sanctuary with the much smaller suite of chambers that makes up the

Dolphin Sanctuary. This is distinguished by having a lustral basin or adyton; it now contains a decorated bathtub but this was actually found nearby, not in the adyton. There is also a lavatory and robing room or vestry at the end of a passage.

If the Dolphin Fresco decorating the main room's north wall seems an irrelevance in a temple, we must remember that the forces of nature were very close to the heart of Minoan religion (see Chapter 9) and that dolphins in particular were symbolic creatures. In the ancient Mediterranean world the dolphin, like the dove, was a symbol of the soul's liberation from the earthly body. The fresco is therefore to be seen at least partly as an expression of the freeing of the human spirit, whether in death or in religious trance. Sinclair Hood has argued (1978) that from their position when found the fragments appear to have fallen from the floor above, where they may have adorned the floor rather than the wall; a comparable fresco-floor has been found in a shrine near Agia Triadha at Phaistos, so it is not impossible. If Hood is right, we should perhaps call the first-floor room the Dolphin Sanctuary, but the name is a convenient tag for the ground-floor sanctuary while the fresco remains on its walls.

In her analysis of well-preserved quasi-Minoan shrines on Thera, Nanno Marinatos (1984) saw the adyton as a focal point and place of separation to which initiates were admitted singly or in very small groups from larger rooms in the vicinity. It may be that the larger rooms of the neighbouring Double-Axe Sanctuary relate to the Dolphin Sanctuary adyton in this way.

THE TRITON SHELL SANCTUARY

To the south of the Dolphin Sanctuary is an even smaller suite, little more than two corridors and three cupboard-like recesses, but with an apparent shrine function even so. Nanno Marinatos reminds us that we have to shed our western ideas of religious architecture when dealing with a culture with a strong oriental element. We cannot judge the function of a chamber by its appearance, only by the equipment it contains. The newly discovered temple at Anemospilia on the northern slope of Mount Juktas is a case in point. As Nanno Marinatos and Robin Hägg (1983) observe, the architecture is distinctly un-temple-like; at first glance, with its three narrow rectangular chambers and three entrance lobbies leading off a central hall or corridor, Anemospilia looks rather like the West Magazine complex at Phaistos. Yet, as we shall see in Chapter 9, the cult equipment and other remains tell us of activities that were unequivocally religious in nature.

The two corridors of the Triton Shell Sanctuary open from the west side of a small courtyard, which may have had some functional connection with the little sanctuary, perhaps as a semi-public space. One corridor is a dead end and when excavated was found to be crammed with beautifully painted lily vases. Opening out of it to the south is a small bath chamber with a bath in it,

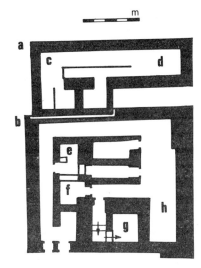

Figure 24 The Triton Shell (a) and Late Dove Goddess (b) Sanctuaries. c – small bench altar, triton shell found nearby, d – small courtyard, possibly used for access by ladder from floor above, e – Late Dove Goddess shrine, f – later walling, sealing shrine off, g – adyton, h – courtyard

possibly though not provably for ritual ablution (Figure 24).

The second corridor, immediately north of the first and separated from it by a thin partition, turns a corner and leads into two cupboard-like compartments which were also full of pottery. At the bend in the corridor there is a small shelf-like ledge which was used, by analogy with the next sanctuary to the south, for cult objects that may have included small statuettes of goddesses. Evans thought so and others have joined him in treating this odd little corner as a 'domestic' shrine.

The most evocative find in the sanctuary was a triton shell. It would have been used, as Evans suggested, for summoning up whatever deity was worshipped there.

THE LATE DOVE GODDESS SANCTUARY

To the south of the Triton Shell Sanctuary lies yet another, built with a slightly different orientation to the rest of the East Wing and evidently built as a separate unit. Several of the sanctuaries give the impression of being designed and built almost as autonomous units within the overall temple-complex. The Double-Axe and Dolphin Sanctuaries, for instance, were obviously laid out as a single architectural design incorporating the Grand Staircase and the East-West Corridor.

Like the Triton Shell Sanctuary, the Late Dove Goddess Sanctuary is small in scale with a small courtyard along its east side. A corridor passes round the sanctuary's north and west sides and leads into an important stairwell, the South-East Staircase.

The sanctuary has an adyton as well as a small shrine, which Evans named

Figure 25 The Late Dove Goddess Sanctuary: reconstruction of shrine

the Shrine of the Double-Axes. On the narrow altar shelf were two sets of horns of consecration, saddle-shaped clay structures with a stucco finish. In the hollow of each saddle was a socket to hold the sacred double-axe, the principal religious symbol of the whole temple-complex. But the figurines Evans found on the altar are of far greater importance. One was the goddess, an opulently dressed, bare-breasted goddess with huge braceleted hands raised in generous benediction. On her head perched a dove. Near her were two priestesses, attendants or lesser divinities with their hands clenched to their collar bones, apparently in a gesture of respect, adoration, or supplication (Figure 49). A naked female worshipper, or possibly sacrificial victim, is a rather pathetic figure. A man approaches bearing a dove as an offering. This repetition of the dove symbol – dove as sacrifice, dove as the goddess's symbol – is the reason for proposing that the area be renamed the Dove Goddess Sanctuary.

The idols found there actually date from around 1360 BC, after the Labyrinth as a whole is supposed to have been abandoned. The continuing worship of the goddess in this little shrine (Figure 25) among the deserted sprawl of ruins bears eloquent testimony to the continuing sanctity of the Labyrinth; it was still regarded as a holy place, even in decay.

In this brief tour of the Labyrinth, we have scrutinized it room by room, suite by suite, and found that the temple-complex hypothesis has stood up well to examination. When we look at the distribution of Minoan religious cult objects and furnishings, we find that the evidence pervades practically every part of the Labyrinth: double-axes, altars, benches, stone thrones, snake tubes, votives, religious frescoes depicting cult scenes and signposting the uses of the chambers, communion chalices, idols, shells, water-worn pebbles, red pigment, animal rhytons, adyta and horns of consecration. The great majority of the finds make far more sense interpreted as part of an orientally derived temple-complex than as part of a royal palace. The architecture too is easier to understand in these terms, the enclosed shrines as centres for esoteric rituals, the open courts as arenas for congregational ceremonies and ritual dances.

8
Beyond the Labyrinth walls

As for us here, I live in the temple area. You know the conditions in
which we live. I live all alone with the scribe Zaroy and the scribe of
the soldiers, Penta-hit-nacht. I hope you will cause the men of the
labyrinth to be captured and returned to me on this bank of the river.

Letter from a depressed overseer at the Labyrinth of
Medinet Habu, *c.* 1100 BC

THE 'PALACE DEPENDENCIES'

If we accept for the moment, however provisionally, that the so-called 'Palace
of Minos' was a temple-complex, we may have to revise our interpretation of
the other Minoan buildings in its vicinity. Evans and his followers have seen
them as princely residences for important officials or members of the
Knossian royal family, and some of them do seem to have fulfilled an
ancillary or satellite function in relation to the main building. If the main
building was a temple, the satellite buildings too may have had a religious use.

The South House was seen by Evans as a very important private residence
and he may have been right, but there is some slight evidence that it may have
been a sanctuary instead. Its walls encroached on the foundations of the
colonnaded south-west approach to the temple, indicating that it may have
been part of the temple-complex, and therefore possibly an outlying
sanctuary. It has a fine location overlooking the Vlychia valley and with a
view across to Mount Juktas, the sacred mountain of the Labyrinth (see
Chapter 9). In its original state, the South House would have been the first
sanctuary that pilgrims arriving from the south or from the pilgrim hostel
would have passed as they entered the Knossian temple-complex.

It had a foundation block that consisted of a stone box containing tesserae
made of a whole range of exotic materials: plain and smoked crystal, beryl,
amethyst, lapis lazuli, bronze, and gold. There was a pillar crypt which
originally had a columnar shrine containing a double-axe stand above it. On

an upper floor a hoard of silver vessels may, to judge from their thinness, have had a ritual use. The building also had its own adyton which, as we have already seen, strongly suggests a religious cult use.

On the south-eastern edge of the temple-complex, the House of the Chancel Screen has architectural features that are shared with the Royal Villa and the High Priest's House. In each case there is a pillar crypt and a principal chamber with a pillared balustrade separating off a part of the room as an inner sanctum. A central gap in the balustrade allows passage up a few steps to a throne or altar. The architectural effect is distinctly religious in feeling. The House of the Chancel Screen had a square rostrum at its focal point, where Evans felt a wooden throne might originally have stood. He may have been right, and a priestess may have sat on it, an oracle among many oracles to be consulted in the Labyrinth; he may have been mistaken, though, and an altar or some other object of veneration may have stood on the dais instead. Evans' workmen may have had a better instinct about this building than did Evans himself when they named it 'the House of the Priest'.

Like the rest of the southern edge of the Labyrinth, the site of the Chancel Screen Sanctuary is badly eroded and its plan is difficult to interpret in detail (Plate 9). The rectangular chamber in front of the balustrade opens into a central, public chamber by way of a pier-and-door partition. This central chamber had a passage leading to the South-East House or to an independent entrance; a second door led south to what seems to have been an adyton; a third exit led west to a pillar crypt. The layout suggests a religious cult use.

Close beside the Chancel Screen Sanctuary and similar in size and style is the South-East House. There are differences in detail and orientation, but once again the sanctuary was designed as an architectural entity, just like the sanctuaries incorporated in the main complex. In one room, a pair of limestone horns stood on a small platform-altar covered in water-worn pebbles, reminiscent of the shrine in the Late Dove Goddess Sanctuary. The South-East House also had its pillar crypt.

Further off to the north-east of the temple is the 'Royal Villa' or Balustrade Sanctuary. This has a spacious pillar crypt, a shrine-like main chamber (Plate 7), and a spacious, ceremonial staircase apparently giving access to the building at first-floor level on the west side. Visitors must have approached the gloomy ground-floor rooms much as they approached the Double-Axe Sanctuary in the East Wing of the temple, from the west and down flights of stairs. Evans found the remains of what he thought was yet another throne, though it may have been an altar, in a curious light-well. It was possible to look down onto it from a balcony on the first floor; this odd arrangement may have been designed to allow people on both floors to have a sight of the image of the goddess or whatever idol stood or sat on the throne-altar.

The High Priest's House on the road out of Knossos to the south has a sanctuary layout reminiscent of the architecture of the Chancel Screen and Balustrade Sanctuaries. Evans' reconstruction drawing of the balustraded

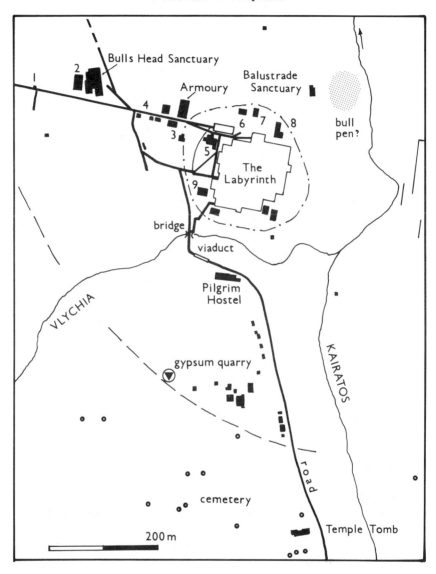

Figure 26 Map of Minoan Knossos. The Labyrinth was built on the ancestral settlement site. The dot-and-dash line shows the extent of the late neolithic village; the dashed line shows the southern limit of intensive occupation by 1400 BC. The Labyrinth was roughly in the centre of Minoan Knossos. 1 – House of the Sacrificed Children, 2 – Unexplored Mansion, 3 – House of the Frescoes, 4 – Royal Road, 5 – North-West Treasure House/Sanctuary, 6 – North House/Sanctuary, 7 – North Pillar Hall, 8 – North-East Sanctuary, 9 – South-West House

altar area of the High Priest Sanctuary unequivocally shows a shrine with a square stone altar flanked by double-axes.

Some 230 metres along the Royal Road from the north-western entrance to the temple-complex is a much larger building than any of those so far considered: 85 by 30 metres, it is the most substantial Minoan building so far discovered at Knossos outside the main temple-complex. Not surprisingly, Evans named it 'the Little Palace'. In it there was an adyton equipped with strange cult objects that prove its use as a chthonic shrine. There was also, across the southern end of the building, a suite of pillar crypts supporting cult rooms on the floor above. An extraordinary collection of religious para-phernalia was found in this area; it was in disarray, apparently having fallen from the floor above.

The most remarkable of these objects is a bull's head rhyton made of smooth black steatite. The rhyton is a special type of vessel used for pouring libations, so there is no ambiguity about the object's religious function. The bull's head as reconstructed has curving horns of gilded wood, eyes of inlaid crystal and jasper, and nostrils of mother-of-pearl; it is one of the finest pieces of artwork found at Knossos, virtually emblematic of the Minoan culture (Figure 38).

In addition to the steatite rhyton, there was a black double-axe stand, a ewer, another bull's head rhyton made of painted clay and a lead figurine of the snake goddess. It was a collection that could only be interpreted as the cult equipment of a sanctuary dedicated to the chthonic deities. Evans himself declared that most of the southern end of the Little Palace was given over to this cult; in fact he described the building as a whole as a practically uninterrupted suite of sanctuary chambers and said that it had 'every appearance of a religious foundation'.

We should therefore see it as another temple, perhaps naming it the Bull's Head Sanctuary after its distinctive libation jug. The sanctuary was built straight after the major earthquake of 1700 BC, the earthquake that destroyed the first temple-complex and led to its rebuilding. It is tempting to see the building of the Bull's Head Sanctuary as an act of propitiation to the earth deities as a direct response to the earthquake disaster.

On the south side of the Labyrinth is a very different sort of building, which Evans called the Caravanserai. We can agree with Evans that this was a reception area for travellers arriving from the south along the Minoan road leading to the Stepped Portico at the Labyrinth's south-west corner. At one end of the road frontage was a square building, the Fountain Chamber, which housed a spring. Near it was an elaborate footbath, now beautifully restored, where travellers might wash the sweat and dust from their feet before entering the hostel (Plate 6). An adjacent room had several clay bathtubs. This room did not have any of the characteristics of the sacred lustral basins or adyta within the temple and we should assume that its function was for purely secular cleansing, not for ritual.

The Caravanserai was essentially a public, secular building and from its position, architecture, and equipment it seems virtually certain that it functioned as a pilgrim hostel. Very similar buildings were provided at the edges of the later, classical Greek sacred places. At Nemea, for example, in 350 BC, a guesthouse and bath-house were provided in a 100-metre-long range not far from the Sacred Grove of cypress trees and the Temple of Zeus.

ATHENS, THEBES AND HATTUSA

The parallels between Knossos and the sacred places of classical Greece should not be pressed too far. A thousand years and the wide waters of the Aegean separate them. Yet it is not by any means impossible that some of the religious and social customs of the Minoans survived in classical Greek culture. Examples are many of ancient practices that have been subsumed, often to reappear in disguised forms in later cultures, so we may be able to identify some quasi-Minoan features. The bath-house and guesthouse facilities at the approach to the Labyrinth may be one such. The sacred precinct with its aggregation of sanctuaries may be another. The temple hypothesis reveals the Knossos Labyrinth as a sequence of related but fairly separate sanctuaries, very probably dedicated to different deities or different aspects of deities. The Acropolis at Athens occupies the site of the ancestral settlement, a small hill-top refuge, and became a sacred precinct as the city spread out across the surrounding low ground. The Labyrinth at Knossos also stands on the site of its ancestral settlement: as we saw in Chapter 4, the low Kefala mound is a neolithic and early bronze age tell.

The Acropolis had its Panathenaic Way, a processional approach road; the Labyrinth had its Royal Road and its Corridor of Processions. The Acropolis' major sanctuary, the Parthenon, contained a colossal statue of the goddess Athena, 10 metres high, encrusted in ivory and gold and costing a thousand talents; the Labyrinth too had its spacious Great Goddess Sanctuary with a large statue of the deity at one end. The Athena portrayed by Pheidias had a python half-hidden behind her golden shield; many of the goddess figurines at Knossos held snakes. Beyond the south parapet of the Acropolis lay the Theatre of Dionysos, a place designed for religious dramas; at Knossos, the Theatral Area and the West and Central Courts served this public ceremonial function. The temples and open spaces on the Acropolis were embellished with many statues, carved reliefs, and painted images; the walls of the Labyrinth were equally lavishly decorated with frescoes.

Obviously it would be unwise to press the parallels too far, or to read too much into them. Minos' Crete in 1600 BC and Pericles' Athens in 438 BC were two very different places, but there are resonances of the Knossos Labyrinth in the Athenian Acropolis. We might perhaps regard the Labyrinth as an early forerunner of the Greek temple-precinct idea.

There are admittedly many respected and experienced researchers who adhere to the view that the Labyrinth was a centre of secular administration and a palace in the full sense of the word, but there is an increasing literature which converges on the temple-complex interpretation. As we have already seen, Evans' *Palace of Minos* contains countless references to the religious function of the building. Bogdan Rutkowski has recently (1986) commented that Evans' insistence that the building is saturated with sacred elements poses a complicated question, although he rather frustratingly does not develop the idea.

Nicolas Platon feels, after the excavation of the smaller 'palace' at Zakro, that the primarily religious function of the palaces has been confirmed (1971). The West Wing at Zakro was given over to a shrine and ancillary chambers dedicated to cult use. Geraldine Gesell (1985) sees the balustrade room as an unusually elaborate type of bench sanctuary: the offering bench or altar is set apart behind a low wall with columns on it. In other words, the Balustrade Sanctuary, Chancel Screen Sanctuary, and High Priest Sanctuary were in her view probably all dedicated to religious cult activity.

The double-axe symbol has been generally acknowledged as the principal and most potent religious symbol of bronze age Crete; the profusion of double-axe signs in the Labyrinth must be held to reinforce the idea of the Labyrinth as a sacred place.

Maitland Edey (1975), along with several other writers, has drawn attention to the curious *absence* of temples on Minoan Crete. The artefacts and the artwork show an obsession with religion, and yet there were no temples or other large centres of worship. Rutkowski (1986) is convinced that temples, as a major element in every civilization, were a universal feature of the bronze age Aegean, yet he cannot point to any examples of temples on Crete and he is evidently puzzled by this. He identifies some sanctuaries in the Labyrinth, such as the Early Dove Goddess Sanctuary found underneath the remains of the Great Goddess Sanctuary and its cellars and the Late Dove Goddess Sanctuary (Evans' Shrine of the Double-Axes). Rutkowski also draws the significant conclusion that it is very likely that rooms and spaces adjoining shrines were also used for worship; the Tripartite Shrine in the west façade of the Central Court strongly implies a sacred use for the open space directly in front of it – the Central Court itself.

We come closer still to the point of convergence with the work of Paul Faure, who in 1969 interpreted the 'villa' at Niru Khani as a temple and in 1973 interpreted the Palace of Minos at Knossos as a 'great sanctuary'.

The main problem remaining is really that the Labyrinth does not look much like a temple to eyes and minds conditioned by the aesthetics of classical Greece and Rome, where the external appearance, the visual identity of the building, becomes part of its function. The apparent informality and asymmetry of the Minoan temples should not deceive us. It is simply that more important considerations to the Minoans were the specific requirements of religious cult practices.

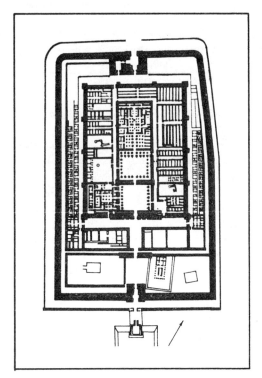

Figure 27 An Egyptian labyrinth: the mortuary temple of Rameses III at Medinet Habu

There are nevertheless parallels in contemporary religious architecture. As we saw in Chapter 6, the Hawara Labyrinth built in Egypt in about 1800 BC was in many significant respects a similar building to the Knossos Labyrinth. It had hundreds of chambers, colonnaded courtyards, winding passages, and limestone walls covered with carved figures. The Hawara Labyrinth was a temple with a cult connection with the pyramid that stood at one end of it; in Herodotus' day it was still a taboo place and only the Labyrinth's guardians were allowed to descend to the lower storey where the mummified crocodiles lay.

The Labyrinth of Medinet Habu at Thebes has survived in a rather more recognizable but still ruinous state. Built in about 1160 BC, it is significantly later than the Labyrinth at Knossos – it post-dates the abandonment of the Labyrinth by two hundred years – so we must not attach too much importance to any parallels we may find. This labyrinth was built as a very special kind of temple. It was a temple to commemorate the Pharaoh Rameses III and as such it was built in the form of a royal palace, but it was lived in by only ten people: an overseer, two scribes and seven servants, who carried out the daily service for the dead. The labyrinth was so haunted by the spirits of the powerful dead that the servants frequently ran away and had to be brought back by force.

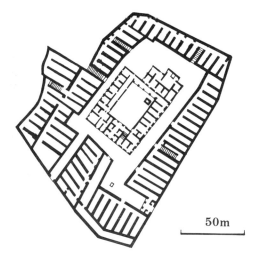

Figure 28 The Great Temple at
Hattusa, capital of the Hittite
empire

50m

A more significant parallel than either of these Egyptian labyrinths is to be
found in Turkey. Just as the Minoan sea-empire, if we may call it that,
reached its peak around 1600 BC the capital of what was to become the Hittite
land-empire was being built. The ruins of the city of Hattusa, capital of the
land of Hatti, can be seen at the village of Boğazkale (formerly Boğazköy),
some 150 kilometres east of Ankara. The second temple was built at Knossos
in about 1700 BC and it was finally abandoned in 1380 BC; the city of Hattusa
was rebuilt after invasion-destruction in about 1650 and was destroyed by the
mysterious Sea-People in about 1200 BC.

Knossos and Hattusa were roughly contemporary cities. The city of
Hattusa developed outwards, from a core area round its Great Temple, into
an urban area over a kilometre across, making it about the same size as
bronze age Knossos. It was different from Knossos in being a great military
stronghold surrounded by massive walls. It had a monumental stone gateway
guarded by carved lions and in this respect it anticipated Mycenae. But it is
Hattusa's temples that are our main concern. There were smaller, subsidiary
temples scattered through the lower city, but the Great Temple that was the
city's focal point was a large and impressive building, 160 by 135 metres,
about the same size as the Knossos Labyrinth. The sanctuaries were located at
the centre in a courtyard completely enclosed by extensive store-rooms. The
store-rooms were long and narrow, and they contained huge earthenware
jars.

There is no broad and spacious court at the heart of the design, but apart
from this there are many points of similarity with the Knossos Labyrinth. The
store-rooms at the Hattusa Temple were designed to accommodate the
sacrifices offered to the deity: in other words, they had the same function that
I am proposing for the store-rooms at Knossos. A peculiarity of the Great
Temple at Hattusa is its complete lack of symmetry; even the individual

rooms often lack symmetry, with corners that are not right angles. The Labyrinth at Knossos is, in a sense, a half-way house between the total asymmetry of Hattusa and the formal classicism of the Parthenon.

Whether the architecture of the Labyrinth is a conscious development, a borrowing, from that of Hattusa is impossible to say. The architectural concept of the Labyrinth and the other temples on Crete seems to have grown by a process of largely indigenous evolution, out of the cellular layouts seen at earlier sites like Myrtos and Vasiliki (2400–2300 BC). The concept seems to have evolved towards a form very like that of Anatolian and Mesopotamian temples, but that does not necessarily mean that it was copied, even though we know that Hittite influence extended to the Aegean. The two buildings, the Knossos Labyrinth, and the Great Temple of Hattusa, may have been separate products of a common fund of ideas and customs.

Either way, there was a great and labyrinthine building in the Hittite capital that was a temple dedicated to the Weather-God and there was a great and even more labyrinthine building at Knossos, the principal Cretan city; from the mounting evidence, it is reasonable to infer that it too was a temple.

But a temple to what deities?

9
The Lady of the Labyrinth

I come from the pure, pure Queen of those below,
And other gods and demons:
I have paid the penalty for deeds unrighteous,
Whether it be that Fate laid me low or the gods immortal,
I have flown out of the sorrowful, weary circle.
I have passed with swift feet to the diadem desired.
I have sunk beneath the bosom of the Mistress, the Queen of the
  Underworld.
> Funerary tablet from Thurii, Southern Italy, *c.* 350 BC.

THE GODDESSES AND GODS OF CRETE

It was, perhaps more than any other single phenomenon, the worship of goddesses that gave the Minoan civilization its distinctive character. From 2300 until 1100 BC, nearly 300 years after the temple at Knossos was abandoned, goddesses preoccupied the Cretans. Exactly what these goddesses were in the Minoan mind is very difficult to know. From the enormous number of religious artefacts, idols, frescoes, and seal impressions, we can deduce a good deal about their function. We even know the names of some of them although we cannot match up the names with specific icons.

One goddess at least was concerned with fertility and abundance and with the procreative acts that produced them, a role later to be assumed by Aphrodite. The dove as proverbially the most amorous of birds was her symbol, and she was often depicted with doves perched on her. The dove is absent from scenes depicting wild or orgiastic behaviour, so the implication is that the Goddess of Doves was a homely, household goddess.

Another was a Goddess of Renewal and she was connected with the central rites of the vegetation cycle. Often the annual death and rebirth were acted out by a young male deity, a Year-spirit who took the roles of both son and consort. This small but heroic figure who died and was born again every year, just like Adonis, seems to have been the prototype for Zeus, although in the Minoan period he was subordinate to the goddess whom he served. The cult

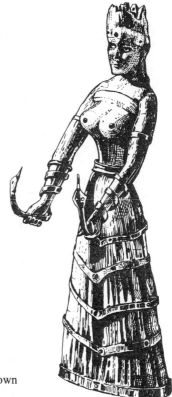

Figure 29 Snake Goddess, known
as 'The Boston Goddess'

surrounding this proto-Zeus continued after the Minoan civilization came to
an end and it seems that his original Minoan name survived in one of the titles
attached to Zeus on Crete – Velchanos.

Velchanos was always subject to the goddess and always depicted in
worshipful attitudes. The crowned 'Divine Child' figurine in ivory, described
by Evans as probably from the Labyrinth, may well have been intended as an
image of the pre-pubertal Velchanos, hands upstretched in adoration. The
even more remarkable ivory figure known as the Boston Goddess (Figure 29)
is thought to be the other half of the tableau. Both may have been stolen
from the surface layers in the area of the Great Goddess Sanctuary, which had
been picked over well before the Evans excavations started. Evans found
another ivory figurine, showing a slightly older Velchanos with shorter hair
and a small cap which may have been designed to cover a tonsure. We know
from other evidence, such as carved locks of hair and altars with plaits carved
on them, that youths grew their hair long in preparation for a ritual offering
of a lock of hair to the deity. The older boy has evidently gone through this
lock-giving initiation. He still stands erect, with arms raised in the same
gesture of worship.

Velchanos was leader of the young Kouretes, the nature spirits who together with their female companions, the Kourai, caused the flowers to bloom. Sometimes, when the worship of the goddess became more orgiastic, he seems to have become the Minoan prototype of Dionysos with his wild rout of maenads. In a gold signet ring from the New Temple of Knossos we can see the goddess calling the young Velchanos down from the sky.

The Great Goddess or Mother Goddess held sway until the very end of the Minoan civilization and was even for a time in a dominant position in the Mycenean pantheon, until her position was supplanted by Zeus. The Great Goddess seems to have been called Potnia, at least in the final decades of the Labyrinth's history. The name recurs in place after place, not just on Crete but throughout the Mycenean world. Meaning no more than 'The Lady' or 'The Mistress', it nevertheless carried powerful connotations and resonances: it was clearly the proper name of an important goddess.

We find the Great Goddess named in the Labyrinth itself (see Appendix B). On tablet Gg 702, the inscription refers to an offering made to 'da-pu-ri-to-jo po-ti-ni-ja'. Professor John Chadwick (1976), who has worked on the decipherment of the Linear B script for over forty years, explains that these symbolic signs give an approximation only of the original pronunciation; probably in the original the phrase would have been something close to 'laburinthos potnia', meaning the Lady of the Labyrinth, or Potnia of the Labyrinth. Potnia appears again and again as the main goddess. 'Potnia' was still in use in the classical period as an honorific title in addressing women of rank, such as queens, goddesses and mothers; it seems to have had the same flavour of archaic deference as the phrase 'my lady'.

Potnia had a domestic aspect as a guardian of households and cities. In classical times, resonances of Potnia can be felt in goddesses such as Athena, Rhea, and Hera. She was the wife and mother, the dependable figure of order and reason. In a sense she represented the conscious mind. Hers, probably, was the double-axe symbol that we find at so many Minoan sanctuaries on Crete, but possibly the pillar and the snake were her symbols too. The hearthside crevices where snakes liked to sleep suggest that the snake may have made a natural symbol for the chthonic, Earth-mother aspect of Potnia. Since the name 'Labyrinth' derived specifically from the Labyrinth at Knossos and the tablet Gg 702 was found in the Labyrinth, we can be absolutely certain that at least one sanctuary within the Labyrinth was dedicated to Potnia. We know that 'houses', i.e. temples or sanctuaries, on mainland Greece were dedicated to the same goddess.

There were wild goddesses too, associated with untamed landscape and consorting with wild beasts. Ariadne, the licentious wild goddess, was later often shown sitting under a vine with her husband Dionysos. It is no accident that in the classical legend Ariadne came from Knossos and was able to help Theseus find his way in and out of the Labyrinth. Whether the Minoans called this impulsive goddess Ariadne or used some other name is not known.

A chaste and free wild goddess, who was a huntress and tamer of wild beasts, is now often referred to as the Mistress of Wild Animals or Queen of Wild Beasts. It seems that the Cretans called her Britomartis, said to mean 'sweet virgin', and she became the Artemis or Diana of the classical period. If the Goddess of the Doves represented the ethereal or celestial aspect of the cosmos, the Goddess of Wild Beasts represented its terrestrial aspect. This goddess was worshipped at peak sanctuaries, where we know that ritual pyres were lit; the later cult of Artemis involved similar mountain bonfires, so it is possible that there was real continuity of ritual and belief into the classical period. One of the many Minoan seal impressions that have survived shows a male counterpart for this goddess, a Master of Animals, who may have been the goddess's son or consort. In much the same way, the classical Greek Artemis had a young consort called Hippolytos. It is, incidentally, now thought that the many breasts of the statue of Artemis at Ephesus were bulls' testicles and that bulls were both castrated and sacrificed in her honour; this link further strengthens the link between the classical Artemis and the Minoan Potnia, who also had a connection with bulls. Another link is that Artemis Ephesia, worshipped from about 600 BC onwards, was *epiphanes*, a divinity who was normally invisible but could appear in order that worshippers could see and revere her. Artemis succeeded and developed out of an older deity, Cybele, the mother-goddess of the Phrygians. Cybele too was usually invisible, but present in the rocky mountainsides. Sometimes she was manifest in a stone pillar flanked by lions or took on human form between her animals: sometimes she was seen in a special 'window of appearance'. There are close connections here with the Minoan goddess, who was also thought of as residing in the stone of the mountain peaks (hence the peak sanctuaries), as manifesting herself in human form between pairs of animals, or even – as powerfully shown by the Lion Gate at Mycenae – as a pillar flanked by two lions.

Possibly there was a Goddess of Gardens, recognizable as Antheia, the Goddess of Flowers, in the period immediately after the Minoan civilization ended. Possibly there was a Goddess of the Sea too. The sea shells used to mantle the altars of some shrines suggest that one or more of the deities was associated with the sea. Jacquetta Hawkes (1968) speculates that there may once have been shrines dedicated specifically to a Sea Goddess but that they have been eroded away by the sea. On the other hand, it may be that the marine references were simply covert, indirect references to the god Poteidan, or Poseidon, who seems to have presided over the Labyrinth as a whole.

There is stronger evidence of a Goddess of Caves. She was associated with childbirth and the underworld and may have been regarded as the primeval Earth Mother. She may be recognizable as Rhea in the later myths, but we know that in the final centuries of the Labyrinth's use she was known in Crete as Eleuthia. She was named in the temple records at Knossos and her nearest sanctuary, the Cave of Eileithyia as it is known today, is at Amnisos. The

Cave of Eleuthia was an important centre of worship from neolithic times right through the bronze and iron ages, into the Roman period. It is even mentioned in Homer's *Odyssey*, Book 19. Inside the Eleuthia Cave is a natural stalagmite protected by an artificial stone wall, the focus of the cave cult and probably regarded as the manifestation or dwelling of the goddess Eleuthia.

In Greek religion, Eleuthia was sometimes identified with Artemis, although she was often treated as a separate deity. On Minoan Crete, Eleuthia may have had an entirely independent existence in her cave sanctuaries, yet there is a possibility that she may have been regarded as the same goddess who dwelt at the peak sanctuaries. The discovery in 1974 of the sacred cave in the peak sanctuary of Mount Juktas shows that it was possible to combine

Figure 30 Cult objects from the Temple Repositories. A selection of objects found in the two large stone-lined safes sunk in the floor of the Snake Goddess Sanctuary

peak and cave sanctuaries. It may also be significant that often the same inscriptions are found on stone offering tables in both sacred caves and peak sanctuaries. Perhaps the Minoans, like the later Greeks, worshipped a two-sided goddess, Artemis-Eleuthia. We should bear in mind John Pendlebury's view (1939) that there was a tendency in Minoan Crete to combine the goddesses into one deity.

The Snake Goddess is another deity representing the underworld. Snakes wriggling up out of crevices are easily understandable as symbols of the life within the earth. In the Snake Goddess Sanctuary two beautiful figurines depicting the Snake Goddess were buried with all their cult paraphernalia, much of it broken, in cists under the floor. The nature of some of the cult objects found with the Snake Goddesses implies a connection with the fertility of the land and the sea. This creates problems for us, because we have already identified a Dove Goddess as a fertility deity and speculated that there might have been a Sea Goddess too. Now we have a Snake Goddess whose concerns seem to overlap with those of the other two goddesses.

A temple at Kannia near Gortyn had a sanctuary that contained four goddess figurines, all with snakes on their crowns. One of them had snakes on her arms as well and a dove on her cheek. So, at Kannia too, it looks as if there was an overlap between the Snake and Dove Goddesses. Perhaps the situation can be explained in a similar way to the Christian Trinity; perhaps some of the Minoan goddesses were aspects of each other, transformations of a single deity representing different cosmic functions. If this is so, identification of the various deities and their transformations is going to prove extremely difficult. For our present purposes, it is enough that the Minoans clearly recognized the goddesses by different names, accorded them different attributes and areas of concern, and gave them separate sanctuaries.

The Snake Goddess figurines form one of several links between the Minoan religion and the maenad cults known from later Greek culture. The maenads remembered in the classical period handled snakes during their ecstatic dances, apparently regarding them as incarnations of the god Dionysos. There are curious modern parallels too. The Holiness Church of Leslie and Perry Counties in Kentucky is reported to have indulged in ecstatic dancing and snake-handling, ostensibly based on Mark 16:18, 'They shall take up serpents', as part of a Christian service. The same association between snake-handling, ecstatic dancing and epiphanies existed in Minoan religion; all the ingredients are present in the artwork that survives from Knossos. The Snake Goddess statues brandish snakes, pottery snakes decorate the storage jars and the Isopata ring (Figure 33) shows priestesses dancing with wild abandon to produce an epiphany of a goddess.

It would seem that maenadism had antecedents in a cult that was important at Minoan Knossos. The later Greek writers explained the maenads' appalling ritual of tearing live victims to pieces and eating them raw as a rite commemorating the tearing asunder of the god Dionysos. In fact a simple, savage form of homeopathy explains it better. By eating your sacrificial victim, you acquire his qualities; to be god-like, you must eat god. The 'priestess' burial of the Lady of Arkhanes has curious undertones of the maenad's tearing-asunder rite. The horse buried with the priestess was dismembered, although after it had been sacrificed.

A two-yearly festival of maenads consisting of all kinds of open-air revels was held across a significant part of the Aegean world: it was reported in Arcadia on mainland Greece, on Rhodes and on Crete too. We can visualize ecstatic dances by day at Knossos, such as those shown in the Sacred Dance Fresco, followed by nocturnal mountain dances. At classical Miletus, which significantly originated as a Minoan colony, the priestesses of Dionysos 'led the women to the mountain'; we can imagine the priestesses of the Labyrinth leading similar processions up to Juktas for dancing by night at the peak sanctuary. The ecstatic tossing and swaying of the head characteristic of the later bacchanalian dancers is clearly shown in the Isopata ring.

Deities appeared in the form of snakes, animals or even, it seems, trees, stalagmites and pillars: all were reverenced in Minoan artwork. Given this preoccupation with the supernatural, it is odd that we find so little in the Minoan religion about male deities. From the Linear B tablets found in bronze age archives at Knossos, Pylos, Mycenae, and Thebes, it appears that at least in the period 1470–1380 BC the same deities were worshipped on Crete as on the mainland of Greece. The same names of goddesses and gods appear repeatedly. The principal god was, at least as far as the mainland was concerned, Poseidon. In Mycenean Greek he was called Poseidaon and this was derived from an original form 'Poteidan', according to Chadwick, or 'Potidas', according to Platon.

This ancient god, whose power was originally far greater than that of Velchanos-Zeus, was made offerings of very large sacrifices at Pylos. As Lord of the Earth, it was appropriate, yet there is no evidence so far from Knossos that his cult was anything other than minor on Crete. At Pylos, during the final century of the Temple at Knossos, Poseidon the King, as he was often called, was the most important single deity. Among the other Pylian deities there were at least three more gods: Tris-Heros, the 'Thrice-Hero', Drimios, who seems to have been a son of Zeus, and Diktaian Zeus, who was in effect Velchanos from the Minoan pantheon. There were goddesses too: Ma-na-sa, Pe-re-swa, Posidaeia, Iphemedeia, Diwya, and Rhea. Posidaeia was Poseidon's queen; Iphemedeia was Poseidon's mistress. Diwya was a female counterpart of Di-we, or Zeus, while Rhea was the Divine Mother or Mother of the Gods.

How many of the mainland, 'Mycenean' deities were worshipped at Knossos? Some at least are actually named in the offering archives found in the Labyrinth. Potnia, the Lady of the Labyrinth, Eleuthia and Diwya have already been mentioned as Knossian goddesses; Qe-ra-si-ja, Pi-pi-tu-na, A-ju-ma-na-ke, A-ro-do-ro-o and Pa-de were also worshipped at Knossos or in the immediate neighbourhood, although we know little more of these shadowy deities than their names. Among the gods worshipped at Knossos were Erinus or Erinys, who seems to have been a personal agent of destiny, enforcing the fulfilment of a moira, Hermes, Marineus, Diktaian Zeus, and Hephaistos. The worship of Hephaistos has been inferred from a man's name, Hephaistios, which has been derived from the god's name. One tablet which lists several deities, including Potnia, mentions Enualios, a name frequently used in Greek literature as an alternative to Ares, the war-god. This same tablet, reassembled from the fragments labelled V52, 52b and 8285, also has what seems to be the first part of Poseidon's name, 'Po-se-da', but the expected ending '-o' is broken off. On the same line, sandwiched between Enualios and Poseidon, is the name Pa-ja-wo-ne or Paiawon, which several centuries later was used as an alternative name of Apollo, presumably offering Apollo attributes of the older god. In addition to these, it is likely that the other deities mentioned at Pylos were also honoured: Posidaeia, Ma-na-sa, Tris-Heros, Pe-re-swa, Iphemedeia, Drimios and Rhea.

The series of Linear B tablets called Fp makes it very clear that offerings at the Labyrinth were dedicated to gods and goddesses, although not necessarily all in the temple-precinct itself (see Appendix B). Table Fp 1 begins, 'In the month of Deukios: to Diktaian Zeus one [measure] of oil'. The second entry on the tablet is in its way one of the most interesting of all; it reads, 'to the Daidalaion two [measures] of oil'. Some writers have interpreted this to mean that Daidalos the legendary engineer was himself worshipped, just as the Posidaion at Pylos was a sanctuary dedicated to the god Poseidon. But if the word 'Daidalaion' is taken at face value, 'the building of Daidalos', we can see that what is meant is the building that Daidalos himself designed and erected, the Labyrinth at Knossos. In other words, the tablet records a gift made to the temple, presumably for its upkeep and glorification.

On other tablets, the Gg series for example, a frequent entry is 'for all the gods'. This phrase confirms, if we had not already deduced it, that there were many deities in the Minoan pantheon. It seems very likely that shrines with this dedication existed in the Knossos Labyrinth as well as at Amnisos and other places; a catch-all offering 'for all the gods' would have made sure that no deity could take offence. On line 7 of Fp1 there is an entry for Amnisos; on line 10 there is an offering to a special wind sanctuary, which may or may not have been at the port of Amnisos; the dedication, 'to the priestess of the winds', is evocative and mysterious. Other Fp tablets mention this priestess too. One locates her in the town of U-ta-no, which may be Mallia: as yet we do not know what the Minoan name of Mallia was, so it may have been something like Utanos.

We might reasonably have expected the Labyrinth, or indeed other Minoan temple sites, to have thrown up evidence of a powerful father-god. The absence of evidence of a powerful god suggests that the bull, central to one of the Minoans' most exotic rites, symbolized the male creative force and aggression, and that the god was worshipped through this medium. It is significant that the classical myths feature bulls very conspicuously in the Cretan episodes. Europa is abducted and seduced by Zeus in the form of a bull; Minos fails to sacrifice a bull given to him by Poseidon; Pasiphae develops an unnatural lust for a bull; she gives birth to a monstrous bull-man; Theseus frees the tribute-children by killing the bull-monster. In these myths there is a clear memory of a Cretan preoccupation with the bull as a mythic archetype, a surrogate god.

In the celestial sphere, the Bull God, if we can call him that, was represented by the sun and crescent moon. In the subterranean sphere, the god manifested himself in earthquakes and tsunamis and showed himself to be master of both earth and sea. In the tablets he is called Poteidan, Lord of the Earth. It may be that the sea shells and beach pebbles scattered on some of the altars at Knossos were intended as a reference to Poteidan's sea-kingdom and to his ever-present power; the beautiful sacred anchor found in the Labyrinth, carved out of fine porphyry and complete with clinging octopus, almost certainly is.

It is difficult to match names with specific idols and shrines, but the general picture that emerges is one of great diversity. The bronze age Knossians were worshippers of many gods; we can name over twenty likely deities just from the very incomplete tablet-archives that survive, and it is possible that there were many more. A pantheon as large as this would have required many shrines and sanctuaries. An extensive temple-complex with a wide range of variously equipped sanctuaries and cult rooms is exactly what we should expect. The Labyrinth, or Daidalaion if we prefer to call it that, precisely suits the needs of the complexities of Minoan religion.

How in detail the minor gods and major goddesses were honoured at Knossos is nevertheless of great importance. The appropriateness of the Labyrinth's architecture to its sacred function is established, but we need an image, and something better than an impression, of the rites that were carried out there. Evans made much of the Priest-King, a figure he invented because of the King Minos element in later legends, but no firm evidence has been recovered at the Labyrinth, as far as I am aware, that indicates his existence, let alone his pre-eminence. As we saw in Chapters 5 and 7, the Priest-King Fresco was Evans' best piece of evidence and that does not depict a king at all. The longest section of the Procession Fresco that is susceptible of reconstruction clearly shows a female, presumably a deity, as the central and focal figure, standing between two approaching lines of men bearing tribute. The Palanquin Fresco and the Grandstand Fresco similarly show female figures as the most important: in these instances they were priestesses. There is no sign of Evans' king and no sign of any important male officials. The Lady of the Labyrinth and other deities honoured in the temple were, it seems, attended by an elite of powerful priestesses.

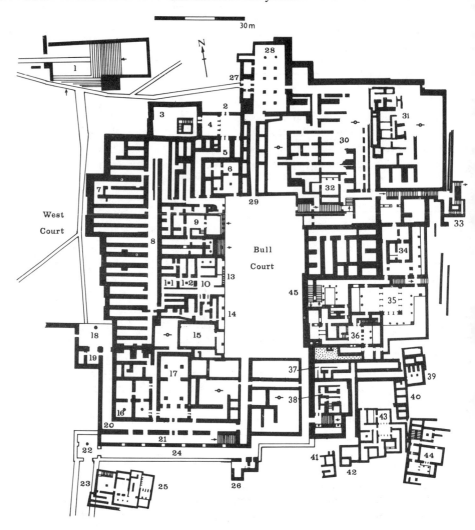

30m

N

West
Court

Bull
Court

Figure 31 The Minoan Temple at Knossos: a reconstruction of the 'ground-floor' plan.
1 – Theatral Area, 2 – North-West Portico, 3 – Initiation Area, with adyton,
4 – Induction Hall and Vestibule, 5 – North-West Entrance Passage, 6 – Lotus Lamp
Sanctuary, 7 – West Store-Rooms, 8 – Lower West Wing Corridor, 9 – Throne
Sanctuary, 10 – Snake Goddess Sanctuary, 11 – West Pillar Crypt, 12 – East Pillar
Crypt, 13 – Tripartite Shrine, 14 – Colonnade of the Priestesses, 15 – Destroyed
Sanctuary, 16 – Columnar Shrines (South-West Pillar Crypts below), 17 – Cupbearer
Sanctuary, 18 – West Porch/Entrance, 19 – West Porch Shrine, 20 – Procession
Corridor, 21 – South Terrace, 22 – South-West Porch/Entrance (at lower level),
23 – Stepped Portico or paved ramp, 24 – South Corridor (at lower level),
25 – South (or Silver Vessels) Sanctuary, 26 – South Porch/Entrance, 27 – North
Entrance, 28 – South Pillar Hall, 29 – North Entrance Passage, 30 – Service Quarter:
North-East Store-Rooms and Kitchens, 31 – North-East Kamares Pottery Store,

32 – North-East Sanctuary, 33   East Entrance, 34 – Temple Workshops, 35 – Double-
Axe Sanctuary, 36 – Dolphin Sanctuary, 37 – Triton Shell Sanctuary, 38 – Late Dove
Goddess Sanctuary, 39 – Monolithic Pillar Crypt, 40 – Pre-Temple buildings,
41 – House or Shrine of the Sacrificed Oxen, 42 – House or Shrine of the Fallen
Blocks, 43 – Chancel Screen Sanctuary, 44 – South-East Sanctuary, 45 – Grand
Staircase.
Arrows on staircase indicate 'down' direction, asterisks indicate temple repositories
(stone-lined strongrooms for religious cult objects), and stippling indicates tell
material not quarried away at this level. The winged circle indicates that the site was
too badly damaged at the time of excavation for reconstruction to be more than
tentative

THE PRIESTESSES OF KNOSSOS

There is evidence of male priests from bronze age Crete, such as the fifteenth-
century green jasper seal showing a cloaked and robed priest holding a bird,
or the master of ceremonies on the Harvester Vase (Figure 42). But, at least as
far as the Labyrinth was concerned, the priestesses were pre-eminent. Evans
rightly inferred that women achieved high status. From Arkhanes comes the
evidence of a female burial of great splendour and wealth; the woman
concerned may have been a queen or a princess, but she may equally have
been a high priestess.

The fragmentary Palanquin Fresco shows a major public ceremony
attended by large numbers of warriors. In the middle of it all is the figure of a
woman in a simple (i.e. unflounced) dress being carried along on a litter. The
fact that she is on a litter indicates her high status, but does it indicate that she
is a priestess? A collection of cult objects from the Great Goddess Sanctuary,
cascaded down into the Loom-Weight Basement, suggests that it does. The
collection consists of terracotta models of a black-and-white checked shrine,
an altar base, an altar surmounted by horns of consecration, bell-shaped
masks, miniature triton shells, a three-pillared shrine with doves perching on
its roof, and a palanquin with the remains of a priestess sitting on it (Figure
47). Since the collection as a whole represents a sacred group, it is reasonable
to assume that the woman seated on the palanquin is a priestess on her way to
perform a religious ceremony.

On the Agia Triadha sarcophagus, the priestesses are shown as the key
figures in funerary ceremonies. On Side A (Figure 32), priestesses or temple
servants carry pitchers of liquid to tip into a large vessel standing between two
double-axes; they are followed by a man, significantly dressed in a priestess's
robe and playing a lyre. There was evidently a subordinate caste of priests
who wore women's clothes, presumably becoming nominal priestesses in the
service of a goddess; they were probably eunuchs. The Camp-Stool Fresco
shows some males in long robes as well as priestesses seated on folding chairs
and being offered chalices containing the kykeon.

On Side B of the sarcophagus, two richly dressed priestesses (their upper
bodies defaced) are following a third priestess who wears a plumed red crown

and stretches her hands out in front of her at waist level in what may have been a conventional processional posture (Figure 45). In front of the three priestesses a man plays a flute as a bull with its throat cut, trussed on a sacrificial table, bleeds its life away into a two-handled pitcher. At the head of the procession, another priestess places an offering bowl on a low altar. Three men on Side A are shown carrying calves or calf-models and a boat-model towards a male effigy, but it is the women who dominate the sarcophagus scene.

In the Grandstand Fresco, as we have already seen, it is the groups of women, whom we now see as priestesses, who are very obviously the most important figures. There is still no sign of Evans' king and no sign of any male officials.

Jacquetta Hawkes, in her book *Dawn of the Gods* (1968), has drawn attention to the essential femininity of Minoan culture, which makes it essentially different from the Mycenean or other later European development. Much of the artwork does have a feminine grace, refinement, and fastidiousness suggesting strongly that it was primarily women's tastes that were being satisfied by the temple craftsmen and artists. Even so, the point should not be overstressed, as the culture was by no means as soft-centred as Evans would have us believe.

The many votive offerings found in shrines include model robes, often elaborately decorated. These evidently represent the sacred vestments which priestesses put on when they conjured up and greeted the goddesses they served. It is probable that by putting on these special clothes and performing certain rituals a priestess was believed to turn into an epiphany of the goddess. A seal impression shows a priestess apparently on her way to such a ceremony, carrying a double-axe and an elaborately flounced dress. It may be that she is about to wear the dress herself, or alternatively drape it over a wooden cult image so that it, instead of she, will somehow 'become' the deity.

One way or another, the deity had to be induced to appear before the worshippers. The theophany might take many forms, forms that we today

Figure 32 Religious ritual, from the Agia Triadha sarcophagus (side A)

Plate 1 Pillar in East Pillar Crypt with double-axe carvings (Ashmolean Museum)

Plate 2 The reconstitution of the Grand Staircase (Ashmolean Museum)

Plate 3 Sir Arthur Evans at Knossos (Ashmolean Museum)

Plate 4 The Throne Room immediately after excavation and before any restoration work; the Antechamber in the foreground and the Lustral Area to the left (Ashmolean Museum)

Plate 5 Store-rooms in the West Wing; West Wing Corridor in the foreground, West Court in the background

Plate 6 The footbath in the Pilgrim Hostel as reconstructed by Evans

Plate 7 The main chamber in the Balustrade Sanctuary (or Royal Villa)

Plate 8 Part of the West Wing first floor
as restored by Evans

Plate 9 The south-east corner of the Labyrinth. The reconstructed building in the
centre is the Chancel Screen Sanctuary

Plate 10 The principal chamber of the Double-Axe Sanctuary, showing pier-and-door partitions

Plate 11 The cave at the peak sanctuary on Mount Juktas

Plate 12 The east front of the Labyrinth. The reconstructed cornice of the Double-Axe Sanctuary can be seen beyond the high boundary wall

Plate 13 The South Propylaeum as reconstituted by Evans, with the new staircase (built on Evans' instructions) in the background (see also Figure 7)

Plate 14 The bull-vaulting block at Phaistos

Plate 15 The ground floor of the Double-Axe Sanctuary: colonnade and L-shaped light-well

Plate 16 The East Entrance seen from outside

Plate 17 The West Entrance seen from the West Court, with the beginning of the Procession Corridor on the left

Plate 18 The Dolphin Sanctuary

Plate 19 Paving in the south-west corner of the Central Court

Plate 20 The Unexplored Mansion, showing the masonry supports for the bridge which originally connected the mansion with the Bull's Head Sanctuary

would not regard as remotely divine, and forms of bizarre variety – snakes, boulders, trees, or shaped pillars in shrines. An epiphany in human form would nevertheless have had the greatest impact. The later goddess Artemis Ephesia was expected to show herself in special windows of appearance positioned high in the temple's pediment. Precisely what happened during one of these appearances is not clear, but it seems likely that a priestess took on the role of Artemis and in some way became the epiphany of the goddess. This type of ritual appearance was already an ancient convention by the time of the Temple of Artemis around 600 BC: it had been a common practice in Syria, Anatolia, Mesopotamia, and Egypt (Trell 1988). Nanno Marinatos (1984) has argued persuasively that windows of appearance were a feature of Minoan religion on Thera, and it may be that windows overlooking the West and Central Courts of the Labyrinth were used in this way. It is likely that we are dealing with a common fund of religious customs which prevailed across the eastern Mediterranean region.

We can be sure that the priestesses of the Knossos Labyrinth were pre-occupied with inducing the deities to appear. If a priestess resorted to robing herself as the deity, no fraud was intended since this was only undertaken in the appropriate ritual context; with the right ritual preparations, the priestess for a time became possessed by the goddess. If analogies between the Knossos Labyrinth cult and the Ephesian Artemis cult seem strained, it is as well to remember the wide frame of reference in which they existed. We know, for example, that the great Temple of Artemis at Ephesus, one of the Seven Wonders of the World, was built by Khersifron and his son Metagenis. Not only were they Cretans, they were Knossians, born and bred within sight of the Labyrinth's crumbling walls.

Priestesses were involved in religious dances which were important elements of worship. Men were dancers too, as a simple clay model from Zakro shows; four men naked except for their caps are dancing a ring dance inside a small circular enclosure. Usually, though, it is women who are shown dancing and in all sorts of locations, in sacred groves, in flowery meadows, in wild rocky places or mountains, and apparently on the West Courts of the temples.

The dancers are shown with raised arms, swaying bodies, leaning heads, often in complete abandonment to the music. Dionysos was certainly worshipped at Pylos in the Mycenean period and his orgiastic cult was possibly preceded by some proto-Dionysian cult in Minoan Crete. It has been suggested that wine may have helped to produce the euphoric states apparent in some of the dancers and worshippers: drugs also may have been used. We know that poppy-growing began very early in Anatolia; there is a Minoan seal showing a goddess holding three poppy seed-heads; there is a famous late figurine depicting a goddess, inevitably known as the Poppy Goddess, wearing three seed-heads, cut as if for the extraction of opium, set in her crown. Opium-taking as part of religious worship could explain the curious

Figure 33 The Isopata Ring.
Priestesses perform a ritual dance to
produce an epiphany of the goddess

transformations of deities; it could also explain the exaggerated surrealism of some of the mythic imagery, the strange beasts, the demons.

Perhaps the image which best conveys the religious aspect of this ecstatic dancing is the one on a gold ring from a Minoan tomb at Isopata, just north of Knossos (Figure 33). It shows four opulently dressed priestesses, their breasts bared, their arms raised as they dance. One of them, the central one, seems to be doing some sort of solo dance: she leans her head right over to one side and her right arm points down at the ground. It is the abandoned dance of a maenad. Above, almost unnoticed, is the tiny figure of a goddess appearing out of the sky. This visitation by the goddess is obviously the purpose of the ritual dance.

Priestesses were also involved in rituals connected with sacred trees Growing, living trees or boughs torn from them are quite often shown decorating altars, sometimes planted upright in slots and sometimes laid horizontally, as on the peak sanctuary rhyton from Zakro (Figure 37). The tree was a central element in the Goddess of Renewal's annual vegetation drama. There was an actual or a symbolic uprooting of the sacred tree, accompanied by lamentation from the priestesses. The uprooting symbolized the death of the young god Velchanos. This tragic ritual was counterbalanced by a spring festival to celebrate his resurrection as evidenced by the new growth in the vegetation. The most vivid image in the cycle is of a young man pulling down the sacred tree and a priestess/goddess collapsed in a state of grief. Is the young man Velchanos himself? Is this a very early example of the Year God's ritual complicity in his own destruction, an example that would go through many later transformations, as Samson, Odin, and Jesus?

DEATH AND SACRIFICE

This inference of the gods' approach to death leads naturally into a consideration of the Minoans' attitude towards death. The sarcophagus found at Agia Triadha gives us the most complete picture we have so far, and there is the exciting possibility that there are further painted sarcophagi in the same cemetery, as yet unexcavated, that will eventually tell us even more about the Minoan religion at the close of the Labyrinth's heyday.

On Side A, in addition to the lyre-player and the two priestesses pouring libations, there is an all-male scene in which two priests in sheepskin skirts carry calves or models of calves and one carries a boat model to offer up to a curious limbless figure in front of a shrine. Most prehistorians are content to identify this as a conceptual depiction of the dead man. Although this is a plausible explanation, it is important to keep an open mind on the matter; the figure could be intended as a presiding priest or as the draped xoanon of a god. The green bough planted beside the mysterious figure could be seen as a piece of sympathetic magic, an attempt to bring new life back to the figure. Yet this clue does not really solve the problem. If the figure is the dead man, then resurrection or continued life in the next world might well be wished upon him. Equally, if the figure is an armless xoanon of Velchanos, his annual resurrection would be sought: seeking the god's well-being implies also seeking the well-being of the cosmos and the Minoans' interest in that would be self-interest. In other words, propitiating the annually dying Velchanos might have been seen as a natural part of the funerary rites for a recently dead mortal.

The shrines depicted show double-axes mounted on high, tapering posts or pillars that stand on pyramidal stone bases painted red and white. A large black bird perches on one of them, perhaps to show that a divinity is present or perhaps to indicate the dead person's freed spirit. There is a large vessel between two of the double-axes. The third double-axe has a spiral-decorated altar in front of it and a spiral-decorated shrine behind; this shrine is surmounted by four pairs of horns and a palm tree. This is the vocabulary of Minoan cult scenes.

Most vivid of all is the scene of bull sacrifice itself. From the great emphasis on the bull and on sacrifice, it is surprising that depictions of the bull sacrifice are so rare. Perhaps it was a rare event. Or perhaps there were religious or ethical reasons that we cannot guess at for not showing it. Below the sacrificial table, two tethered goats await their fate. The bull's blood is collected in a pitcher of the same type that the three priestesses are using on the other side of the sarcophagus to pour libations into the large vessel.

This may have led on, although the Agia Triadha sarcophagus does not show it, to a sacred communion, a special meal at which initiates, perhaps only priests and priestesses, consumed the offerings. A scene like this is shown in the Camp Stool Fresco, fragments of which fell from an upper floor of the West Wing of the Labyrinth. The libations would have been undrinkable if they had consisted of nothing but blood; probably they consisted of several liquids, like the Kykeon consumed at Eleusis, where milk, honey, and wine were mixed in with the blood of sacrificed animals. Certainly bulls' blood was involved and this would give extra point to some of the special libation-pouring vessels' being designed in the shape of a bull's head. Given the proposition that the bull was seen as a manifestation of the god Poteidan, drinking some of his blood would have been seen as a means of sharing and participating in the life of the Lord of the Earth. It is not so very far removed from the idea of the Christian communion.

The communion consists of partaking of bread and wine, body as well as blood, and equally it may have been the practice to eat part of the sacrificed bull at the ritual feast. Sacred meals of this type may have taken place in the temple refectories or in some special sanctuary. Platon (1971) thinks a sacred banquet hall was provided; if so, the most likely location for it in the Knossos Labyrinth would be above the South Pillar Hall (Evans' Custom House).

Wine was probably consumed as well. We tend to associate ritual wine-drinking with the worship of Dionysos, but Platon feels that the roots of this orgiastic cult will eventually be found in Minoan Crete. The most horrific rite associated with the Dionysiac cult was the *diaspasmoi*, the tearing-asunder rite, in which a victim singled out to represent the god was torn to pieces and eaten by maenads. If this has its roots in a Minoan practice, we are presumably to suppose that from time to time a youth was sacrificed, dismembered and eaten by the priestesses of the Labyrinth. As we shall see, such practices are not beyond the realms of possibility. Although we must not take the events of the myth of Theseus and the Minotaur as historical facts, the Labyrinth at Knossos was a place that inspired horror as well as awe in the Greek imagination; the Athenian tribute-children were offered up to the Cretan king and his bull-monster to be devoured. There may be a folk-memory in this of an exotic cult in which a bull-god was worshipped and young people were sacrificed.

EVIDENCE OF HUMAN SACRIFICE

In recent years, startling new evidence has been discovered near Arkhanes and at Knossos itself, evidence which clearly points towards human sacrifice. It was in 1979 that a small sanctuary was discovered at Anemospilia on the hillside 5 kilometres north-west of Arkhanes (Figure 35). It consisted of three narrow, oblong rooms ranged along the uphill side of a 10-metre-long hall, which itself served as an area where sacrifices were prepared: there were auxiliary altars in the hall. The narrow shrine rooms were littered with fine pottery and ritual vessels including a chalice and a large stone basin. In the central room a pair of life-sized clay feet were found, probably belonging to a wooden idol (Figure 34). It has been argued that such 'feet of clay', which have been found in other sanctuaries as well, could not have supported an image of any kind, but there is no reason to suppose that they ever had to carry the weight of an idol. The use of long and elaborate sacred vestments on cult images meant that the wooden framework of the xoanon needed only to be the simplest type of tailor's dummy. No doubt a carefully modelled head

Figure 34 Clay feet found at
Anemospilia

made of wood or clay coated with painted plaster was fixed on top. The clay
feet were placed under the hem of the robe to complete the illusion.

The image of the god or goddess stood on a low bench altar against the
southern wall. At its feet, a low knob of living rock jutted up through the
floor, probably a holy rock on to which libations were poured.

In the southern shrine there was a stepped altar of a similar general type to
the one in the Late Dove Goddess Sanctuary in the Labyrinth. In the
northern shrine there was a low, free-standing altar rather like a table tomb,
but about a metre long. On it were found the remains of a 17-year-old youth.
His ankles had evidently been tied and his legs folded up to make him fit onto
the table; we can imagine that his wrists too must have been tied. He had been

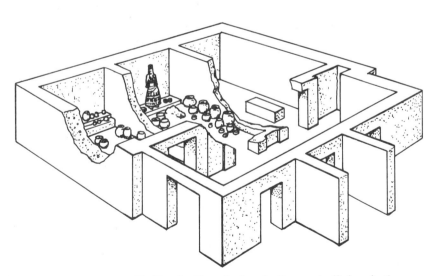

Figure 35 The Anemospilia Temple. Note the bench-altars and offerings in the
central and southern shrines, the goddess statue in the centre and the stone altar in
the northern shrine where the boy was sacrificed

ritually murdered with the long bronze dagger engraved with a boar's head that lay beside him.

The bones of three other people participating in the youth's sacrifice were found nearby. One had apparently been carrying a bucket vessel with a white bull painted on its side; his or her skeleton was found sprawled through the doorway into the central shrine where the sacred stone and the image of the deity stood. It is reasonable to speculate that the vessel contained blood freshly drained from the youth's cut throat and that the attendant was carrying it in to make a blood offering to the deity at the moment when the building collapsed.

A second figure, a tall and powerfully built man perhaps in his thirties, had stood beside the boy, supervising the ritual. This man was evidently a person of rank and consequence: he was wearing a ring made of silver and iron – extremely rare in those days – and carrying an agate seal-stone. A woman's body, perhaps that of a priestess, lay nearby. The youth had been sacrificed just minutes before the building collapsed on the priests who murdered him. The powerful priest was felled by the falling roof timbers and dropped onto his back on the floor beside the sacrificial table, as dead as his victim.

The inference from this vivid and dramatic evidence is clear. Earth tremors of increasing severity caused the priests at the Sanctuary of Anemospilia to offer a sacrifice. They were attempting to propitiate the deities of the underworld – whether Poteidan or Potnia or some other deity we cannot tell – at the very moment when the climactic earthquake of 1700 BC brought the sanctuary down. It was almost certainly, from its date, the same great earthquake that caused the destruction of the Old Temple at Knossos.

Professor Peter Warren (1987) believes that human sacrifice was rare and exceptional in Minoan culture, that the Anemospilia boy-sacrifice was a unique and desperate attempt to avert a major catastrophe. But in this he may prove to be wrong: it may be that human sacrifice was an integral part of the Minoan belief-system.

In the Labyrinth at Knossos, temple archives were found which seem to record human sacrifices; at any rate, they can be interpreted in that way. One includes a dedication to a god followed by a human offering: 'for Marineus, one female servant' (Gg 713). Another entry begins with a list of men's names and then goes on to the dedication, 'to the house of Marineus, ten men'. The word 'house' is invariably used for sanctuary or shrine, which implies that Marineus was a god; his name also comes up in other Aegean sites in a similar dedicatory context. It may be that wealthy slave-owners offered tribute to the temple in the form of temple servants, but they may alternatively have been offering troublesome slaves for sacrifice. Perhaps it was a way of keeping the male slave population down.

In 1978–80, Peter Warren was excavating a Minoan house in the western part of the city of Knossos, about 100 metres from the Bull's Head Sanctuary (Evans' Little Palace), when he found a mass of children's bones. There were

299 of them, all carefully butchered and carved, to judge from the knife marks on them. It appeared that a sheep had been sacrificed by having its throat cut at the same time that the children had died. Warren was reluctant to conclude that the children had been sacrificed and then eaten but the conclusion seems inescapable. The idea of human sacrifice and ritual cannibalism adds an altogether new and unpleasant dimension to the picture of Minoan religious practices but – given the mythic horror story of the tribute-children and the all-devouring Minotaur – perhaps we should have been prepared for this.

MOUNT JUKTAS

Another dimension that has been long known but is often overlooked is the link between the temple-worship in the Labyrinth and the rites conducted in the peak sanctuaries. Homer wrote of the 'great city of Knossos' where 'Minos was nine years king, the boon companion of mighty Zeus.' There is also a tradition that Minos went up to Mount Juktas to converse with Zeus, and since the remains of an important Minoan sanctuary still stand on its northern summit it is possible that the Minoan king really did go up periodically from Knossos to confer with the gods.

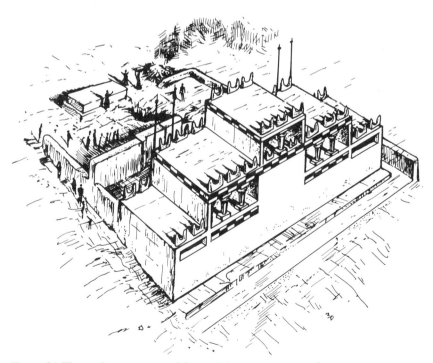

Figure 36 The peak sanctuary on Mount Juktas: a reconstruction

Figure 37 A peak sanctuary: drawing on a rhyton found at the Zakro temple

The peak sanctuary on Mount Juktas was the nearest one to Knossos and its cult was almost certainly linked with the cults practised in the Labyrinth below. The peak sanctuaries were not so high up as to be inaccessible; most were 400–800 metres above sea-level. The highest peaks on Crete were not sanctuaries in the Minoan period, just as Mount Olympus on the Greek mainland was not a cult place in the Mycenean period: they were only developed later.

But the massive precinct wall on Mount Juktas, 730 metres in circumference, originally 3 metres thick and 4 metres high, was built early on. It is thought to date from around 2100 BC, two hundred years before the First Temple was built at Knossos. The holiest part of the sacred precinct was at the edge of the steep, west-facing cliff. There, an area was marked off by two built terraces and a row of five small cult rooms. Between this small temple and the precipice was the ragged entrance to a cave-cleft, an altar, and a pyre (Figure 36).

The small temple was probably, from the evidence of the Zakro rhyton (Figure 37), elaborately embellished with parapets, rows of horns, flag-poles and altars. Somewhere on the site, no one knows quite where, fragments of the head of a large statue of a deity were found. It seems likely that the statue of a Weather-god or Ruler of the Heavens stood inside one of the cult rooms, presiding over weather-magic rites, receiving offerings and caring for the crops and animals of the surrounding hill slopes.

In the early days of the peak sanctuary, it seems to have had only a local significance as a focus for the pastoralists of the immediate area. Later, as the towns on the plain below expanded and, perhaps, as the demand for temple-tribute became greater as well, there was an increased demand for agricultural produce. That in turn accentuated the need for supernatural support: subsistence output was no longer enough. Eventually the temple priestesses reached out and took control of the peak sanctuaries. The peak sanctuaries could not be allowed to continue as potential rivals to the temples, nor as potential seed-beds of heresy. It may also have suited the political situation in Knossos to weave the peak cult into the Labyrinth's ritual calendar.

The tradition of a great king or dynasty of kings of bronze age Crete is very strong, and yet much of the evidence at the Labyrinth points to a powerful priesthood. The solution to this paradox is probably that in domestic affairs the king was a puppet of the temple priestesses, relying on them for his wealth and position, relying on them for divine approval of his reign to consolidate his position in the eyes of his subjects. We can imagine the temple priestesses organizing periodic (perhaps annual) royal processions from the Labyrinth up to the summit of the sacred mountain to receive divine blessing for his continuing reign. The back of the stone throne in the Throne Sanctuary at Knossos is shaped like a stylized Minoan mountain; it was therefore certainly intended as a token or symbolic mountain-top sanctuary for the god or goddess or priestess, a mountain within the temple. The link between the Labyrinth and Mount Juktas was a very natural one.

The poles ranged in front of the façade of the peak sanctuary may have been intended to honour the young male god Velchanos. The poles would have attracted lightning, often the harbinger of rain: erecting them may have been a simple piece of sympathetic magic. At intervals, perhaps twice a year, pilgrims came up the hillside to the precinct to place their offerings in front of the little temple. Priestesses took the offerings and put them on altars while attendants lit bonfires. Music of lyre, sistrum, and triton shell accompanied ritual dances while the pilgrims went forward to throw their offerings into the flames. After it was all over, the temple attendants collected the charred remains of the offerings – small human figures with their hands raised in supplication, clay figures of bulls, rams and sheep – and pushed them down into the sacred cleft.

Seen across the plain, from the Minoan settlement of Ghazi, the mountain has the shape of a reclining human face in profile. Tradition has it that this is the face of Zeus himself and that Zeus was buried on Mount Juktas. In classical times and later, the grave of Zeus was pointed out on the mountain, but it seems likely that in the Minoan period the choice of site for the sanctuary had much more to do with the fact that it would have been visible – and majestically so – from the chambers and corridors on the south front of the Labyrinth. Looking south from Knossos we still see the almost volcanic-looking horned peak of Mount Juktas dominating the skyline. Peculiar, dramatic and distant-looking, it must have seemed the ideal location for a 'magic mountain' cult centre for the Labyrinth.

DEVELOPMENT OF MINOAN RELIGION

How or where the religion of the people of Minoan Knossos originated is too large a question to attempt to explore in this book. Probably we should think of many threads with separate and obscure origins woven gradually together. Probably the cults of the cave and peak sanctuaries started off as purely local practices, and they seem to have begun early, well before the building of the temples.

The cults of the peak sanctuaries sprang into life around the year 2100 BC, before Knossos and the other temple sites became major foci of religious activity. Gradually, from 2000 onwards, religious power gravitated to the lowlands. The early temples were built in about 1930 BC and from that time on the temple authorities were anxious to extend the power of the temples to the outlying sanctuaries. In the beginning, the peak sanctuaries were catering for the local pastoral populations only; as time passed they became geared increasingly to cater for urban and lowland rural populations as well.

From the Knossos Labyrinth, the peak sanctuary on Mount Juktas was seen as a focus for pilgrimage, a place where the sky deities could be confronted, where kings might converse with them. A link was made with the key idea of divine authority, the kings ascending to the peak sanctuary to have their authority validated and renewed. Wherever the idea came from, divine renewal of secular authority was a stroke of genius: it supplied the kings with credentials and gave the priestesses a significant amount of political power. Probably by 1650 BC the peak sanctuaries were closely controlled from the lowland temples; the priests who presided over them were very likely appointed by the temple priestesses. Solomon, king of the Israelites at the time the first temple was built in about 930 BC, extended his power over the Israelite 'high places'; we should visualize a similar process taking place on Crete, with a well-organized urban priesthood systematically extending its power to embrace the peak sanctuaries.

An enduring link between temple and peak was forged, a link which can be glimpsed elsewhere in the Aegean during the following centuries. On Crete, as elsewhere, priestesses led periodic wild processions of women up to the mountains for nocturnal dancing. The bizarre and little-understood cult of maenadism was undoubtedly one aspect of the Labyrinth's ritual life. The brandishing of live snakes during the climactic ecstasies of the rite doubtless led to the attribution of supernatural powers to the temple snakes, at Minoan Knossos just as at classical Epidaurus. The Epidaurian Record tells of miraculous cures at the temple, such as infections healed by the snake's lick. The legend of the Labyrinth includes the story of Polyeidos the seer; as we saw in Chapter 1, the temple snakes of the Knossos Labyrinth assisted him in bringing Minos' son Glaukos back to life. It looks as if the Labyrinth may have been visited as much for its divine snakes as for its bull dance.

What precise role the priestesses of the Labyrinth had we can only speculate. The frescoes show them dominating, presiding luxuriously and imperiously over every ceremony. But they may have had other functions besides. They may have been regarded as prophetesses, like the 'belly-talkers' or pythons of the classical period; they had a second voice, a daemon, within them with which they carried on a dialogue. It was a hoarse and distorted voice like that of a modern medium, and these seers functioned in a similar way, revealing aspects of the unseen present or the unknown future. Prophecy was only possible after careful preparation by a series of ritual actions, including incantation, meditation, drinking from a sacred spring, and making contact with the god by holding a branch from his sacred tree, by inhaling the smoke from its burning leaves, or by drinking the blood of his sacrificial victims. All these things were performed in that still-archaic world of the classical Aegean, and they were probably performed in the twilit world of the Minoan Labyrinth long before.

The classical Greek preoccupation with significant and symbolic dreams is similarly rooted in an earlier age, and we can be sure that Minoan Crete, hung half-way between ancient Egypt and classical Greece, both preoccupied with dreams, was also dream-oriented. Much of the fresco, seal, and ring art contains imagery of an unreal, dream-like quality. It is as if the Minoan priestesses dwelt on dreams for their inspiration. Doubtless they deliberately stimulated and provoked them. There were standard procedures for doing so among the ancients: isolation, prayer, fasting, sleeping on the skin of a sacrificial animal, touching a holy object and – most potent of all – sleeping in a holy place. This curious act, called incubation, may have led priestesses and their initiates to sleep in the shrines, on the peaks and even in the caves in order to induce powerful dreams. We are told in the saga of Epimenides, the famous Knossian seer, that he slept for fifty-seven years in one of the Cretan cave-sanctuaries. Even if this is an exaggeration, it shows how long periods of sleep or trance in a sacred spot were regarded as essential to the prophetic insight.

It is possible that Epimenides' prestige sprang at least in part from his origins in the shadow of the then-deserted Labyrinth, crumbling, mysterious, and hugely suggestive of reserves of ancient mystic power. The Cretan culture generally was regarded by classical Greeks as redolent of religious mystery and power. It was Cretan shamans or seers who were particularly prestigious in the archaic period. It was Karmanor the Cretan shaman who purified Apollo, they said, after the slaying of Python. This reputation for spiritual power extended also to Egypt. There is a carved tablet, now in Cairo, found in the Serapeum at Sakkara, which dates from the Ptolemaic period. It carries a drawing of a bull standing beside an altar surmounted by a pair of sacral horns – in itself a powerful reminiscence of the Minoan past. The inscription above is an advertisement commissioned by a Cretan seer. It reads, 'I interpret dreams, for I am entrusted to do so by the god, with good fortune. It is a Cretan who interprets.'

But all this was to come much later, long after the Labyrinth fell. At around the time the New Temples were built to house the priestesses, seers, and dream-interpreters, i.e. 1650 BC, a new style of pottery decoration was developed, the Marine Style. Its beguilingly attractive designs, including delightful octopus, starfish, seaweed and shell patterns, may cause us to overlook its possible symbolic significance, especially given the time of its appearance. The decoration amounts to an exhortation to the fertility of the sea and may be taken as an implicit invocation to Poseidon; as Nanno Marinatos (1984) has shown on Thera, it would be unwise to treat a Minoan decorative scheme as purely decorative. Sinclair Hood (1978) comments that most of the Marine Style and other richly decorated vases produced at Knossos during the New Temple Period (1700–1470 BC) were ritual vessels made for cult use.

As the New Temple Period began, the sacred cave at Arkalochori was the centre of a major cult dedicated to warriors. The cave's deity was a protector of soldiers. Many specially made offerings of very thin bronze swords were found there. Bronze swords tended to break far too easily, so they needed magical protection of some kind to make them effective in battle.

By the time the temples had all been abandoned, from 1380 until 1200 BC, over thirty grottoes were in cult use in Crete. Curiously, the late cave cults combined elements of the sky-god cults deriving from the peak sanctuaries with those of the underworld cave-deities to make a single supreme deity with universal characteristics. It is almost as if, with the transfer of religious power from peak to temple, and then the destruction of the temple, the cave had to become the mythic repository, the night-safe, of Minoan religion. It may also be that out of this sequence of events came the extraordinary myth of the birth and sheltering of the infant Zeus in a cave.

It is also significant that a major religious development followed the fall of the Labyrinth in 1380. The Labyrinth with its highly organized priesthood and its seemingly universal control over Minoan religion was a major force for conservatism. The priestesses of the Labyrinth promoted the dominance of the goddess in all her many manifestations. It looks as if the fall of the Labyrinth so weakened the old goddess cult that the newer cult of Zeus was able to emerge from its smoking ruins. In the century immediately before the Labyrinth fell, the cult of the goddess was at its peak. Signet rings from this phase show an archetypal image of her poised, tense with power, gesturing with a staff, flanked by heraldic lions on a mountain top (see chapter title illustration). By this late stage the great days of the peak sanctuaries were over: the real power and drive in Minoan religious life already resided in the temples. Even so, the peak sanctuaries were still regarded as awesome places where the authority of gods, goddesses, priests and kings originated. Perhaps it was already a nostalgic, backward glance by the time the signet rings were made, but they nevertheless unmistakably show the overriding and commanding authority of Potnia, the Lady of the Labyrinth.

The eruption of Thera in about 1470 BC (see Chapter 11) may have resulted in a major dislocation of Minoan values. The religious practices designed to order the natural environment demonstrably failed; the eruption was catastrophically destructive. It is reasonable to assume that it led to a loss of faith either in the gods themselves or in the old rites for propitiating them. In fact the decline of the peak sanctuary cults seems to date from the Thera eruption; from then on people seem to have focused more on the temples and cave sanctuaries. From the sky, the Cretans turned to the underworld for help in their appeal to new deities to save them from disaster.

Turning to new gods, new places, and new rites brought new life to the subterranean cults of the caves – and those of the temples too. For one major feature of the Labyrinth is the pseudo-subterranean quality of many of its chambers, and this quality will have reinforced its role as a religious centre in the final phase, between Thera and its abandonment in 1380. Mount Juktas was not abandoned entirely. Some ceremonies were still conducted there, doubtless because of the momentum of tradition and because the king's authority was tied up with pilgrimages to the peak sanctuary, but the archaeological evidence shows that it was at a more subdued level than before the Thera eruption. The Temple at Knossos, the Labyrinth, the Daidalaion, was now the hub of the religious life of much of Crete. Other temples had fallen and been left in ruins, but the Labyrinth was restored and continued to function: it alone represented the temple cult.

Nevertheless, the priestesses of the Labyrinth went on looking back to Mount Juktas as a celestial reference point, modelling thrones on the mountain's idealized shape, setting the commanding figure of Potnia on the mountain top among shrine buildings, setting her above the less important figure of the boy-god Velchanos, with her staff thrust forward in command of the cosmos. It is almost as if she is defiantly and consciously holding back the forces of religious change, trying to stem the creeping incoming tide of Zeus-Velchanos worship, the cult that would eventually prevail after her temple fell.

10
The bull dance

There were bulls which had the run of the temple of Poseidon; and the ten kings, being left alone in the temple, after they had offered prayers to the god that they might capture the victim which was acceptable to him, hunted the bulls without weapons but with staves and nooses; and the bull which they caught they led up to the pillar and cut its throat over the top of it so that the blood fell upon the sacred inscription.

Plato's description of the capital of Atlantis, *Critias, c.* 380 BC.

EVIDENCE OF BULL-LEAPING

The cult of the bull, one of the central symbols in the Minoan belief-system, was a major ingredient in the religious practices conducted in the Labyrinth. Bull sacrifices alone would not amount to proof of a bull cult. The Agia Triadha sarcophagus shows us a bull trussed and sacrificed, but two goats are pathetically awaiting their turn beneath the sacrificial table and they are not offered as evidence of a goat cult. J. T. Hooker (1983) takes a fairly extreme position: for him, neither bull sacrifices nor bull-leaping are enough to prove a bull cult. But the evidence of a preoccupation with bulls is pervasive. Mythological evidence quoted in Chapter 9 showed that the bull was regarded as a theriomorphic transformation of Poteidan, the most powerful male deity in the Minoan pantheon. There is also archaeological evidence in and round the Labyrinth: the magnificent bull's head rhyton from the Bull's Head Sanctuary, the skulls of slaughtered bulls forming a foundation deposit in the 'House of the Sacrificed Oxen' on the Labyrinth's southern margin, frescoes showing bulls in the Northern Sector and East and West Wings, a miniature crystal painting of a bull in the Throne Sanctuary, and the stylized bull's horns incorporated into the architecture. The portrayal of bulls and bull-leaping on the walls of the temple appears to have been unique to Knossos. We should not read too much into this, because the wall decoration schemes have not survived at all well at any of the temples and there may have been many more bull-leaping frescoes than the handful that survived in fragments

Figure 38 Bull's head rhyton

at Knossos. Nevertheless, on the existing evidence, the bull cult does seem to have been more important at Knossos than at the other temples.

The frescoes and seal stones can tell a great deal about the nature of the bull games, but these representations have to be treated with caution. Nevertheless, it is possible, by putting the images carefully into a sequence, to assemble a likely course of events. At Vaphio on the Greek mainland, two

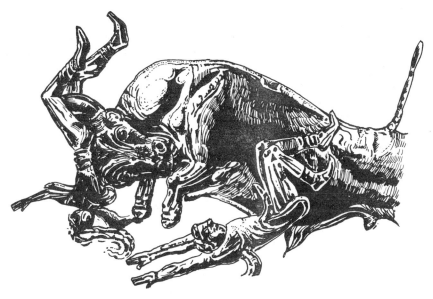

Figure 39 A bull gores its hunters. The Vaphio Cup I, made in about 1500–1450 BC

gold cups were found which certainly came from Minoan Crete. The first cup shows violent scenes of a bull hunt; one bull is caught in a net while another escapes and tramples his would-be captors (Figure 39). The second Vaphio cup, in contrast, shows a bull being caught by cunning; a beautifully drawn Minoan man – the most vivid and animated impression so far found – tethers the bull while he is preoccupied with a decoy cow. Once the wild or half-wild bulls were captured, they were taken to the temples for the bull games.

Some scenes show bull-leapers being tossed by a bull. The Boxer Vase from Agia Triadha shows a mishap of this kind. It may be that onlookers were thrilled at the prospect of gory accidents, just as in the later classical world one of the attractions of chariot races was the death-risk involved; it still seems to be an element in modern car racing, to judge from the morbid interest in racing car crashes shown by television news editors. This is not to say that the accidents were an intentional part of the bull games, dangerous though they were.

The head-on encounter between bull and bull-leaper was the most dangerous. The leaper dived between the bull's horns – whether he touched them or not on the way is open to discussion – and landed hands and face downward on the bull's back. Seal impressions from Zakro and Sklavokampos show this.

The famous Bull-Leaping Fresco from the Great Goddess Sanctuary in the Labyrinth shows what happened next. The bull-leaper's hands and forearms are safely down on the bull's back and his legs continue involuntarily over towards the beast's tail. The fact that the youth's arms are so far down on the bull's back means that there would have been no spring available to push him clear, so this particular detail must be stylized.

With hands pressing firmly down on the bull's spine and the assistance of the continuing momentum of the legs, the leaper's body arched backwards over the bull's tail, as shown in a gold ring from Asine. This sequence of movements is known as 'the Diving Leap'. The Bull-Leaping Fresco has sometimes been held to show three separate stages in a bull leap. The figure on the left has grappled the bull from in front and is hanging on to its horns, apparently relying on the bull to toss its head vigorously upwards to carry the leaper over to the second position, on the bull's back. The third figure alights safely on the ground behind the bull (Figure 40).

The acrobat's utilization of the toss-back of the horns is often mentioned, by Graham for example. In reality, bulls shake their heads erratically. They tend to lower their horns vertically and then twist them sideways as they jerk them up again to inflict the maximum injury. If Cretan bulls 3,500 years ago behaved in the same way as modern bulls, the acrobats could never have cleared the horns if they were holding onto them. No bull-leaper, however experienced, could use an unpredictable and possibly diagonal toss to get him or her safely over the bull's horns. It is hard to believe that it was ever done. The alternative and more likely explanation for the Bull-Leaping Fresco is

Figure 40 The Bull-Leaping Fresco

that it shows some of the members of a bull-leaping team at work. Such feats were surely only performed with assistance from other acrobats, like many a modern circus act. The figure at the front, grappling with the bull, is distracting it, keeping its head down and its back fairly still for the vault. There are clay models that show as many as three bull-grapplers hanging on to a bull's horns. A manoeuvre like this would be essential to lower and, in effect, pad the lethal horns while the leaper, the star performer, dived over. The third figure on the Bull-Leaping Fresco, the figure at the back with outstretched arms, similarly represents a group of helpers waiting behind the bull to catch the leaper after his successful vault.

It seems likely that, if three consecutive stages of a bull leap had been intended, all three figures would have been the same sex; in fact the leaper is a youth and the assistants are girls. It is also significant that the figure on the right is facing the wrong way to have landed from the vault shown.

A fine bronze statuette, thought to have come from Rethymnon, shows a bull-leaper landing upright on his feet on the bull's back. To have reached this position, the acrobat must have gone through a different sequence of movements. Somehow, this daring acrobat has somersaulted over the bull's head, and it is not possible that the horns could have been used. The most likely way of gaining the height and impetus required would have been to use the energy of the team to propel him up and over the horns, ideally while two or more grapplers held them low. From a standing position on the bull's back the leaper could simply have stepped or jumped off over the tail; maybe a really accomplished leaper would attempt a second somersault for extra effect. It certainly appears that there were variations in the repertoire of feats.

Ever since Sir Arthur Evans first uncovered evidence of bull games on bronze age Crete, controversy has surrounded them. Sceptics have said repeatedly that bull-leaping as shown in Minoan works of art simply could not have happened: it was physically impossible. Many traditional cultures that have made use of cattle have had bull sports of some kind; there is evidence not just in Crete, but in Turkey, Syria, Thessaly, China, Portugal, southern France and of course Spain, where bull sports survive as a major element of the culture. It is possible that the bullfights of modern Spain are ultimately derived from the Minoan bull games, but there is no hint in any of the portrayals of Minoan games that any infuriating injury was inflicted on the Cretan bulls: as a result, the behaviour of the Cretan bulls would have been significantly different from that of the Spanish bulls.

Although bull-leaping is rarely reported as being part of the modern Spanish bullfight, it certainly was at one time an element in the bull-baiting. There is film footage of Spanish bullfighters jumping over bulls and, moreover, not by grasping the horns. In the days before film, vaulting over the bull from a chair or table was a recognized trick in many Spanish bullfights.

In the Portuguese bull sport, the bull has its shoulder muscles weakened by having *bandarilhas* stuck into them. Then the leader of a team of eight *forcados* throws himself on to the bull's head as it charges, landing between the padded horns. If he is successful, the rest of the team helps to immobilize the beast by hurling themselves on top of him; one man goes round behind and hangs on to the bull's tail. This is still regarded as a dangerous feat, even though the bull is in a weakened state when it is attempted.

In the little-known 'vâche-fights' of southern France, a feat very similar to the diving leap is still performed today. At St Jean de Luz in the 1970s, an experienced leaper was seen to dive between a cow's horns and on to its back while the animal was distracted by a troupe of assistants. Risk is involved, but the feat can be performed. The accumulating evidence from present-day bull sports and from a careful interpretation of the Minoan artwork suggests that bull-leaping *did* take place in Crete in the bronze age.

Some scholarly observers of the Minoan scene remain sceptical. J. Pinsent (1983) reminds us that it is unwise to treat bronze age art as if it was a photographic representation of life. 'Realism', if an equivalent word existed in the Linear A language, would not have meant the same thing to a Minoan as it does to us. Some drawings may show, in an idealized way, what ought to have happened in certain situations. The running bull, for instance, is usually shown with all four feet off the ground at once. This artistic shorthand, known as the flying gallop, was a common image in European art in the eighteenth and nineteenth centuries. It is not how quadrupeds actually run: it merely shows the concept of galloping, an impression. Similarly, we may have to make allowances for the way in which the leapers, grapplers, and catchers are depicted.

One possibility that may be kept in reserve is that far less daring feats were performed. Perhaps the bull was vaulted from side to side rather than from end to end. Perhaps the skill of the teams of acrobats, performing all kinds of diversionary handstands and somersaults on the ground between the bull and the spectators, convinced those watching that they were seeing something far more dangerous and spectacular. As we know from watching the acts of

professional conjurers, the power of suggestion in a sympathetic audience is
not to be underestimated.

The scenes depicting bull games provide very few clues about their location.
The Knossos Labyrinth was designed round a spacious rectangular Central
Court and many people have understandably assumed that this court was
where the bull games took place. The priestesses and onlookers in the
Grandstand Fresco are watching a major spectacle in the Central Court which
may well be the bull games. The curiously isolated section of colonnade to the
south of the Tripartite Shrine may have been some sort of spectator box for
priestesses of the Snake Goddess. The present concrete reconstruction is
incorrect, with too low a ceiling and access only from the Central Court.
Fyfe's manuscript plan shows that originally there was a doorway through
from the southern chambers of the Snake Goddess Sanctuary, which would
have been essential if bull games were in progress in the court (see Figure 15).

Evans ruled out this possibility early on because of the large number of
doorways and corridors which open onto the Central Court: with so many
exit points, it would have been too difficult to contain a bull and unthinkable
that the beast would have been allowed to charge off into the maze of
chambers on all four sides of the court, wreaking havoc wherever it went.
Another objection is that the court is rather small compared with a Spanish
bullring and that it would not have allowed enough space for the bull-leaping
manoeuvres. If the Knossos Central Court was used for bull games then so,
logically, were the equivalent courts at Phaistos, Mallia, and Zakro. The
court at Mallia has some sort of altar at its centre and this, it has been argued,
would have been an obstruction to the bull games.

An additional problem is that the Central Courts were originally paved
over. At Knossos, only a small area of the paving has survived (Plate 19), but
enough to indicate that the whole Central Court was paved. James Graham
(1987) suggests that this surface would have been too smooth and slippery for
the performance of bull games and that sand may have been sprinkled on it.
This would have made it worse; if anything was sprinkled on the stone
pavement it must have been something like wet sawdust.

Other possible locations have been sought, outside the temple precinct.
Some think the building lay on the flat floor of the Kairatos valley
immediately to the east of the Balustrade Sanctuary (Royal Villa); certainly a
compound or pen close to the temple would have been necessary, and the site
in front of the Balustrade Sanctuary is a probable one for this purpose, but
the bull games themselves are more likely to have taken place in the Central
Courts. Graham points out that the Central Courts seem to have been built
like games pitches to standard specifications: all paved, all with one or more
porticoes and with (probable) upper viewing galleries, all with north-south

long axes and all roughly 24 by 52 metres. They are a standard feature, designed for a specific, disciplined ceremonial activity. But if Evans rejected their use for bull games, why should we reconsider them? What Evans had not allowed for – and this is where his reconstitution of the site caught him out – was that the margins of the Central Court at Knossos were particularly badly preserved. The situation looks very different if we allow that some continuous barrier ran along the four edges of the court.

At Phaistos there is clear evidence of doors that closed off all openings on to the Central Court. The four doorways into the Lobby of the Magazines near the north-west corner of the court could be closed during the bull games by large doors. The outer two doorways were later sealed up, possibly to a height of only a metre, by mud-brick walling. The inner doorways continued to be closed by two massive wooden doors which, uniquely, closed against a central round timber column.

At Mallia a broad staircase leading up from the west side of the Central Court was closed off by a set of double doors. Along the north side of the court ran a columned portico with a distinct threshold, implying a doorway, between the two westernmost columns; this implies that the gaps between the other columns were not left unobstructed, but what formed the barrier here is open to speculation: possibly a low mud-brick wall like the one at Phaistos, possibly a wooden rail socketed into the columns. On the east side is a well-preserved portico of alternating columns and pillars. In the stone sill separating each column and pillar are three circular sockets, evidently for wooden posts that originally supported a rail. Since the portico is at ground level, there was no need to install a stout rail to stop people falling down into the courtyard. The alternative is that it was put in to stop some large animal in the court from getting into the portico.

Similar wooden balustrades very probably ran round the perimeter of the Central Court at Knossos too; a fresco fragment from the Labyrinth actually shows us a strongly made three-rail fence with a female attendant or priestess leaning on it as she watches.

THE BULL-VAULTING BLOCK

One of the finest representations of the bull leap is on a seal (Figure 41). It shows the bull with its forelegs up on a large rectangular block, sometimes identified as a water tank: a bull-leaper is vaulting over the horns. Graham has cleverly connected this image with the large, oddly shaped stone block built into the north-west corner of the Central Court at Phaistos. Its top stands about a metre above the ground. At its eastern end it narrows off and drops half-way down to ground level. It looks like two large steps, and the treads are worn down as if by repeated clambering up and down, but it makes no sense at all as a staircase since it leads into a blind corner.

Figure 41 Bull-leaping scene on a
sealstone

Graham supposes that one of the acrobats' tricks was to tease the bull into cornering one of the team on the block. As the bull succeeded in getting his forefeet on to the narrow end of the lower step, where there was no room for him to toss his head without unbalancing, the acrobat dived between his horns and somersaulted off his back onto the ground.

The distinctive criss-cross pattern drawn on the block as shown on the seal was also found close to the Phaistos bull-vaulting block as part of the design of the north wall; just a few metres away there are two niches that were painted with the criss-cross pattern. Perhaps the bull-vaulting block itself was originally painted with this design: we know from the frescoes that other stone ritual structures were painted.

The main north-south axis of the Bull Court at Phaistos is aligned directly on the double peak of Mount Ida, which must have suggested, even more to the Minoans than it does to us today, a felicitous symbolic reference to the sacral bull horns, one of the most powerful and resonant religious symbols. The north-south axis of the Bull Court at Knossos is roughly aligned on the peak sanctuary of Mount Juktas which, from Knossos, also appears to be twin-peaked. At Mallia and Zakro the twin peak is missing, so the landscape symbolism cannot be pressed too far.

When the bull games were over, presumably in a climactic feat of daring, like a multiple somersault leap, the bull may have been sacrificed. In the Knossos Labyrinth this may have taken place on the pavement in front of the Tripartite Shrine decorated with its many horns of consecration. At Phaistos, Graham suggests that the sacrifice took place in the Lobby of the Magazines, but I think it more likely that, as at Knossos, the ritual took place in the Bull Court itself, in front of what seem to be the cellular remains of a Tripartite Shrine in the north-east corner.

Graham tries to identify stalls for the bulls used in the bull games, but there is really not enough evidence to do this. His identification of Room vi 12 at Mallia in particular seems an odd choice, in that the beast would have to be steered through four narrow doorways to get it there – a great deal of unnecessary trouble.

THE BULL FROM THE SEA

The phrase 'bull games' has been used repeatedly. It is unsatisfactory in that it implies that they were for entertainment or sport, which they clearly were not. Most scholars are agreed that they were religious and symbolic in intent. Obviously the term 'bullfight' would be inappropriate as well. If we could see the bull games, the impression would be much more that of an elaborate and carefully choreographed dance.

Certainly there were elements of stress and danger, and a struggle of wills between the team of acrobats and the bull, but nevertheless we would have seen something akin to the ritual dances that we know were performed by priestesses on the West Courts. We would have seen an *agon* of physical strength, daring, and skill, an aesthetic struggle that bears comparison with other scenes of struggle familiar from Minoan artworks. There is the Boxer Vase from Agia Triadha, which shows bull-leaping, boxing, and wrestling; there is the bee pendant from Mallia, which shows two bees or hornets in combat; there are the many seals showing pairs of animals in conflict, such as the one showing a confrontation between a wild goat and a collared hound found at Arkhanes.

The ritual *agon* was a religious rite and the bull in particular was strongly associated with Poteidan. Much of the evidence from the Knossos Labyrinth points to a dedication of that building to goddesses. The use of the Central Court as a Bull Court and the presence of frescoes depicting bulls elsewhere in the temple-complex imply covert references to Poteidan. There may seem to be an inherent paradox in a sanctuary-by-sanctuary dedication to goddesses, but a central dedication to a god. Similar apparent clashes of allegiance are

Figure 42 A rural ritual: harvest celebration from the Harvester Vase

nevertheless to be found in some Christian churches, where there may be a nominal dedication to a saint, a central focus on an implicitly male Trinity, and representations with varying emphases of male and female saints, disciples and a quasi-goddess, the mother of Christ.

There is a clue to the specific problem of the Labyrinth's dedication in the myth of King Minos. The fine white bull from the sea, Poseidon's gift to Minos that was intended to be offered back in sacrifice, was described as having a silver circle on its forehead and horns like a crescent moon. The circle may be taken to symbolize the sun and the two symbols together, sun and moon, were the symbols of Poteidan in the celestial sphere. We have to remember always that the deities inhabited three worlds, the celestial, the terrestrial, and the subterranean. Poteidan might manifest himself as sun and moon in the first of these worlds, as a bull in the second, as earthquakes and tsunamis in the third. The fact that Minos' bull carried the sun and moon symbols on its head meant that it carried Poteidan's signature, his seal. The same sun and moon symbols hover above the goddess Potnia in several of the seal impressions. The bull's head rhyton from the Bull's Head Sanctuary has a suggestion of the sun-disc on its forehead. They are not mere decorations. Poteidan is apparently, if the ciphers are read correctly, a cosmic background presence in the epiphanies of the goddess.

It is important to see the deities of bronze age Crete as related and even overlapping with one another. It may be wrong to try to deal with them separately, and it is very likely that the Minoans themselves attributed family relationships of some kind to them. It may be that Poteidan was then, in these pre-classical times, seen as the primeval father, the father of the gods, and as such he would have his central place in the Knossos Labyrinth. He would have his sacrifices. And he would have his bull dance, the ritual bull dance that expressed the interweaving of human and divine destinies, the bull dance that intimated human collusion, struggle, and collaboration with the god.

11
The Thera eruption

I mean to say [the Egyptian priest replied] that to my mind you [Athenians] are all young; there is no old opinion handed down among you by ancient tradition, nor any science which is hoary with age. And I will tell you why. There have been and will be again many destructions of mankind arising out of many causes; the greatest have been brought about by the agencies of fire and water.

Plato, *Timaeus*

THE DESTRUCTION OF 1470 BC

The circumstances in which the Labyrinth was finally ruined and abandoned are shrouded in mystery. The building was repeatedly damaged by earthquake, possibly earthquake-induced fires and perhaps by other agencies as well. Each time, the priestesses caused the damage to be made good, often using the opportunity to alter the structure and its décor.

In about 1700 BC there was a major destruction at many Minoan sites. It marked the end of the Old Temple Period on Crete (in conventional chronologies the boundary between Evans' Middle Minoan II and Middle Minoan III and between Platon's Proto-Palatial and Neo-Palatial Periods). There was at least one major earthquake and maybe a whole series of earthquakes which shook and severely damaged both the temple-complex and the city of Knossos. Afterwards, the Labyrinth was repaired and modified. The Procession Corridor, instead of running straight across from the West Court to the Bull Court, was diverted south to make it longer and, presumably, to make the delayed entry to the Cupbearer Sanctuary and the Bull Court the more dramatic: the former entrance passage was converted into a store-room, Magazine II. The temple at Phaistos was so badly damaged that the ruins of the old temple were demolished and levelled; a new temple with a different plan was built on the rubble at a slightly higher level.

Other Minoan sites were also damaged in the 1700 BC earthquake but such was the strength of the Minoan civilization at this time that the destructions in no way impeded its development: rather, they seem to have stimulated it to reach new heights. The two hundred years that followed were the most flourishing and vigorous in the development of the culture. The population of Crete may have increased at this time, resulting from improving living conditions and a lower death-rate. Following on from this, there was expansion: the establishment of colonies in the Aegean, such as Akrotiri on Thera and Phylakopi on Melos.

The first destructions, those caused by earthquakes in 1700 BC, are the subject of general agreement among scholars. The second major disaster remains a matter of heated controversy among archaeologists and geologists Sir Arthur Evans changed his mind, in the end favouring a date for the final destruction of Knossos at the close of his Late Minoan II period, which would now be put at about 1400 BC. There are many differing views on the later stages of the Labyrinth's history and the issues are far from being resolved.

Nicolas Platon (1968) puts the second major destruction of Knossos at about 1450 and feels that it was likely to have been associated with the eruption of Thera which is known to have happened at about that time. Platon feels that the evidence points unequivocally to the 'total and universal destruction of the New Palaces by geological upheaval'.

Sinclair Hood, like Platon, has the benefit of a long experience in Minoan archaeology; he too sees evidence of widespread destruction at Minoan sites in 1450 but attributes it to invasion. In addition, though, he points to evidence of the catastrophic eruption of Thera, in the form of earthquake damage, in about 1500 BC. Earthquake damage in 1500 may have disrupted the Minoan economy severely; Hood detects a phase of noticeably poorer, devitalized artistic activity in its aftermath (1978, p. 24). Mervyn Popham (1984) too refers to evidence of damage done to the Labyrinth and other Minoan buildings at Knossos in the 1500 earthquake: it interrupted work on the 'Unexplored Mansion', which was being built at that time.

We may be dealing with two alternative dates for a single disaster or with two separate disasters. Some scholars have attempted to close the time gap between 1450 and 1500, with the idea that all the damage was done during the course of a single large-scale catastrophe. John Luce (1969) in particular has offered a persuasive scenario along these lines, with a sequence of closely connected geological upheavals beginning in 1500 and culminating in about 1470 BC.

The nature of this '1470' destruction, if we can provisionally refer to it in that way, is in itself controversial and virtually every aspect of the Labyrinth's mazy history from this point on has been challenged by one researcher or another.

Destruction by invaders, most likely from Attica or the Argolid on the Greek mainland, is one possibility. In his enthusiasm for the newly discovered civilization, Evans advanced the view that Minoans spread across the Aegean and eventually dominated parts of the Greek mainland. It was Wace who in

Figure 43 The bronze age Aegean world. 1 – Attica, 2 – Argolis, 3 – Messenia, 4 – the nearest approach to Crete of the Hittite empire. Asterisk = Minoan colony

1939 first argued in favour of a reverse process, an invasion of Crete by Mycenean Greeks; it was a proposal which counteracted the excesses of Evans' Minoan Empire theory. Although the damage done to the temples in the 1470 destruction may have been inflicted by invaders, it seems unlikely (Warren 1975). At the Zakro temple, massive stone walls were overturned, suggesting a geological upheaval rather than a bronze age conquest. In any case, invaders intending to settle and exploit a new land would have had little to gain from severely damaging the main administrative and storage buildings: they would have been more likely to treat them with care so that they could use the buildings themselves. On the whole, a major earthquake seems more likely. Peter Warren favours an earthquake associated with the big Thera eruption, which may have inflicted destructive aerial blast waves on Knossos and a fall-out of volcanic ash as well.

In 1939, Spyridon Marinatos first proposed that it was the Thera eruption which brought to an end the Minoan civilization on Crete. The idea had begun to take shape as early as 1932, while he was excavating the remains of Minoan houses on the seashore at Amnisos. He found pumice and beach sand among the ruins and large blocks of masonry pulled out of place as if by the powerful suction of a mass of water. Marinatos reflected that this might be construed as specific evidence of the nature of the general cataclysm that had laid Crete waste. Crete had been devastated by the tidal waves generated by the Thera eruption. Marinatos' article was published with a disclaimer from the editor of the journal (*Antiquity*), saying that more evidence was needed to support the theory. Nicolas Platon, who excavated the newly discovered temple at Zakro, again on the seashore, was convinced by the pumice-stone and thick layers of volcanic ash which he found there that Marinatos was right. John Luce has taken these ideas and developed them further and we will return to his comprehensive explanation of events later.

Other possibilities include revolution and systems-collapse, but it would be unlikely that we would find archaeological evidence to support either of these explanations. That is not to say that they did not happen. It is possible that the Minoan economy collapsed because of some internal and archaeologically invisible failure, leaving the island open to Mycenean invaders. Nevertheless, the volcanic eruption theory has solid geological and archaeological evidence to support it, so it needs to be taken very seriously. As Peter Warren (1975) has said, it makes sense to correlate the Thera eruption, which is known to have been catastrophically violent, with the greatest destruction level ever detected on prehistoric Crete – and several other Aegean islands as well. The economic, social, religious, and political repercussions of the Thera eruption would have been far-reaching, and it is easy to visualize that this axe-blow to the roots of Minoan culture could well have led on to revolution, civil war, systems-collapse or, when the mainlanders of Attica or Argolis got to hear of the situation on Crete, invasion. It is possible that all these things happened in turn.

Whatever the detailed scenario of the 1470 destruction, all the Minoan temple-complexes were destroyed by it. All were left in ruins and abandoned except for the Knossos Labyrinth. Only the Knossos Labyrinth was repaired and restored. The final phase of the Minoan civilization, the post-Thera phase here called the Late Temple Period, 1470 to 1380, turned out to be the Labyrinth's zenith, when its power extended widely to east and west across most of Crete. It alone of the major temple-complexes survived, although only for a further ninety years. During this phase power was highly centralized, with Knossos controlling the whole of central Crete from Rethymnon right across to Ierapetra (Chadwick 1976). The eastern and western extremities of the long island, which had previously been controlled

from the Kydonia and Zakro temples, seem to have remained independent of
Knossos, presumably freed by distance.

According to John Luce (1969), the key to the mystery of Knossos'
destruction is on Thera, the volcanic island 120 kilometres to the north of
Crete, where the ruins of Minoan houses complete with frescoes have been
found, smothered by thick layers of white volcanic tephra. Thera's peculiar
shape, a ragged ring of islands like a shallow cone with the centre blown out,
is almost entirely due to the colossal eruption which engulfed the Minoan
town at Akrotiri.

The geological stratification on Santorini, the ancient Thera, gives the very
clear, precise evidence needed of the sequence of events that produced the
complex evidence of disaster on Crete. The Thera evidence points to a series
of volcanic eruptions early in the fifteenth century BC and culminating in a
cataclysmic caldera eruption which completely blew out the centre of the
originally circular island in around 1470. To judge from the ash and pumice
layers preserved on the flanks of the island, the sequence started with an
eruption that produced a grey pumice layer 4 metres thick (at Phira). In the
ruins of Minoan houses engulfed by this pumice there are few human remains
or valuables, implying that the inhabitants had some warning from
premonitory earthquakes which allowed them to escape. The tephra layer
ejected in this initial eruption had sufficient time to be criss-crossed by
erosional gullies before the next layer, of ash, was deposited; in addition,
some of the ruined houses were adapted and re-used by squatters, so we can
infer that a lengthy quiescent phase of some years or decades followed. The
remains of a tree buried in the first layer have been radio-carbon dated and
the date is consistent with an eruption between 1500 and 1550 BC. Pottery
discovered at Akrotiri suggests that the eruption occurred at the end rather
than the beginning of this period. Significantly, it was in the years around
1500 that major earthquakes damaged Knossos, so it seems very likely that
the 1500 earthquake damage at Knossos can be linked directly with the 1500
eruption of Thera.

After the quiescent phase there were several separate minor eruptions, each
producing a layer of volcanic ash or pumice of a different colour: five distinct
volcanic eruptions can be identified. After this warming-up phase came the
caldera eruption, a gigantic explosion which tore the heart out of Thera and,
where once had been an imposing mountain peak perhaps 1500 metres high,
left a deep basin, the bottom of which was as much as 400 metres below
sea-level. Where the mountain had been, there was a bay 8 kilometres across.
On the lower slopes of the cone, sheltered from the main force of the eruption,
a layer of fine white volcanic ash up to 66 metres thick was deposited on top
of the earlier ash and pumice layers. Some of this white ash, blown south-

eastwards by the wind, settled on the Mediterranean sea-bed and can still be traced almost as far as the coasts of Cyprus and Egypt (Figure 44).

The exact date of the big Thera eruption is not known, but it is thought to have been around the year 1470 BC. In 1470 the great temple-complexes at Knossos, Phaistos, Mallia, and Zakro were destroyed together with their towns. Outlying mansions at Tylissos and Sklavokampos and the temple at Niru Khani were destroyed. The houses Marinatos excavated at Amnisos were levelled, so we can assume that the harbour town of Knossos was destroyed. The Minoan towns of Gournia, Palaikastro, Pseira, and Mochlos were destroyed. The roof of the sacred cave of Arkalochori collapsed.

It seems logical to correlate this widespread devastation on Crete in about 1470 with the final caldera eruption of Thera, which we know was very violent and which we know happened at about the same time. The large scale of the Thera eruption may be judged from a modern analogue. The Krakatoa eruption of 1883 produced a caldera crater about 7 kilometres in diameter, roughly the same size as the Thera crater. Ash from Krakatoa fell over an area 3,000 kilometres across, in places forming layers 60 metres thick; the Thera ash layer reached a maximum thickness of 66 metres. Krakatoa formed a crater in the sea-bed and a great tsunami drowning 36,000 people: rafts of pumice 30 kilometres across drifted about on the sea. Thera too was a very deep-seated eruption which cratered the sea-bed; it too must have created a tsunami which swept outwards at high speed through the deep water to the south of Thera.

In deep water, the tsunami may have travelled as a broad, low and deceptively unobtrusive wave at 150 kilometres per hour. As the sea-bed shelved sharply up along the north coast of Crete, and on the Thera-facing coasts of other Aegean islands, the wave narrowed and towered up perhaps 30 or 50 metres into the air before smashing across the coastal lowlands. These projections are not mere speculation. Twenty-four kilometres east of Thera there is a small island call Anaphi. Deposits of pumice at 200 metres at the head of a valley leading down to a bay imply that water from the Thera tidal wave swept inshore up to that height.

Nor were the awe-inspiring tsunamis and earthquakes all that Minoan Crete had to withstand. The aerial shock waves or 'blast' from the eruption will have cracked and demolished the upper, mud-brick walls of many of the buildings, including the Labyrinth, just as blast from the Krakatoa eruption cracked open walls as much as 160 kilometres away from the volcano. The ashfall, probably the last of Poteidan's trident-thrusts, was at the same time the quietest and deadliest result of the Thera eruption. A study of Icelandic ash eruptions indicates that an ashfall of only 10 centimetres may cause farmland to be abandoned until the ash is washed or blown away. The sea-bed between Thera and Crete is still coated with ash from the 1470 eruption. One core taken from the sea-bed 120 kilometres south-east of Thera shows an ash layer 78 centimetres thick. Knossos is the same distance from

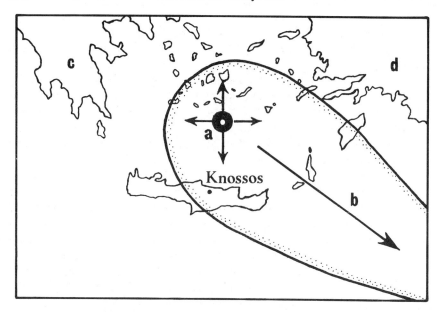

Figure 44 Area affected by ashfall from the Thera eruption. The centre of the 'bull's eye' shows the position of Thera and the arrows marked 'a' show the initial radial dispersal of ash by the eruption itself. Ash was carried by a north-west wind (b) across the eastern half of Crete and 500 kilometres further to the south-east

Thera but was not directly downwind at the time of the disaster; it is reasonable to estimate that the ashfall at Knossos was between 20 and 30 centimetres thick. The whole of the eastern half of Crete would have been coated to a similar depth with the fine, white, sterilizing ash. The silent fall of white dry dust, darkening the sky, choking the livestock and smothering the crops, was easily enough to put all the farmland of the centre and east out of production for several years and cause widespread famine.

Luce's chilling account of the effects of the 1470 Thera eruption on Crete is as convincing as it is horrific. The Minoan economy was assailed by earthquakes, fires, aerial blast, towering tidal waves and the thunderous bull-roar of Thera exploding. Knossos and its territory were finally wrecked by a white pall of slowly falling dust, blanketing and paralysing the countryside, cutting off the life-blood of the Labyrinth.

KNOSSOS: THE LOST ATLANTIS

Soon after Evans rediscovered the Minoan civilization it was suggested that memories of the ancient culture formed the basis of the Atlantis legend. K. T. Frost, in a *Times* article in 1909, pointed out some parallels between the descriptions of the island of Atlantis given by Plato in the *Timaeus* and the *Critias* and the picture of Minoan Crete then emerging from Evans' excavations. Interest in his theory was slight, and Frost himself was killed shortly afterwards in the First World War, but his work set down some useful guidelines for an interpretation of the Atlantis legend based on bronze age Crete.

Frost drew attention to the important point that the Atlantis legend makes sense historically and geographically if its elements are viewed from an Egyptian point of view. Plato, who was an Athenian living from 427 to 347 BC, described how he had acquired the story from Solon, a friend of his great-grandfather. Solon in turn had heard it from priests in Egypt when he had been there in about 590 BC.

From time to time the Atlantis legend has been revived and linked with one ancient culture or another. Luce has added the important point that the Greek (i.e. Plato's) version significantly altered the original geographical and historical perspectives. The classical Greeks lived in a larger world than their ancestors, so the Minoan culture which had actually flourished a thousand years before was put back nine thousand years into the past. The location of Atlantis was altered too. Crete was actually 720 kilometres north-west of Egypt across the Great Green, which to the Egyptians was in the far west. The Greeks, putting the lost island in their own far west, located Atlantis beyond the Pillars of Hercules. To the Egyptians, Crete had seemed a very large island – it was the largest in the Aegean, certainly – so Plato made his Atlantis large by the standards of his own day, 'larger than Libya and Asia put together'.

The conventional view of Plato's Atlantis is that it is an allegory, a noble lie, an elegant literary device to convey a specific moral point. Plato himself insisted that the story was 'certainly true', that it had the great advantage of being fact and not fiction, and there are many details in the *Critias* that are too close to what we have learned of Minoan Crete to be mere coincidences. The following list is a sample of the parallels.

1 *The* Critias *mentions strife between the city of Athens and 'all who dwelt within the Pillars of Hercules' on the one hand and the kings of Atlantis on the other*. There was a struggle for cultural and possibly political supremacy in the Aegean between Crete and the mainland Greeks.

2 *Atlantis was a large island, sunk by an earthquake.* Crete was a large island, whose economy was wrecked, according to the Luce hypothesis, by earthquakes and the Thera eruption.

3 *'The allotments of the gods ... they divided the earth into portions of varying extent, made for themselves temples and instituted sacrifices.'* The temple-complexes were divided up into separate sanctuaries, each allotted to a specific deity. There were indeed temples and sacrificial offerings.

4 *'Half-way down the length of the whole island there was the fairest of all plains and very fertile.'* Half-way along the island of Crete are two fair and fertile plains, one the Plain of Messara and the other with Knossos as its focus: either or both considered jointly could be intended.

5 *'Near the plain, and also in the centre of the island at a distance of about fifty stadia (about 8 kilometres) there was a mountain not very high on any side.' Folklore surrounding this mountain associated it with Poseidon and his union with Cleito; Poseidon 'enclosed the hill in which she dwelt'.* Mount Juktas is about 8 kilometres in a straight line from Knossos. At 800 metres, it is not very high. The remains of its major peak sanctuary can be seen, together with the ruins of a precinct wall. Juktas was the Labyrinth's 'holy mountain', the dwelling-place of its chief deities.

6 *Atlantis was divided into ten territories.* Minoan Crete was divided into several territories, each with its own temple-complex. Five major temples are known to have existed, at Khania, Phaistos, Knossos, Mallia, and Zakro: it is possible that several more await discovery.

7 *The rulers of Atlantis were immensely wealthy.* Enormous wealth was channelled through the temples and we can assume from their rich burials that members of the Minoan ruling elite, whether religious or secular, were personally rich.

8 *Atlantis was a sacred island.* Minoans were preoccupied with their nature-deities: to outsiders it may have seemed as if the whole island was a sacred precinct.

9 *'They went on constructing their temples, palaces and harbours.'* The Minoan temple-complexes were major building projects: maintaining, repairing and redecorating them was a continuing preoccupation.

10 *'At the very beginning they built the palace in the habitation of the god ... which they continued to ornament in successive generations ... building a marvel to behold for size and beauty.'* There seems to have been confusion even in Plato's time about the function of the Labyrinth. Was it a palace, or a temple, or a palace within a temple? The Labyrinth was elaborated over several successive generations, making it a marvel to behold for its size and beauty.

11 *'In the centre [of the capital] was a holy temple dedicated to Cleito and Poseidon, which remained inaccessible.'* At Knossos, the principal city of Minoan Crete, there was the Labyrinth, a sacred temple apparently dedicated to many deities, the chief of which were Potnia and Poteidan. Access to certain sanctuaries would have been restricted to initiates.

12 *'The people annually brought the fruits of the earth [to the temple] to be an offering.'* People brought offerings to the Labyrinth as sacrifices to deities; the offerings were stored in the extensive store-rooms.

13 *'Poseidon's own temple was a stadium in length and half a stadium in width, and of a proportionate height ...'* The Knossos Labyrinth is roughly square and approximately one stadium each way. It was a lofty building: the East Wing may have been four or five storeys high.

14 *' ... having a strange barbaric appearance ... [with] pinnacles.'* The Labyrinth would have looked very strange and barbaric to the classical Greeks, who liked clean lines and symmetry. The building is known to have

been embellished with sacral horns, which are in effect double pinnacles.

15 *'The walls and pillars and floor they coated with orichalcum.'* Orichalcum, to the Greeks, was an exotic, legendary, reddish metal. The pillars, some of the walls and some of the plaster floors of the Labyrinth were painted with a reddish pigment, the colour of orichalcum.

16 *'In the temple they placed statues.'* There were statuettes in the Snake Goddess and Late Dove Goddess Sanctuaries, and at least one large statue, in the Great Goddess Sanctuary.

17 There were also in the temple *'other images left by private persons'*. It was characteristic for Minoan worshippers to leave votive objects in sanctuaries: many hundreds of these have been discovered.

18 *'In the next place they had fountains . . . they constructed buildings over them.'* At the Pilgrim Hostel next to the temple-complex, there were springs. One was ducted into the roofed footbath; another was turned into a shrine with a separate building over it.

19 *'There were many temples built and dedicated to many gods.'* The Labyrinth contained many sanctuaries dedicated to various deities.

20 *'The entire area was densely crowded with habitations.'* Minoan Knossos was a densely crowded city.

21 *'The order of precedence among them and their mutual relations were regulated by the command of Poseidon.'* The Minoan society dates to a period before the rise to pre-eminence of Zeus: Poteidan was the chief god in those days. Minoan society was theocratically controlled.

22 *'These were inscribed on a pillar, which was situated in the middle of the island, at the temple of Poseidon.'* Pillars inscribed with double-axes in the pillar crypts were the focus of religious reverence. There is probably some mixing of traditions here. The idea of laws inscribed on a pillar suggests the Codex of Gortyn, carved in the fifth century BC at Gortyn near Phaistos; the codex is thought to represent the earliest codified legislation in Europe. If Plato borrowed this irrelevant piece of later history from Crete to incorporate into his description of Atlantis, the identification of Atlantis with Crete is once again reinforced, if inadvertently.

23 *'There were bulls which had the run of the temple of Poseidon; and the ten kings, being left alone in the temple, after they had offered prayers to the god that they might capture the victim which was acceptable to him, hunted the bulls, without weapons but with staves and nooses; and the bull which they caught they led up to the pillar and cut its throat over the top of it so that the blood fell upon the sacred inscription.'* Bulls were released into the Bull Court at the Labyrinth. A team of bull-leapers, grapplers and acrobats, perhaps ten in all, performed extraordinary feats in a ritual, religious bull dance. The bulls were captured in weaponless hunts and no weapons were used during the bull dance either. At the end of the bull dance the bull may have been sacrificed and its blood poured as a libation over pillars and sacred horns.

24 *'When, after slaying the bull in the accustomed manner, they proceeded to burn its limbs, they filled a bowl of wine and cast into it a clot of blood for each of them [the ten kings].'* The sacrifice was followed by a ceremonial burning or cooking and a ritual meal, in which parts of the bull's flesh were eaten and some of the bull's blood was drunk, diluted in wine.

25 *Each of them offered up prayers, 'at the same time drinking and dedicating the cup out of which he drank in the temple of the god'.* This detail may explain the large numbers of cups and other drinking vessels found in the Labyrinth: many must have been left as votives after worshippers had drunk the sacred *kykeon* out of them.

26 *'After they had supped and satisfied their needs, when darkness came on and the fire about the sacrifice was cool, all of them put on the most beautiful azure robes and, sitting on the ground at night, over the embers by which they had sworn and extinguishing all the fire about the temple, they received and gave judgment.'* Minoan priestesses and others officiating at certain religious ceremonies wore special robes. Some rituals were deliberately conducted in nocturnal gloom.

27 *'And when they had given judgment, at daybreak they wrote down their sentences on a golden tablet and dedicated it together with their robes to be a memorial.'* The Linear B clay tablets in many cases record offerings to gods and goddesses. Special robes were dedicated and donated to the temple, either for the priests and priestesses to wear or to adorn the statue of a deity.

28 *The kings of Atlantis 'possessed true and in every respect great spirits, uniting gentleness with wisdom. They despised everything but virtue. Nor did wealth deprive them of self-control.'* Plato's description of the perfect, just and wise philosopher-kings of Atlantis is remarkably like the apparently separate classical tradition of a perfect, just and wise King Minos of Crete; and they, like him, were destined to fall mightily.

29 *'Zeus, who rules according to law and is able to see such things, perceiving that an honourable race was in a woeful plight and wanting to inflict punishment on them that they might be chastened and improve, collected all the gods into their most holy habitation.'* Unfortunately the *Critias*, which is the more detailed of the two accounts, breaks off unfinished at this point, but it is clear that dire consequences are to follow. Minos too made a serious error of judgement in trying to keep the white bull given him by Poseidon to sacrifice; falling foul of Poseidon, King Minos suffered divine retribution.

The parallels between Plato's fourth-century description of Atlantis and the realities of sixteenth-century Knossos are very striking, and really too numerous to be written off as coincidences. A certain degree of distortion will have crept in over such a long lapse of time but, even allowing for this, there are still many recognizable features of Minoan Knossos in Plato's description. Even the covered springs of the Caravanserai and the correct distance between the Labyrinth and Mount Juktas are there.

Figure 45 Religious ceremony involving animal sacrifices, from the Agia Triadha sarcophagus (side B)

It is tantalizing not to have the full and detailed account of the final collapse of Knossos as Plato might have told it in the *Critias*; we might have been given even more conclusive evidence of the identity of the Atlanteans and their extraordinary Poseidon-Cleito temple with its rampaging bulls. Even so, there is enough to permit a glimpse of many of the rituals performed at the Knossos temple-complex as they were remembered and reported to Solon in about 590 BC, nine centuries – not mine millennia – after the Greeks thought they were swept away by the god-sent Thera eruption.

It is in the *Timaeus* that Plato tells of the disappearance of the Minoan-Atlantean civilization, vanishing from the face of the earth in a paroxysm of 'violent earthquakes and floods ... in a single day and night of misfortune the island of Atlantis disappeared into the depths of the sea.' In reality neither Crete nor even Thera disappeared into the depths of the sea, but the 1470 disaster may have sufficiently traumatized the Cretan economy to allow invaders in. Certainly the Greek folklore version of the Minoan civilization may have attributed its collapse to the Thera eruption. Nevertheless, it was not the island which disappeared, but rather the pre-eminence of the civilization in the Aegean world.

12
The fall of the Labyrinth

At the end of a dynasty there often appears some show of power. It lights up brilliantly just before it is extinguished, like a burning wick the flame of which leaps up brilliantly a moment before it goes out, giving the impression that it is just starting to burn, when in fact it is going out.

Ibn Khaldun, *An Introduction to History*, AD 1377.

The ferocity of the caldera eruption on Thera suggests that Knossos and the civilization that produced it would have been destroyed utterly in 1470, yet they were not. The nature of the post-Thera Late Minoan II period, the Late Temple period (1470–1380), is the subject of heated controversy. Were the cultural developments of this phase Cretan but post-Minoan, or were they the result of Mycenean invaders implanting their mainland culture, or was there some sort of Minoan revival? What kind of phoenix was it that fluttered up out of the volcanic ash?

Much of the controversy surrounds pottery sequences, their cultural implications and their dates. The evidence and arguments are very difficult for the non-specialist to follow; they are often difficult for archaeologists to evaluate, when it is no longer certain precisely where the pottery was found. There is, for example, uncertainty about whether Sir Arthur Evans accurately reported Duncan Mackenzie's finds at Knossos. Evans' 'West Court Section', published in an excavation report of 1904, was the basis for his threefold division of Minoan prehistory into Early, Middle, and Late Minoan which he communicated to an international congress in Athens in the spring of 1905. By the autumn of that year Mackenzie was writing to Evans, 'As regards an Early Minoan series, I cannot understand how you came to imagine such a series either from the West Square Section or anywhere else at Knossos.' According to Mackenzie's account, the workmen had missed the floor levels, and the Early Minoan deposit, occupying only a cubic metre in all, had no clear upper or lower limit. The problem was that Evans had not been at Knossos when the test pits were dug and, it was later alleged (by Leonard Palmer), had misunderstood the sketch section Mackenzie sent him.

Leonard Palmer, an Oxford philologist, has been at pains to show (1969) that Evans inadvertently or deliberately misread or misrepresented Mackenzie's findings, that floor levels were drawn in where none showed in the excavations. The situation is not quite that simple, though. Less than two years after Mackenzie wrote that the workmen had missed the floor levels, he was referring to floor-deposits in a very positive way. His Daybook for 5 May 1907 reads: 'Discovery of MMI floor-deposits in the West Square' and later it refers to 'the important MMI floor-deposit'. In view of this entry, Palmer may be wrong to dismiss Evans' earlier, though possibly premature, interpretation of the excavation: there *were* floor-deposits, or at any rate Mackenzie thought so in 1907.

Mackenzie did not always agree with Evans' view of the dig. He later admitted to one visitor to Knossos when looking at some area of the excavations, 'I don't mention this to Sir Arthur, but I have my own ideas about it' (Powell 1982, p. 64). Understandably, Mackenzie felt that he, who was at Knossos all the time and closely supervising the excavation, knew more about it than Sir Arthur. Understandably, there was sometimes friction between the two men, and Mackenzie went so far as to say that Evans 'had imperfect control and knowledge of the operations'.

In some important ways, Evans distorted the evidence. He even invented a period of decadence, a squatter phase at the very end of the Labyrinth's days, to explain a lot of pottery that did not fit in with his scheme.

A 'MYCENEAN' LATE TEMPLE PERIOD

On the question of the cultural climate at Knossos during the 1470–1380 period, Evans had no doubts. He was convinced that his powerful new civilization dominated the Aegean and that Knossos was the home of Cretan Minoans right up to the time the Labyrinth was abandoned in 1380 BC. But Carl Blegen and Alan Wace (1939) argued that this Late Minoan period on Crete was Mycenean. Their view remained a minority view during Evans' lifetime, but after Evans died and the Linear B inscriptions were identified as an early, Mycenean form of Greek in 1952 many more changed over to the Blegen-Wace view. Nowadays the orthodox view among scholars is that the Late Temple Period, 1470–1380, was a period when Myceneans occupied Knossos.

Several arguments can be marshalled in favour of a Mycenean invasion of Crete and Mycenean overlordship at Knossos. The temple records at this time were kept in Mycenean Greek, implying that the ruling elite at Knossos were of Mycenean origin. The Labyrinth seems not to have suffered serious damage – nothing that was difficult to repair – so it looks as if the invaders were planning to use the city and temple of Knossos as their headquarters for the administration and control of Crete.

The Late Minoan II 'warrior graves' at Knossos seem to represent a completely new type of burial with daggers, spears, swords, helmets as grave goods: the tombs consist of whole armouries of superb weapons. These are found on the Greek mainland and close to Knossos. They are seen by some as compelling evidence of the arrival of an important military contingent from the mainland and the establishment of Knossos as a Mycenean garrison town.

There was a change of style in wall decoration. The frescoes of this period at Knossos depict figure-of-eight shields (in the East Wing) similar to those seen at Tiryns, and griffins (in the Throne Sanctuary) similar to those seen flanking the later Mycenean throne at Pylos. It seems that these artistic changes affected Knossos but nowhere else on Crete, which could be interpreted as a cultural implant associated with the new Mycenean elite. The Throne Sanctuary as a whole is seen by some as a completely Mycenean work, because of its entirely alien, non-Minoan style.

There is also the oft-quoted evidence of ancient Egyptian tomb paintings showing Keftiu bringing offerings to Egypt that are identifiably Minoan, such as a distinctive Late Minoan IB collared rhyton and a bull's head rhyton. Two panels on the Tomb of Rekhmire, dating to about 1470 BC, show Keftiu bringing offerings. They are curiosities in that the Minoans' clothes were overpainted to indicate a change of fashion. First the men were painted with typical Minoan codpieces, then they were overpainted in about 1460–1450 with patterned kilts of a type that was fashionable at Mycenae from 1560 onwards. According to Schachermeyr (1964), Rekhmire was giving diplomatic recognition to the new, Mycenean regime at Knossos; he was Vizier and one of his responsibilities was to receive so-called 'vassal' princes or their representatives. The significant change of costume on the painted Minoans is seen as confirmation that an important change of regime had occurred on Crete (Figure 10).

The arguments presented by the pro-Mycenean camp seem overwhelmingly convincing, but they – and the conclusion that they lead to – are too often presented as fact. Sinclair Hood (1978, p. 24), for example, refers to 'the mainland conquest of Crete c.1450'. Yet there are those who believe that Knossos remained under native Cretan control until the end came in 1380 (e.g. Niemeier, 1983).

A 'MINOAN' LATE TEMPLE PERIOD

Knossos may have continued under Cretan control, even if the rising star of Mycenae in the Aegean world meant more and more cultural borrowings from Greece. Artistic influences and fashions are not always linked with political control. The influence of the United States on European popular culture in the twentieth century has been very great, but it has nothing to do

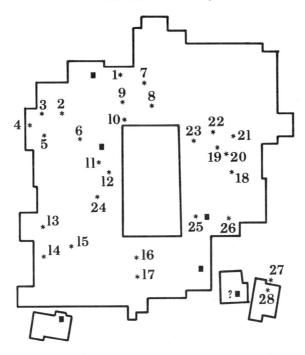

Figure 46 Findspots of frescoes, tablets, and cult objects in the Labyrinth.
1 – North-West Fresco Heap, 2 – Hieroglyphic Deposit, 3 – Linear B Tablets,
4 – Camp Stool (or Sacred Communion) Fresco, 5 – Pillar Shrine Fresco, 6 – Griffin
Fresco, 7 – Bull Relief Fresco, 8 – Great Deposit of Tablets, 9 – Saffron-Gatherer
Fresco, 10 – Grandstand and Sacred Grove Frescoes, 11 – Jewel Fresco, 12 – Snake
Goddesses (Temple Repositories), 13 – Bull-Grappling Fresco, 14 – Procession
Fresco, 15 – Cupbearer Fresco, 16 – 'Priest-king' Relief Fresco, 17 – Palanquin
Fresco, 18 – Bull Grappling Relief Fresco, 19 – Town Mosaic and Miniature
Sanctuary Equipment, 20 – Great Goddess locks of hair, 21 – Bull-Leaping Fresco,
22 – Gaming/ Divination Board, 23 – Ladies in Blue (Priestesses) Fresco,
24 – Central Treasury (first floor), 25 – Treasury (first floor), 26 – Dolphin Fresco,
27 – Ivory sacral knot, 28 – Double-axe stand and ritual pillar. Black square = adyton
(lustral area)

with political sovereignty, everything to do with cultural dynamics. So,
although the Tomb of Rekhmire shows a very significant change in fashion, it
may mean only that the Minoan culture was losing its dominance and that
Knossians were accepting fashions from Attica and the Argolid.

The assertion that the Throne Room or Throne Sanctuary was a piece of
Mycenean architecture grafted into the Labyrinth may be false. Helga Reusch
(1961) feels that its architecture is that of a distinctively Minoan cult chamber.
Hutchinson and Platon excavated the antechapel to the sanctuary in 1945 and
showed that its conception went right back to the very beginning of the
Labyrinth's history; the sanctuary as a whole was therefore emphatically not

the late, revolutionary intrusion that Evans and others subsequently have assumed (Hutchinson 1962, pp. 165 and 292). As we saw in Chapter 3, the restored Griffin Fresco has given a false austerity to the sanctuary's principal chamber and there were almost certainly not two opposed griffins flanking the throne in the original design. The décor has, in effect, been made to look Mycenean, or rather Pylian; it is obviously unwise to use it as evidence of a Mycenean origin.

There are signs of change in the Late Temple Period, but there is still more evidence of continuity than of intrusion in cult practices.

Lydia Baumbach's sample study (1983) of people's names in a series of clay tablets from Knossos shows another aspect of the society of this phase. There are some identifiably Greek names among them, but they are outnumbered three-to-one by non-Greek names. More significantly, the Greek names are accorded no special status, which is odd if they were really members of an assertive, conquering elite.

The arguments seem slightly weighted in favour of a Minoan Late Temple Period. It must be left as an open question until some new line of evidence emerges. The arguments hinge on small and esoteric details from an archaeological record which is very disturbed and incomplete. With more data about the decades leading up to the alleged Mycenean take-over and about the years following, it would be easier to interpret what happened. If there was a Mycenean dynasty establishing itself at Knossos at this time, it went out of its way to assimilate a great number of the local customs; but then, perhaps those customs were familiar because of the earlier Minoanization of the mainland Greeks: perhaps at this time there were fewer cultural differences between Cretans and mainlanders than has generally been thought. Another possibility is that the changes occurring at Knossos were the result of a major yet unrealized threat from Mycenae. The adoption of Linear B Greek as the language of officialdom at Knossos may reflect a shift in the Aegean generally, a shift towards the use of Greek as the lingua franca.

There were shifts of other kinds too. In the Late Temple Period the pottery style changed. The relaxed exuberance of the Marine and Floral Styles gave way to a grandiose and formal 'Palace' Style. The impressive Palace Style amphorae were at first peculiar to the Labyrinth, where it is assumed they were initially designed or made to the designs introduced from the mainland; the style quickly spread from Knossos to other urban centres on Crete.

THE ABANDONMENT OF THE LABYRINTH

In 1380 came the decisive destruction of the Labyrinth which led to its abandonment. In some ways, this event is a greater mystery than the destruction of ninety years earlier; the Knossos Labyrinth was abandoned, never to be reopened until Minos Kalokairinos sank his trial trenches across the West Wing over three thousand years later. The abandonment of the

Labyrinth seems to have been absolute and complete, with the exception of one sanctuary, even though a thriving classical Greek city grew up just a stone's throw to the north and west. It was as if a curse had fallen on the place, as if it had become taboo, so completely was it shunned.

The fall of the Labyrinth was a turning-point in Cretan prehistory. There are rich objects, some Cretan, some Egyptian in origin, that appear in tombs in the Knossos area down to the year 1380, but they are generally missing after that date. The implication is that some major cultural or economic change took place at the time when the Labyrinth was abandoned. It may be significant that there were changes in the world outside Crete at about that time; Mycenean goods had been traded across the length and breadth of the Aegean until 1380, but after that date they spread across the whole of the eastern Mediterranean. In other words, when the Labyrinth fell, the influence of Crete seems to have imploded leaving the way clear for a new expansion of the Mycenean trading empire.

There is evidence of fires, which could have been triggered off by an earthquake upsetting portable hearths and lamps, but we know that the Labyrinth survived far worse natural disasters than that. Perhaps the Minoan temple culture was already weakened by some other agency – perhaps systems-collapse or a virulent epidemic. Then even fairly minor earthquake damage might have put the temple fabric beyond repair. Evans himself supposed that an earthquake was responsible.

A revolution may have been the cause of the Labyrinth's fall. If the priestesses became tyrannical or rapacious after a long period of unrestricted power, the people may have been goaded into rising up, overthrowing them and burning down their sanctuaries. Platon (1968) argues that revolution is unlikely to be the explanation because the overthrow of the Mycenean rulers would have led to the reinstatement of the Minoan dynasty. But this presupposes three fundamental assumptions. First, it presupposes that the rulers were the alleged Mycenean invaders, whose existence is not by any means proved. Second, it presupposes that the secular rulers were based in the Labyrinth, which they may not have been. Myceneans may have come into the city of Knossos and left the temple priestesses alone. A rising against the temple by the Minoan populace might have been condoned and even connived at by a Mycenean governor; such a rebellion need not have weakened his position and indeed it could have strengthened it considerably. Third, there is an assumption that the rebels wanted to return to subjection to their old Minoan masters – or mistresses. In fact, if the slave and worker classes had revolted, they would have had little to gain from ousting Mycenean overlords and reinstating Minoan overlords. We should be wary of assuming simple scenarios for events that happened in prehistoric times; there is no reason to suppose that changes of regime in prehistory were any less complex events than those of modern times.

Invasion is another alternative. Platon argued that this too is unlikely to be the answer because the use of Linear B in the preceding period proves that Myceneans – or others from the mainland – were already ruling in Knossos. Although this has been widely accepted, it is not actually proved. Perhaps this, i.e. 1380, was the time when the Myceneans invaded and not earlier; perhaps the preceding period was Minoan as Niemeier believes; perhaps the fall of the Labyrinth, with its religious and economic grip on two-thirds of Crete, was a direct result of a Mycenean invasion in 1380. According to Hood, mainland Greeks came flooding into Crete in large numbers in about 1200, to judge from the pottery. In 1150 another wave of mainland Greek settlers arrived to colonize the Knossos and Phaistos territories. The Minoans took to the hills at this time or earlier, or fled overseas. By tradition, the Philistines were Minoans who fled to the Palestine coast in the twelfth century.

Leonard Palmer (1969) takes a very different view, suggesting a final destruction for the Labyrinth in about 1150 BC, with Knossos continuing until then as a major Mycenean political and administrative centre. Palmer's argument is too detailed and complex to quote, and difficult to summarize; it depends largely on assertions about findspots and stratigraphic levels which unfortunately cannot now be verified because they were destroyed during the excavations, and because there are discrepancies between Evans' and Mackenzie's notes.

Palmer's method is to show that one detailed structure after another post-dates rather than pre-dates a particular pottery level. This is deep water, because the evidence Palmer himself quotes shows that we cannot be sure how well-defined these levels were. Nevertheless, Palmer's method leads him

Figure 47 Miniature sanctuary equipment: pillar shrine and (remains of) priestess on palanquin

to the conclusion that many parts of the Labyrinth date to Late Minoan III which makes it contemporary with the (purely Mycenean) 'Palace of Nestor' at Pylos, dating to the thirteenth century BC or Late Helladic IIIB. He also argues that the Linear B tablets at Knossos show later forms than those from Pylos, which was destroyed in about 1200 BC. What Palmer seeks to prove is that the Knossos Labyrinth was, after all, a purely Mycenean palace, exactly as Schliemann and Evans had expected it to be at the outset.

This is an extreme minority view and it has been vigorously opposed by archaeologists such as Sir John Boardman (1963), but it is shared by E. Hallager (1977), who infers from the reports of the Kalokairinos dig that complete Late Minoan IIIB pots were found in the Labyrinth and concludes that the building, reconstructed to an unknown extent, went on functioning until about 1200 BC.

Sinclair Hood sees the controversy crystallizing into a disagreement between two opinion groups. There is one group seeking to prove a late end to the Labyrinth. Carl Blegen (1958) proposed an end considerably later than Evans' 1400; Palmer (1960 onwards) advocated a date as late as 1150; Raison (1969) suggested a middle ground, 1300–1250. The second group of scholars, which comprises a much larger number of Minoan authorities, has settled on the period 1400–1375. On the whole, the current majority view seems the most persuasive; Hood, Popham, Boardman and Warren see the fall of the Labyrinth as occurring around the year 1380.

By now it will be clear that the whole subject is a maze of unreliable evidence; neither side in the controversy can be done justice in the space available here. Even so, it is only by resolving this controversy that we will arrive at a more sharply focused picture of the last days of the Labyrinth. It may take another century of excavation at Knossos, as well as the wholesale reassessment of earlier evidence as new archaeological techniques are developed before a definitive picture of the fall of the Labyrinth can be given. Exactly in what circumstances and for what reason the Labyrinth came to be abandoned is, for the time being, still a mystery.

From the cryptic fragments of archive tablets, a tantalizing glimpse of the last few weeks can be gained. It seems that the end came abruptly and without warning, half-way through a perfectly normal year. The sheep had been shorn, the wool issued to women to spin and weave into cloth, and at least some of the grain had been harvested: these are pointers to a date in late summer. On the other hand the pattern of smoke-blackening on the Labyrinth walls shows that a brisk south wind was blowing and that points to spring. The only time of year that is compatible with the evidence is the end of May or the beginning of June (Chadwick 1976, pp. 188–91). But the tablets recording the steady flow of produce and tribute give no inkling that disaster was about to overtake the Labyrinth.

13
The journey of the soul

The god [Hephaistos] depicted a dancing floor like the one Daidalos designed in the broad city of Knossos for Ariadne of the lovely locks. Youths and nubile maidens danced on it with their hands on one another's wrists, the girls in fine linen with lovely garlands on their heads, and the men in closely woven tunics faintly gleaming with oil, and with daggers of gold hanging from their silver belts. Here they ran lightly round, circling as smoothly on their skilled feet as the potter's clay when he runs it through his hands; and there they ran in lines to meet each other. A large crowd gathered round to watch the delightful dance, with a minstrel among them singing sweetly to a lyre, while acrobats, keeping time with the music, turned cart-wheels in and out among the dancers.

Homer, *Iliad* (Book 18)

The final pages of the Labyrinth's unwritten chronicle are enveloped in mystery. The many questions surrounding the beginnings of the Minoan culture which produced the Labyrinth are also beyond the scope of this book. Its concern is with the Labyrinth itself and its design, the ways in which it was deployed during its 500 years of use, and what was in the minds of its builders when they cleared and levelled the summit of the Kefala hill to make way for it in 1930 BC. It is nevertheless as well to stand back from the detail which is often so baffling and attempt to see the pattern, if there is any, in the rise and fall of the Knossos Labyrinth.

The origins of the Minoan culture seem to lie in a brew of Egyptian, Anatolian, and local Cretan neolithic cultures which fermented through the early bronze age. As it did so, stimulated by the highly individual Cycladic culture emanating from the islands of the Aegean to the north of Crete, the Cretan culture gradually acquired the distinctive characteristics that are recognized as Minoan. In Chapter 4 it was suggested that the smaller size of the islands of the Cyclades put a limit on the level of indigenous cultural development. With its area of 8,300 square kilometres, Crete was easily the largest Aegean island and naturally offered scope for further and more complex developments. It is thus not surprising that an elaborate 'Temple

Culture' should have evolved on Crete rather than on the islands to the north. Mainland Greece offered an even larger area and a larger range of developmental possibilities. In retrospect it may seem inevitable that Minoan Crete should rise and then suffer eventual eclipse by a mainland culture, but we can be sure that it would not have seemed inevitable at the time.

The appearance of a new language, Linear B, at Knossos has been interpreted by some as a clear sign of the shift in the balance of power in the Aegean world. The imagined sea-empire of King Minos collapsed in the face of Mycenean depredations; or Crete was invaded and Knossos itself dramatically seized by a Mycenean army; or, as suggested in Chapter 12, the general cultural influence of mainland Greece became so great that the Cretans, though remaining independent, began to use the mainland tongue, at least for diplomacy and official records. Whichever way the evidence is read, though, the adoption of Mycenean Greek at Knossos marks the pendulum-swing. It tells us that the power of Mycenae and other mainland cities was growing and extending across the Aegean while the strength of Knossos was ebbing away. But the stratigraphy of Knossos is as labyrinthine as its architecture, with academics so divided in their interpretations that it is hard to deduce much more.

There remains the tantalizing possibility that the still-undeciphered Linear A script, apparently in the Minoans' own language, will one day reveal much more to us. When the older tablets at Knossos can be read, it may be possible to answer some of the remaining questions about the Minoans and their world. In particular, the Linear A tablets may tell more about the Labyrinth and its opulently dressed priestesses, the fat cats of Minoan society.

THE LABYRINTH AS A BRONZE AGE TEMPLE

The priestesses bring us back by another turn of the twisting corridor to the central theme of this book, the nature and purpose of the Knossos Labyrinth. Though attractive, the existing conventions for interpreting individual chambers and the overall purpose of the building are unconvincing. Sir Arthur Evans' view of the building as a palace leans unacceptably heavily on what *might* have existed on the missing upper floors, which is no kind of evidence at all. The Wunderlich interpretation is convincing in its negative aspect, showing up some of the defects inherent in the palace hypothesis, but not in its positive proposal for a bronze age necropolis.

In place of these two approaches, a new hypothesis has been put forward, that the Labyrinth was a large temple containing several sanctuary suites dedicated to different deities. The time has come to examine how well that hypothesis stands up, whether the theory harmonizes with the evidence, and whether it is the most natural way of interpreting the evidence. Does the theory make sense applied chamber by chamber, suite by suite? Does it make sense when applied to the building overall? Equally important, does the view of the Labyrinth as a temple fit conformably into the picture of Minoan society and religion from Cretan archaeology as a whole?

Evans himself gave a religious function to a great number of the chambers that he excavated; in spite of its title, his *Palace of Minos* is brimming with references to Minoan religious practices and leads the reader to the natural conclusion that the building was a major religious cult centre. There was a widening gap between the results of the excavations and his expectation that the site would yield the remains of a great bronze age palace. Evans sought to resolve this problem in a daring and ingenious fashion, by inventing a Priest-King to preside over the ambiguous building. This explained the religious flavour of much of the site while at the same time allowing him to hold on to his idea that it was a palace, the seat of a great king.

This idea has been widely supported, not least because of Evans' clever restoration of a relief fresco in a way that suggests a portrait of a commanding and athletic prince with a plumed crown. Tourists and academics alike have been ready to see in this an image of the Priest-King himself. The crown may well belong to the creature the man is leading on a rope tether, and the man himself is just one of what were originally hundreds of attendants, musicians and tribute-bearers who lined the walls of the long Procession Corridor. There is no identifiable representation of the king of Knossos, the man whom Evans imagined to be the original lord of the Labyrinth.

Careful examination of the Labyrinth chamber by chamber revealed that it resolved into several suites of rooms, often very self-contained. These can be interpreted as sanctuaries, each designed for a particular set of cult practices and ceremonies, and each probably dedicated to a particular deity or group of deities. The present ruined state of the building allows the visitor to walk from one sanctuary into another with no difficulty; in some places the walls have been eroded down to floor level or very near it so that one can step easily from sanctuary to sanctuary, as in the East Wing where it is possible to walk from the Dolphin Sanctuary to the Triton Shell Sanctuary and on into the Late Dove Goddess Sanctuary. But if we were able to visit the Labyrinth in its heyday, when the walls were complete, we would have had a very different experience. Blind walls would have separated these sanctuaries from one another. In some instances, as on the boundary between the Triton Shell Sanctuary and the Late Dove Goddess Sanctuary, there was a double wall separating them. The Labyrinth was a maze with an enormous number of gloomy, unlit dead ends. On the whole, they make sense only as spaces for secret, esoteric rituals, each one with its own labyrinthine entrance route.

In some of the sanctuaries it is possible to identify shrines with altars or offering-benches. There are several very obvious examples: the Late Dove Goddess Sanctuary, the Throne Sanctuary, the Snake Goddess Sanctuary, the Balustrade Sanctuary and the Chancel Screen Sanctuary. The Late Dove Goddess Sanctuary was discovered with all its ritual furniture still in place, including statuettes of the goddess and her attendants on the bench-altar.

Figure 48 The reconstructed first floor. A suggested alternative to Sir Arthur Evans' 'Piano Nobile'. A – West Wing sanctuary chambers inferred from the form of the west front, B – Great Sanctuary, C – Columnar Shrines, D – Upper West Wing Corridor, E – light-well (gap in ceiling allowing light in), F – Upper Initiation Area, G – Upper Lotus Lamp Sanctuary, H – Upper Throne Sanctuary, I – Portico Staircase (from Bull Court to West Wing first floor), J – Staircase up to second floor? K – Staircase down to Lower West Wing Corridor, L – Upper Destroyed Sanctuary, M – Upper Cupbearer Sanctuary, N – Refectory, O – Bull Chamber, P – Great Goddess Sanctuary over, Q – Store-rooms below P, R – Upper Temple Workshops, S – Grand Staircase, T – Upper Double-Axe Sanctuary, U – Upper Dolphin Sanctuary, V – Lavatories. * = treasury or repository of religious cult objects for use in neighbouring sanctuaries, identified from rain of material into floor below. b = pillared balcony for viewing bull games in Bull Court.

Figure 49 The Late Dove
Goddess with worshippers

Leading into or out of these shrines there are often sacristies or vestries for robing and other preparations for ritual, inner chambers for more secret rites and stone safes let into the floor for storing sacred vessels. By looking carefully at the ruins of Knossos, it is possible to recognize a style of temple sanctuary-suite that is distinctively Minoan. This aspect of the Labyrinth's architecture may have been overlooked before because in the main the sanctuaries abut directly on one another: it is not immediately obvious from the ruins or from the published plans where one suite of chambers ends and another begins. It is only by careful examination of the accessibility or otherwise of each of the chambers that the distinct suites begin to emerge. Had the Minoans built their sanctuaries as separate entities scattered within a walled precinct, a kinship with the Athenian Acropolis might have been recognized sooner.

Comparisons of that kind can be fruitful, and it is useful to draw a parallel between the Knossian 'Caravanserai' or Pilgrim Hostel and the guesthouses with baths that were regularly provided at sacred precincts during the classical period a thousand years after the fall of Knossos. Viewed in this way, the building and the facilities it offered are very compatible with a temple-precinct interpretation.

The immediately 'post-Temple' period, from 1380 to 1300, gives us two further clues. When the great days of the Labyrinth came to an end and it was burnt, abandoned and left to crumble, there was a time when the building remained – blackened, slighted and derelict – as an eerie monument to its own past. During this time we can be sure that the people who lived nearby had not forgotten what the Labyrinth's purpose was, so it is highly significant that, in a dark chamber among the ruins of its East Wing, they continued to worship the Dove Goddess. Equally significant is the fact that the adyton in the now-deserted Bull's Head Sanctuary was walled off and equipped with some primitive idols to make it a shrine in its own right. In each case, although the building as a whole had ceased to function as a temple, one small chamber was maintained as a shrine, as if to honour the sanctity of the place and propitiate its presiding deity.

Approaching the problem from a different angle, it is possible to see a wealth of significance in the comment made by several authors, including Graham (1987) and Rutkowski (1986), that the Minoans had no temples. It would be quite remarkable for an advanced bronze age civilization in the eastern Mediterranean to have produced no temples. Ancient Egypt was and still is famed for its spectacular temples. The less well-known Hittite culture also produced a grandiose temple in Hattusa, its capital city. It would be extraordinary if a civilization as sophisticated and theocratic as the Minoan civilization of the twentieth to sixteenth centuries BC had not resulted in the buildings of great temples. Graham suggested that it was because the Minoans were exceptionally devout that they did not build temples, which scarcely satisfies as an explanation. But there is no mystery here: the temples have been under our noses all the time. Identifying the palaces as temples puts right a major cultural anomaly.

The development of the temples also makes sense in the context of religious and political developments on Minoan Crete. It became clear in Chapter 9 that the building and strengthening of the temples was part of the urbanization process on bronze age Crete: that the outlying peak and cave sanctuaries could have been seen as potentially divisive, socially and politically, by the religious and secular authorities based in the towns. Temple-building in the towns meant religious centralization, and that went hand-in-hand with increasing political centralization: first power was concentrated in half a dozen towns with temples, then finally in just one – Knossos.

In the end, the interpretation of the Knossos Labyrinth as a temple seems so natural and unforced an explanation, and so implicit in Evans' findings of nearly a century ago, that it is surprising that it has to be argued for today. It is less surprising that the palace idea, with all its glamour, has taken such a strong hold: people want to believe in 'the old tales' about Theseus and Ariadne, King Minos and the Minotaur.

Yet, in spite of the attraction of the old tales, there is significant movement towards the new idea that the palaces were primarily centres of worship. Platon (1968), in the wake of his excavation of Zakro, still identifies King's and Queen's Apartments even though he admits that a very large area of the building was given over to religious cult. Paul Faure's admirable study (1973) of everyday life in Minoan Crete is convincing in its insistence that the palaces were really temples. If the store-rooms and pithoi of the small rural shrines are admitted to be repositories for offerings to the gods, the similar but more extensive store-rooms of the 'palaces' might also have been dedicated to gods rather than kings. Faure also recognizes the wider implications of identifying the palaces as temples; smaller buildings with palatial characteristics must also have been temples. The 'villa' of Niru Khani, several kilometres to the east of Knossos, must be treated as a temple: even Evans was struck by the large number of religious objects found there and thought it might have been the house of a high priest (Faure 1973, pp. 175–6). Faure rightly pointed out some of the many clues that Knossos itself offers: frescoes of priestesses, sacral horns, tablets with religious dedications, pillar crypts and at least two identifiable shrines. In fact, he is so convinced that the Knossos Labyrinth and the other 'palaces' were temples that he does not pursue all the possible lines of evidence; had he done so, more of his colleagues might have been persuaded. Faure makes the mistake of thinking that the case for Knossos as a temple is self-evident. The numbers of religious cult objects found at Knossos and the buildings analogous to it are so great, he says, that a list of them would read like an inventory of the Vatican treasures. (Faure 1973, pp. 186–92.)

THE CASE AGAINST

The only strong argument against the temple hypothesis is that the Labyrinth was a major gathering-place for produce, a storehouse, and an administrative centre of regional importance. The extensive store-rooms, especially in the West Wing, and the Linear B tablets prove that the Labyrinth authorities, whoever they were, involved themselves in collecting produce on a very large scale. The tablets indicate that redistribution was a major role of the Labyrinth too.

The administration that was based in, or at any rate recorded in, the Labyrinth ranged widely. Some tablets record details of flocks of sheep. One, as an example, tells us that the name of the man responsible (possibly the shepherd) was Aniatos, that his flock was kept in the Phaistos district and that the sheep were dedicated or allocated to someone (an official, nobleman, or priest) called Werwesios. Aniatos had 63 males, 25 females, 2 'old' sheep and fell short of his quota, a hundred, by 10 (tablet Dg 1158). Other tablets show flocks that were exactly the right size, '50 rams and 50 ewes' (Db 1227). The round numbers suggest an element of idealization. How could flocks be kept at exactly one hundred animals, and why should there be an insistence on this number? It is possible that the notion of a hundred sheep may have had some ritual value as a tribute or sacrifice, a hecatomb.

Other tablets list foals, mares, and stallions. Others list details of grain production or grain tribute: 'Men of Lyktos 246.7 units of wheat; men of Tylisos 261 units of wheat; men of Lato 30.5 units of wheat.' Still others list rations for groups of workers. Tablet Am 819 tells of a working party of 18 men and 8 boys and their ration of 97.5 units of barley, though it is not clear how long this amount was meant to last them. Incredibly large quantities of wine arrived at the Labyrinth. One entry, on tablet Gm 840, mentions a measure equivalent to 4,800 litres. On the other hand, very little seems to have been redistributed. One inference is that large quantities of wine were consumed in the Labyrinth itself; another is that sets of tablets recording the redistribution have been destroyed.

The tablet scribes were busy recording all the many different types of production. As many as seventy different scribal hands have been identified in the Labyrinth tablets and it seems that some at least had specific areas of responsibility. Just one official, judging from the handwriting, dealt with wool, cloth, and the female workers: he or she seems to have been concerned with the organization of the textile industry.

Yet, at the same time, there is more to the Labyrinth's archive of clay tablets than mere secular administration. Some of the tablets, as noted in Chapter 9, record offerings to deities, priestesses and temples. There are also offerings of small quantities of figs which can only be treated as token gifts, votive offerings. There are allocations of single pigs to particular, named individuals, presumably for sacrifice. It is known that pigs were offered as sacrifices. The named individuals may have been nobles, officials, or priests. These tablets point to the Labyrinth's sacral function in recording the administration of religious tributes.

The one area where the archive seems to point emphatically and uncompromisingly towards the traditional idea of a palace and away from the idea of a temple is in military equipment. The references on some of the tablets to weaponry, chariots and armour seem conclusive proof that the Labyrinth was the seat of a king – until the evidence is looked at more closely. A collection of tablets (the Ra series) was found in the south-east of the temple; it appears to have fallen from an upper floor into the area of the Late Dove Goddess Sanctuary. The tablets include a dagger-like symbol with the word pa-ka-na, which is close to one of Homer's words for swords and daggers, phasgana. The conventional explanation is that an armoury would have been needed close to the royal apartments, so that the king's bodyguard could arm themselves when they went on duty. Although this is possible, the references to daggers can be explained in a temple context. It may be that the priestesses felt it necessary to arm themselves or their attendants against emergencies. As we saw earlier, one or more of the destructions may have been the result of invasion or rebellion; the priestesses may well have needed to arm themselves at these times of violence and unrest. It is also known from clay figurines that men often wore daggers in their belts, and that animals and people too were sacrificed with knives. To find an inventory of daggers in a sacral context should not be regarded as surprising.

Some tablets list arrows and spears. Although these might have been used as weapons of war, they might equally have been used as a defensive precaution or for hunting. The picture overall, when compared with that of mainland Mycenean centres, actually shows a dearth of weapons at Knossos. The Knossos Labyrinth did not have a well-stocked arsenal; nor was any list

Figure 50 Linear B tablet. It records a chariot unit

of troops found in the Labyrinth. Even 'followers', or noblemen, are mentioned rather infrequently on the Knossos tablets. The impression that Professor John Chadwick (1976) gives of his reading of the tablets is that the Knossos Labyrinth was not in any sense a military headquarters; some of the people were armed, certainly, and there were inventories of their weapons, but no more than that.

The chariot tablets found in the West Wing of the Labyrinth are a different matter. This series seems to tell in detail of a chariot force, clearly not something which we would expect to find in a temple at all. Some of the tablets include a man's name, apparently the owner or driver of the chariot. Then there is information about sets of body armour for the charioteers and the number of horses: each chariot required two. On the face of it, the tablets tell of a force of some two hundred chariots, which we can imagine were ready to be deployed on the field of battle.

Yet there are problems with this view, as Professor Chadwick has pointed out. There are curious deletions and repetitions on some of the tablets, as if the symbols themselves were being tried out. The inventory also reveals that very few of the chariot units were ready to take the field; some have no horses or only one horse; some have a team of horses but no chariot; many are missing corslets, the articulated body armour without which no charioteer could have gone into battle. More peculiar still, at some points on the tablets a bronze ingot is drawn instead of the corslet, with the implication that charioteers were supplied with the materials to make their own, an eventuality which seems very improbable.

A possible interpretation is that the tablets represent a preliminary inventory designed to detect the shortcomings of the chariot force with a view to making them good. There are some small tablets which carry little more than a name, and these could record complete and satisfactory chariot units. Even so, the chariot force would have been woefully under-equipped. It is hard to visualize an army with any level of organization at all having two-thirds of its chariot force in this state of disarray.

The peculiarities of the chariot tablets have led Chadwick to interpret them as scribal exercises, not authentic archival documents at all. There are several scribal hands, each apparently copying a single, master scribe's signs. Why use chariots for a writing exercise in the midst of the temple? I suggest that, because the temple authorities were not in any way involved with military organization, there was no danger that any of the finished exercises, even if they found their way into the wrong chamber, could be mistaken for real inventories. The alien nature of the subject matter made it a perfectly safe one for teaching purposes.

The tablets reveal a complex bureaucratic organization at work in the Labyrinth, and a broad interest in the many aspects of the economy of the surrounding area. They are, nevertheless, not at all inconsistent with the Labyrinth's function as a great temple-complex. The temple had to be built, maintained, repaired, decorated, staffed, supplied with sacrificial offerings: all this involved cost and a substantial amount of administration.

The vast amount of produce pouring into the Labyrinth's store-rooms every year were necessary to maintain it and its outlying dependent sanctuaries; revenues collected at Knossos provided for the upkeep of temples, shrines, and holy precincts in a large surrounding area. The produce, including the thousands of litres of wine, however disposed of, should be seen as tithes rather than taxes, required gifts to the temple. The produce was brought in the form of offerings, in the way depicted on some of the frescoes, as gifts offered reverentially to the god Poteidan, the goddess Potnia, or one of the several other deities; some were recorded as specifically dedicated 'to Potnia of the Labyrinth' or to the upkeep of the temple itself, 'to the Daidalaion'.

A PREHISTORIC ABBEY

The Labyrinth functioned as a temple. It also functioned as a major redistribution centre for a wide range of Cretan produce. The role of the Labyrinth was paralleled in the middle ages by the great abbeys of northern Europe. They too were extensive building complexes designed as foci of worship and pilgrimage. They too drew large quantities or revenue from the surrounding areas and became centres of wealth and power.

The scale of Glastonbury Abbey in Somerset was comparable with that of the Knossos Labyrinth, although rather different in shape: Glastonbury is roughly T-shaped in plan, whereas Knossos is an irregular square. The original abbey church at Glastonbury was 200 metres long, if the Lady Chapel and Galilee are included at the western end and the Edgar Chapel at the eastern. Leading some 140 metres away to the south from this main 'temple' structure was a sequence of ancillary buildings, including the Chapter House, Refectory, Dormitory, Latrine, and Monks' Kitchen. The Knossos Labyrinth was more compact, about 140 metres north to south, from the northern wall of the Concourse to the South Porch, and about the same distance from west to east, from the West Porch to the East Entrance and the revetment walls running along the eastern boundary.

Both Knossos and Glastonbury had spaces devoted to religious ritual and

spaces devoted to ancillary services. At the centre of Glastonbury there is a
cloister, a square space for tranquil meditation and prayer. At the centre of
the Labyrinth is the Bull Court, a rectangular arena set aside for ritual
struggle; it is different in conception, but equally dedicated to the service of
the deity.

The two complexes belong to different times and different cultures,
different religions and different architectural styles, yet they had comparable
functions. Each was built, maintained and managed by a well-organized and
highly stratified priesthood. Each had a long and complex history,
assimilating changes in the world outside yet sustained always by its own
powerful mythology. It was the legends of Joseph of Arimathea and King
Arthur which gave Glastonbury its particular mythic flavour, legends that
were doubtless fostered if not invented in order to attract ever-larger numbers
of pilgrims. At the Knossos Labyrinth too we can sense a special and now-
inscrutable myth hanging over the temple's history, woven out of the struggle
to propitiate the god Poteidan, to coax productive harvests from the goddess
Potnia and to establish the temple's mystical inheritance from the peak and
cave sanctuaries where the deities lived. At Knossos too worshippers were
attracted in large numbers, even if only certain parts of the temple were
permitted to them.

Glastonbury provided accommodation for its wealthy abbot as well as a
staff of monks. Knossos sheltered, apparently in some style to judge from the
frescoes, an elite of temple high priestesses, unknown numbers of junior
priestesses, who were sometimes known as *klawiphoroi* or key-bearers in
Mycenean Greek, castrated male priests in female attire, as well as attendants,
guides, bull-leapers and grapplers, acrobats and musicians.

Both religious foundations had multiple personalities. Glastonbury could
be monastic, inward-turned, devoted to private meditation, prayer and the
sung praise of God. But it could also be outward-looking in its thirst for
pilgrim revenue, its opulent and theatrical architecture, its carefully presented
associations with mystic figures from the past and its public religious
ceremonies. A third aspect was the acquisition and redistribution of wealth.
This was closely connected with a fourth aspect, the development of the abbey
into a major centre of secular power. A fifth was its complex and variable
relationship with the secular authorities. Finally the abbey fell, in the 1530s,
along with the other abbeys and monasteries, because of the conspicuous
concentration of wealth and power which it had become. The Knossos
Labyrinth, with its similar multiple personality, may have fallen for similar
reasons. It too had a life which was secretive, revolving round arcane rites
performed by small groups of priestesses, initiates and initiands in the
worship of gods and goddesses. It also had an outward-looking side, catering
for pilgrims with its hostel, attracting the eye with its frescoes and exotic
architecture, offering the sensation of ritual dancing, boxing, wrestling, and
bull-leaping.

The store-rooms and the inventories speak eloquently of the wealth acquired and redistributed. The Labyrinth may well have become a major centre of secular power almost as a by-product of its other functions, just like the medieval abbeys long after it; it too may have existed alongside a competing or complementary aristocratic hierarchy based on a dynastic monarchy.

The parallels cannot be pressed too far, but far enough to demonstrate that it is quite possible for a temple to become large and architecturally elaborate, for it to have several apparently contradictory sides to its nature, for it to exist alongside a monarchical system of government, and for it to develop into a powerful centre of secular administration.

KING MINOS AND HIS PALACE

Revising the traditional view of the Labyrinth means revising the traditional view of King Minos. If the huge building on the Kefala hill was not, after all, the Palace of Minos and the dynasty of Cretan kings but a temple instead, we are entitled to question whether Minos himself existed. It is possible that Minoan Crete was ruled by the priesthood; perhaps the state was presided over by a high priestess. Jacquetta Hawkes has made much of the feminine attributes of the Minoan culture, and a matriarchal society would conform with her view. It may nevertheless be wise to leave the possibility of a matriarchal society run by an elite of priestesses as an open question for the time being.

On the other hand, given the strength of the Greek tradition which seems to go back to the Mycenean period immediately following the fall of the Labyrinth, it is difficult to escape the idea that there was a king on Crete. The Greek view of King Minos was contradictory but nevertheless very strongly drawn. He was seen by Homer as a king who spoke with Zeus and by Hesiod as the most supreme of kings; he was a great ruler and law-giver who earned himself the remarkable distinction of becoming one of the judges of souls in the underworld. Yet he was also seen as vicious and implacable, to the extent that according to Plutarch he was satirized on the Athenian stage. Some, Aristotle among them, tried to redeem King Minos' reputation for bloodthirsty revenge by suggesting that the tribute-children abducted from Athens were not put to death at Knossos but that they lived as servants or slaves, some of them until old age.

It is likely that the contradictions may be resolved by recognizing that Knossos may have had, as the Greek tradition held, a whole succession of kings. One Minos may have been violent and bent on revenge against Athens, but another Minos – an ancestor or descendant – may have been devout and profoundly just, a model of kingship. Whatever the truth of the matter, the strength of the Greeks' belief in King Minos suggests that there were kings in bronze age Crete.

Figure 51 Priestess praying,
summoning a male deity out of a
pillar

King Minos' existence, then, seems probable rather than possible. Yet, the size and evident power of the temple seems to leave little room for a king. It is tempting to see King Minos as forever living in the shadow of the High Priestess of the Labyrinth, just as the worshipful Velchanos always lived in the shadow of Potnia. The king may have been a puppet of the priestesses, dependent on them for the divine validation of his reign and perhaps even dependent on them for material sustenance; a share of the large tribute income of the Labyrinth may have been diverted discreetly into the king's coffers.

The king may have lived in an apartment within the Labyrinth, but there is no indication that he did so. It is more likely that he lived elsewhere at Knossos, but where exactly he may have lived is hard to tell. Of the buildings uncovered so far, the oddly-named Unexplored Mansion is a strong candidate because of the unusual features it possesses which cause it to stand out from the other buildings at Knossos.

At first sight it is unimpressive, a relatively small annexe virtually hidden behind the Bull's Head Sanctuary. It was discovered but left 'unexplored' by Sir Arthur Evans in 1908 and was finally excavated by Mervyn Popham in 1968–73. The mansion was set in a cutting in the hillside and it looks as if an earlier building, dating from the same building phase as the Bull's Head Sanctuary, was demolished to make way for it in 1550 BC. The back (i.e. the west) of the house was built into the hillside; the other three sides have walls of superb ashlar masonry, of a quality which suggests some very special function.

On the east front there are curious buttresses projecting to within a metre of a similar buttress projecting from the wall of the adjacent sanctuary. Evans was right to interpret these features as the remains of a bridge connecting the two buildings (Plate 20). Ledges and bolt-sockets indicate that there were originally two large stone slabs spanning the culvert to complete the bridge on each side, but there was apparently a large rectangular hole in the middle of the bridge, right in front of the door. It may be that this was covered by a wooden drawbridge for security reasons. The rather elaborate and unusual arrangements for entering the sanctuary can easily be explained if the mansion was a secure residence for the king and the sanctuary some kind of chapel royal.

The main surviving room in the mansion is a hall about 9 by 6 metres, again of fine ashlar masonry, with a high ceiling at about 3 metres supported on four well-shaped pillars. Although at first glance it is less than palatial in scale, it is actually not much smaller than the 'throne room' of the later kings of Pylos (10 by 8 metres). It is difficult to adjust to the idea of this modest mansion as a king's residence after thinking of the much larger building on the Kefala hill as the palace, but perhaps bronze age kings lived more modestly than Evans led us to suppose.

It is possible that above the four-pillared hall there was a four- or six-columned hall on the first floor, with windows in the east wall. The excavation evidence suggested that the first floor hall was a living room of some sort for people of high rank: remains of finely decorated vases had fallen from it. The small number of finds in the central area is strongly suggestive of a square light-well. The Unexplored Mansion extended up to at least two storeys, but it is by no means clear how far it extended laterally. The excavation showed clear boundaries to north, south, and east, and the cutting stops abruptly in the hillside to the west, but there is a possibility that the mansion continued at first floor level into another cutting. At present this can be no more than a suggestion, but the western edge of the excavation has left exposed several pieces of walling which may belong to such an extension.

The case for the Unexplored Mansion must not be overstated. All that can be said is that it may be considered as a candidate for the Palace of Minos. It is equally possible that the last kings of Knossos lived elsewhere and that leaves the exciting possibility that a major discovery – the discovery of the real Palace of Minos at Knossos – still awaits us. By no means all of the Minoan city of Knossos has been uncovered. The remains of a large and palatial building may yet be revealed, perhaps to the north of the Labyrinth or even to the east, on the steep valley side across the Kairatos River.

THE LABYRINTH LEGEND

The mainspring of Schliemann's interest in Knossos, and really of Evans' too, was the classical Greek legend of the Labyrinth. It was with legend that the twentieth-century journey through the Labyrinth began, and it is to legend that it returns. From a different vantage point there is an altered perspective, both on the building and on the legend surrounding it. With the Labyrinth reinterpreted as a temple dedicated to bronze age deities and their cults, it is still possible to make sense of the later legends as allegories of what happened there.

The classical Greeks remembered a powerful, implacable Cretan king who demanded Athenian blood sacrifices for his bull-monster at Knossos. This can be interpreted as a fearful memory of a time when Knossos was

Figure 52 Mourning scene: at
Mycenae (above) and Arkhanes
(below)

dominated by the cult demands of a powerful and implacable bull-god,
Poteidan. One of Poteidan's aspects, the terrestrial aspect, was the bull; the
portrayal of the Minotaur as half-bull, half-man hints at the god's power to
transform himself into other manifestations. Poteidan as bull-god demanded
sacrifices, just as the Poseidon of the later myth required a bull sacrifice of
King Minos, and he, Poteidan, was offered sacrifices both of bulls and of
boys and girls. The tribute-children, the seven youths and seven virgins
required by Minos of Athens every year, may truly represent a demand that
was made by a dominant Aegean culture of its weaker neighbours; it may be
that Crete expected its colonies and trading partners to supply young slaves
for sacrifice on Crete's many temple-altars. Whether that demand was
actually made of Athens is another question. It is possible that bronze age
Attica interacted with Minoan Crete in much the same way as bronze age
Argolis. It is also possible that the Athenian setting was a translation to
Athens of an older story told long before in Mycenae, and set in Mycenae.
The story may originally have remembered the days when Mycenean children
(i.e. children from the Argolid cities of Mycenae, Tiryns, Argos, Asine, and
Dendra) were taken away in Cretan ships, bound for an unknown and terrible
fate in King Minos' Labyrinth.

The legendary Theseus may have had a literal forebear in a young
Mycenean folk-hero who was taken along with other tribute-children to the
Labyrinth, where he committed some major affront to the Minoan
authorities, perhaps, in the eyes of the Labyrinth priestesses, an act of
blasphemy which desecrated the temple.

Ariadne, the legendary daughter of King Minos, may have been an historical figure, perhaps a priestess of the goddess Potnia. Her position as a priestess would explain her intimate knowledge of the winding passages of the Labyrinth; it would explain how, in the language of the legend, she was able to provide Theseus with the thread that would help him to find his way out of the maze of dark tunnels and chambers. On the other hand, if Ariadne was a priestess it seems unlikely that she could have been so easily seduced, subverted to treason and abducted. Perhaps love conquers all; or perhaps it is the point where mythic story-telling takes over from an admittedly attenuated version of history.

It is, at any rate, possible to tie the temple interpretation of the Labyrinth in with the elements of the classical legends that revolve round Knossos: the two are compatible. A still more fruitful line of thought is to interpret the leading characters in the legends less as individual historical figures and more as collective personalities, each one a personification of a powerful, large-scale cultural force at work in the Aegean world in the second millennium BC. Daidalos, for example, was not just a clever engineer but represents the Cretan genius for all kinds of crafts in metal, stone, wood, and other materials; he epitomizes the precocity, subtlety, and daring of the Minoan civilization. King Minos is the secular and commercial power of Crete, capable of extension across the whole Aegean Sea and beyond, and seen by the Greeks as the noble precursor of their own trading empire.

Pasiphae, Minos' wife, is the Minoan lust to live as close as possible to the primeval forces of nature, a dangerous, unhealthy, but all-absorbing obsession. She can be taken to represent the love of nature and strength and the intense sexuality of the Minoans. Linked closely with Pasiphae – in the mythic telling, the fruit of her lust – is the Minotaur, the darker side of the same archetype. The Minotaur is the embodiment of the terrifying, sacrifice-demanding, tribute-consuming deities of the Minoan pantheon, the deities whose elaborate cults required peak sanctuaries, cave sanctuaries, hillside sanctuaries and probably wayside shrines (like those erected on present-day Crete near the scenes of fatal road accidents) as well as the huge temple-precincts in the towns.

Theseus, the boy-hero from Athens who is at once godling, prince and sacrificial victim, is the vigorous young mainland culture whose destiny it is to pluck away the heart of the Minoan culture and leave the rest to perish. Theseus is portrayed as having two fathers, Aigeus the mortal and Poseidon the immortal. His descent from Poseidon enables him to know and carry out the god's wishes. This was the later, mainland Greeks' way of saying that their religion was truer to Poteidan-Poseidon than the Minoans' and that therefore their culture as a whole was better founded.

The princess Ariadne, at once Minos' daughter and Theseus' lover, is the mystic, mysterious, feminine heart of Minoan civilization. She is the dark and volatile beauty at the centre of the Labyrinth: princess, priestess, goddess, mistress. She flees from Knossos with Theseus, sailing away at night to meet an ambiguous fate. In some versions of the legend she is abandoned on another island in the Aegean. In some she marries the god Dionysos, in others she commits suicide. Whatever her later fate, she is that heart of Minoan civilization that was borrowed by the growing civilization of the Greek mainland and subsumed by it.

The form of the tripartite shrine that was such a distinctive feature at Knossos, Phaistos and possibly Anemospilia too was taken up in later Mycenean temples at Enkomi, Kition, and Paphos. The Myceneans took over the great goddess too, in her characteristic pose with upraised hands. They took over the horns of consecration as a sacred symbol and the tree, baetyl and pillar as manifestations of deities (Dietrich 1983). The cultic rock outcrops preserved in temples, as at Anemospilia and Phaistos (south of Room 64 and in Room 103), were taken over in later shrines too. The Citadel House at Mycenae has a sanctuary with a similar, deliberately preserved naked rock outcrop. At Eleusis too a spur of natural rock was left protruding out of the floor of the anaktoron; it was associated with a fire ritual and was probably connected with an annual enactment of Zeus' periodic rebirth in a cave accompanied by a great flame of fire.

Ariadne is the pivotal archetype. She represents the fall of the Knossos Labyrinth and the uncertain transference of some of its cultural values to the mainland in the hands of the inconstant Theseus. In this view of the Labyrinth legends, some of the cultural forces at work in the sixteenth and fifteenth centuries BC come more sharply into focus. In the prehistory of Europe, the secular power of the Minoan civilization (Minos) still stands, as it always stood, as an impressive cultural edifice in itself. But the more exotic archetypes, Daidalos, Pasiphae, Ariadne and the Minotaur, represent the dark, rich and complex forces which interacted to produce and sustain the Labyrinth. They produced a building of legendary complexity, one which has drawn an extraordinary range of twentieth-century reactions.

Some have seen the Labyrinth as a confused, illogical and apparently insane jigsaw of chambers, stairs and passages. To those conditioned by classical architectural principles, it is understandable that it should seem so. But there is another view that in its extreme form sees the Labyrinth as a masterpiece of pre-classical design. The excavators of Mallia saw that temple as planned from the centre outwards; the four irregular outer walls with their apparently random juts and indents were really the *back* of the building, whose exterior shape was of subordinate importance: the walls facing inwards, facing onto the Bull Court, were the front. In a similar way, the number and height of the storeys varied from one part of the Labyrinth to another, and with them the level of the roof. The building was thought through from the inside out. This interior, introspective approach, in which the external appearance of the building seems to have been very secondary, is the reverse of that displayed by most classical and classically-derived

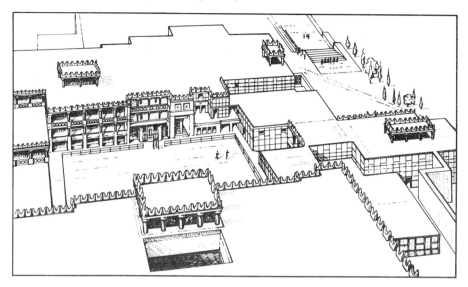

Figure 53 Reconstruction of the Labyrinth. In the foreground, the East Wing roof is perforated by the Grand Staircase light-well (see Figure 8). The Tripartite Shrine can be seen on the far side of the Bull Court and the Theatral Area top right.

buildings where the shape of the shell is of primary importance.

Another reason for the Labyrinth's complicated design (see Figures 31 and 48) is that it had to fulfil many different functions. The finished building incorporates workshops where religious votives and other objects were manufactured, sanctuaries for the worship of a wide variety of deities, special cult rooms for initiation and other ceremonies, spaces for bull games, ritual dances and sacrifices, corridors and courts for religious processions, rooms for oracles, a service quarter and presumably living quarters for the priestesses. With so many functions to accommodate, the building was bound to be complicated.

Even so, the design is not chaotic or disorderly. There is an indication of conscious and deliberate planning in the way the floor levels have been selected. Phaistos is reckoned to be laid out on seven different terrace levels and it is clear that the descent by staircase into the so-called Domestic Quarter in the North Wing was a carefully contrived stage effect. At Knossos, the East Wing is a classic example of the deliberate and artificial creation of a split-level, with two whole sanctuary suites inserted into a two-storey-deep excavation; in this way a dramatic descent by way of the Grand Staircase was made necessary. It is also worth pointing out that the Labyrinth exhibits a degree of symmetry in detail. For instance, the antechapel to the Throne Sanctuary, the Cupbearer Sanctuary, the eastern chamber of the Double-Axe Sanctuary and the Tripartite Shrine were all symmetrical: the Great Goddess

Figure 54 The 'Priest-King' Relief Fresco. A new reconstruction

Sanctuary, as reconstructed here (Figure 22), would have been symmetrical too.

The Knossos Labyrinth has many similarities with the other large temples at Phaistos, Mallia, and Zakro, but it is different from them in one significant way: it is more complicated, more maze-like than any of them. This is partly due to frequent partial rebuilding and alteration. It appears that the Labyrinth was repeatedly damaged, sometimes by earthquakes and perhaps sometimes by hostile attack, and therefore was repeatedly modified. It may also be that, as Knossos was a more important religious centre, its priestesses were inspired by religious zeal or by their higher status to make more frequent improvements to its fabric.

The end result was a bewilderingly elaborate building, cunningly designed to create all kinds of unexpected pictorial effects. Whilst the outer walls were left with their fine cream masonry exposed, the inner walls were richly decorated, sometimes sheathed with alabaster or gypsum veneers, sometimes plastered and painted with religious frescoes. In some sanctuaries entire walls were composed of double doors which could be partially or completely opened to display religious ceremonies to onlookers or closed to preserve secrecy. The arrays of double doors, the light-wells and windows, the piers and columns of colonnaded porticoes all combined to create an endlessly complicated pattern of light, tone, and texture; it was as if the architect had consciously set out to compose symphonically with light and shadow. There were architectural features of great dignity, like the West Porch and Grand Staircase, but they led to some rather disconcerting effects. The West Porch led to an off-centre corridor with two right-angle turns in it: after a formal beginning which created a sense of anticipation, it was a mysterious, suspenseful passage. The antechapel to the Throne Sanctuary led only to the

Throne Sanctuary itself, with a few small vestries and preparation rooms leading off it. At the foot of the Grand Staircase, we feel that we have been led down into a cellar to no purpose: there is no obvious direction to follow, and we find our way almost by accident into the Double-Axe Sanctuary.

The Labyrinth was designed with a thousand pieces of such architectural trickery. The wilful and deliberate irregularity of its layout can be seen as the result of inexperience or cultural *naïveté* or lack of the necessary architectural syntax to bring all the parts meaningfully together; it may be that the Labyrinth is the fruit of an early and not yet perfected system of architecture. Alternatively, the Labyrinth may be seen as part of an aesthetic that has little to do with the classical tradition, one that seeks significantly different effects. The Minoan architect may not have been interested in creating a plastically unified composition, but was instead trying to create a pictorial or narrative experience for the visitor that was unsettling, full of incident, drama, and surprise.

The Labyrinth depends for its effect less on overall structure than on accidentals, modulations, syncopations, and sudden changes of tempo and texture. All is apparent eccentricity, with arresting detail. Symmetry is denied at nearly every turn, with doors often positioned near the corners of rooms as if to provoke curiosity. Everywhere there is something unexpected to look at, something to lead the eye and foot on through the maze: the turning, twisting corridors and cascading staircases, the constantly rising and falling roof lines, the shifting floor levels, the repeatedly and irregularly offset wall lines, the dim light borrowed from deep ventilation shafts reflecting oddly from polished alabaster floors and dados, the symbolic frescoes on the walls, the shadow patterns cast by the tapering painted pillars. The Labyrinth when complete in 1450 BC would have been a profoundly stimulating building to explore.

The Daidalaion, Daidalos' great temple building, seems to have been created as a microcosm of a fluctuating and many-sided universe in which all was complex movement and change, rising and falling, growth and decay, ebb and flow, reassurance and uncertainty, exaltation and fear. It contained within itself some of the polarities that were essential elements in prehistoric religion: light and darkness, optimism and despair, mystery and certainty. It seems as if it was intended to be experienced as a wonder-creating journey of the soul. Or rather, in its many entrances, interlocked sanctuaries and access passages, it set up for the worshipping pilgrim a series of journeys that we can no longer re-create. Only here and there, in the centre of the East Wing for example, are we able to taste what the original architect intended for the Labyrinth's initiands and priestesses nearly four thousand years ago.

Appendix A: Chronological table

Calendar dates BC	Evans' pottery sequence	Platon's chronology (1971)	New chronology (1988)	Events
2000	MMI	Pre-Palatial III	Pre-Temple or Early Shrine Period	Many-roomed buildings on sites of temples.
1950				
1900				First large-scale labyrinths built (though Vasiliki semi-labyrinth was built 2600 BC). Kefala hill cleared: Knossos Labyrinth built c. 1930 BC.
1850		Proto-Palatial I		
1800	MMII	Proto-Palatial II	Old Temple Period	Knossos Labyrinth in use.
1750				Major earthquake destruction of old temples 1700 BC; temples at Phaistos and Knossos rebuilt; temple at Zakro built; Linear A starts?
1700		Proto-Palatial III		
1650	MMIII	Neo-Palatial I		New Labyrinth at Knossos in use.
1600			New Temple Period	
1550		Neo-Palatial II		Earthquake.

Calendar dates BC	Evans' pottery sequence	Platon's chronology (1971)	New chronology (1988)	Events
1500	LMI	Neo-Palatial III		Earthquake damage to Crete as Thera eruption starts; damage to Labyrinth.
1450	LMII	Neo-Palatial IV	Late Temple Period	Major Thera eruption (1470); destruction of all temples; only Labyrinth is repaired and continues in use.
1400				
1350		Post-Palatial I		Abandonment of Labyrinth in 1380 BC. No evidence for cause; Late Dove Goddess Sanctuary continues as minor centre of worship.
1300			Post-Temple Period	Fall of Minoan Knossos?
1250	LMIII	Post-Palatial II		Trojan War?
1200				Mycenean centres on Greek mainland destroyed, apparently by invaders. Fall of Hattusa in Anatolia.
1150		Post-Palatial III		
1100				

Appendix B:
Selected Linear B tablets

Text from the 1986 'Knossos Corpus'	*A tentative translation*

Tablet Fp (1)1

de-u-ki-jo-jo me-no	in the month of Deukios
di-ka-ta-jo di-we OLE S 1	to Diktaian Zeus 1 measure of oil
da-da-re-jo-de OLE S 2	to the Daidalaion 2 measures of oil
pa-de OLE S 1	to Pa-de 1 measure of oil
pa-si-te-o-i OLE 1	to – 1 measure of oil
qe-ra-si-ja OLE S 1	to Qe-ra-si-ja 1 measure of oil
a-mi-ni-so pa-si-te-o-i S 1	to – of Amnisos 1 measure
e-ri-nu OLE V3	to Erinus 3 measures of oil
*47-da-de OLE V1	to – 1 measure of oil
a-ne-mo i-je-re-ja OLE V4	to the Priestess of the Winds 4 measures of oil

Tablet V52+52b+8285

a-ta-na po-ti-ni-ja u(	to Potnia Athena (?) ...
e-nu-wa-ri-jo pa-ja-wo-ne po-se-da-(	to Enualios to Paiawon to Poseidon

Tablet Gg (1) 702

pa-si-te-o-i me-ri *209 VAS 1	to – 1 pitcher of honey
da-pu-ri-to-jo po-ti-ni-ja me-ri *209 VAS 1	to Potnia of the Labyrinth 1 pitcher of honey

Tablet Gg (3) 705

a-mi-ni-so e-re-u-ti-ja (me-ri) VAS 1	to Eleuthia of Amnisos 1 pitcher of honey

Tablet Oa 745+7374

aka- ( ) -jo-jo me-no	in the month of Aka – ios
da-pu-ri- (-to-jo) po-ti-ni-ja	to Potnia of the Labyrinth

Notes on the illustrations

10 The pier-and-door partitions extend round three sides of the chamber. The wooden throne was made and installed at Evans' orders; there is no evidence of the chamber's original focus.

11 The sacred cave-cleft in the centre of the picture was discovered in the 1970s. Remains of the temple building can be seen to the left and an altar to the right. A reconstruction of the site is shown in Figure 36.

12 The section of the east front reconstructed by Evans shows a high wall which must have excluded light from the ground floor of the Double-Axe Sanctuary behind it. The revetment walls in the foreground were probably always fairly low. The steps are modern. The square hole and the duct leading from it are the outfall from the Double-Axe and Dolphin Sanctuaries' sewerage system.

13 This is a piece of 'Tourist Knossos' which did not exist in the bronze age. The piered and pillared space in the foreground was a substantial chamber, the Cupbearer Sanctuary (Figure 20); it may originally have had a lower ceiling. The staircase in the background is an entirely twentieth-century construction (see Figure 19).

14 The block is very well preserved, with signs of wear on the lower step. It stands in the north-west corner of the Central Court at Phaistos.

15 Evans restored the ground floor completely and the floor-plan of the storey above; originally there may have been four storeys (see Figure 8).

16 Itself a minor labyrinth, with a twisting staircase leading up to the East Staircase, this is one of Evans' most successful and evocative reconstructions. The rainwater duct with one of its stilling tanks or (more likely) sediment traps can just be seen on the landing between the two visible flights of steps.

17 In the foreground a covered porch, the West Porch, was supported by a large column, itself an important architectural feature. The Procession Corridor leads out of it on the left. The rectangular room on the right may have been a shrine; Evans' suggestion that the king sat in there to greet visitors seems rather ill-considered.

18 This dark suite of chambers would have been even darker in the bronze age, with walls towering round it. The doorway on the right leads to the small east light-well, the one in the centre to a staircase to the floor above, and the one on the left to the Double-Axe Sanctuary (see Figure 23 for plan). The Dolphin Fresco may have been a floor decoration belonging to an upper storey.

19 This small patch in the south-west corner of the Central Court is the best preserved area of paving, but it does indicate that the court as a whole must originally have been paved over.

20 The bridge was completed with two stone slabs and a wooden drawbridge. From the walling exposed in the section above the site, in the background of the photograph, it appears that the Unexplored Mansion may have extended up the hillside at first-floor level.

FIGURES

1 The roads are inferred rather than proved routes: some are borrowed from Evans, some from Pendlebury. The map suggests a nodal relationship between Knossos and its territory. Note that the distances are short to the sacred caves of Eleuthia and Skotino and to the peak sanctuary on Juktas; it is also a short distance to the ports.

2 The arrows represent proved or likely access routes. The layout was designed to lead visitors to the Central Court by a series of more or less indirect routes and at the same time preserve the privacy and sanctity of large areas of the Labyrinth.

3 Greek vase painting, white on black, sixth century BC.

4 This sketch plan shows in general terms how the site was interpreted in the last two decades of the nineteenth century. Fundamentally, the Labyrinth consisted of the West Wing with courtyards to east and west and was seen as a palace on the mainland model, though at 55 by 43 metres already significantly larger than the palace area at Tiryns.

5 The ground plan of the Vasiliki building appears to be a direct ancestor of the design of the later palaces.

6 Although the summit on the rhyton is a small detail, partly masked by two seated mountain goats, its shape is very distinctive. There is no doubt that the peculiar shape of the throne back was intended as a deliberate reference to the mountain summit; the throne is the throne of a mountain deity.

7 The map is based to an extent on the plan drawn by Theodore Fyfe and published with Evans' *Palace of Minos*, but with some significant alterations. Details such as paving, altars, pithoi, fresco findspots, etc., have been omitted to make the building's outline clearer. Walls marked by Evans or Fyfe as 'conjectural' have been drawn in solid black. Walls not shown by Evans on his plan and yet reconstructed by him on the site have also been added in solid black. The intention is to make Evans' conception of the building's overall architectural plan as clear as possible. Compare this plan with the reinterpretation in Figure 31.

8 The lowest two storeys were inserted into a deep cutting excavated from the tell. The remains of the Grand Staircase implied that one or more storeys existed above the level of the West Court as well. The upper floors may have had identical plans to the ground floor, as shown here.

9 This group is the least restored, the most complete and therefore the most reliable. It shows five priestesses in relaxed and animated conversation. One is shown, unusually, with drooping breasts: the implication is that she may be an older woman.

10 Egyptian wall painting made about 1460–1480 BC. The figures wear decorated kilts similar in style to those worn on the Greek mainland and those worn in the Procession Fresco. When the paintings were cleaned, it was found that the dress of the Aegean envoys (and theirs only) had been altered in antiquity. The original garments were short, tight kilts with prominent codpieces – typical Knossian garments of the New Temple Period. The implication is that the figures were repainted after a subsequent embassy in around 1450 BC. This has been interpreted as indicating the political take-over of Crete by mainland rulers, but it may mean only that there was a shift in cultural influence.

11 Contrary to Wunderlich's assumption, the Minoan burial grounds were located well outside the city. After the fall of the Labyrinth, the classical city of Knossos developed to the north and west of its ruins: the ruins themselves seem for the most part to have been carefully avoided. Source: Hood and Smyth's *Archaeological Survey of the Knossos Area* (1981).

12 A cache of stone and faience ritual vessels, including funnel-shaped and egg-shaped rhytons, dating to before 1450 BC. The alabaster rhyton in the shape of a lioness's head is a superb piece of craftsmanship, as is the Egyptian alabaster rhyton carved in the form of a triton shell. Behind them is an elegant faience jug. Many of the other cult vessels were badly broken. Each sanctuary probably had its own collection of cult equipment.

13 The intention is to show how the plan of the Minoan temple resolves into quite well-defined functional zones. There is restricted access to many of the sanctuary suites, implying relatively separate functions. It appears that there was originally no lateral connection between Q, R, and S: a double wall separates R and S. The separate functions of A, M, T, U, and V are easier to visualize, since orientation and space distinguish them from neighbouring structures.

15 The southern edge was badly eroded when excavated. This reconstruction is based partly on the surviving wall foundations and partly on Theodore Fyfe's plans. The doorway in the south-east corner may have been put in to provide the sanctuary's priestesses with access to the pillared portico, a spectator-box for the ceremonies in the Bull Court.

16 One of the three goddess statuettes whose broken remains were found in the Temple Repositories in the floor of the Snake Goddess Sanctuary. Made in about 1600 BC. Faience, 29.5 centimetres high. Evans had the statuette restored with a seated lion or leopard stuck on the head-dress: there is no reason to suppose that it belonged there. The statuette and other cult objects were finally sealed into the Temple Repositories in about 1550 BC.

17 Reconstruction based on surviving footings, including pillar sockets, and the painted shrine shown in the Grandstand Fresco. In detail it may be incorrect – e.g. more of the stonework may have been decorated with painted images – but it gives a reasonably accurate impression of the structure which formed a focus for the Bull Court.

18 The miniature fresco, painted in about 1450 BC, seems to show the shrine whose footings can still be seen in the west wall of the Central Court. The two outer pillars are blue, the two inner ones red: the colours almost certainly carried some religious symbolism. The back walls of the three cellae were also painted different colours, the left red, the centre blue and the right yellow, to represent the three worlds – underworld, heaven, and earth. The real shrine differed in having two pillars in each of the lower cellae and one in the narrow upper cella, but the fresco shows that the shrine was an elaborately decorated focus for religious ceremony.

19 The original form of this suite is uncertain, but it seems to have consisted of a large principal chamber with a portico opening on to the Central Court and two small vestries or sacristies.

20 The plan shows the early 'temple repository' which is partly concealed beneath the sanctuary wall. A plinth or altar is suggested at the northern end of the sanctuary.

21 The North-West Adyton was the largest in the Labyrinth. Set apart in its own enclosure, it seems to have held some special significance.

22 This follows Evans' reconstruction, a large chamber approached up a flight of steps from the Central Court. It differs in placing the statue of the goddess at the centre of the east wall.

23 The two sanctuary suites were apparently designed and built at the same time, inserted in a deep cutting in the side of the tell. They share an integrated drainage system.

24 The Triton Shell Sanctuary is curious in apparently having had no access door at ground level. It is separated from the Late Dove Goddess Sanctuary by a double wall.

25 Evans excavated the small 'Shrine of the Double-Axes' in 1902 and found it fully equipped with cult furniture dating from the Late Minoan III period, when the Labyrinth as a whole had been abandoned. The wall in the foreground to the right and the substantial door-jambs seem to have been added late, apparently to make

the shrine more secret. The shrine is very small, only 1.5 metres square. Stirrup vases on the floor seem to have held offerings, perhaps of food and drink. On the low step are more offering vessels, small cups and jugs, and a three-legged circular libation table cemented down near the centre. Beyond this is a narrow bench-altar with two sets of sacral horns (stuccoed clay) and an important group of figurines including the Dove Goddess and worshippers (see Figure 49). It is possible that even this small chamber had frescoes, but no attempt is made here to reconstruct them.

26 Data mainly from Hood and Smyth's *Archaeological Survey of the Knossos Area* (1981), but with some additions such as the likely site of the compound where bulls were kept prior to bull games. The roads are shown continuous, although they are known only in short sections. The lines on the eastern side of the Kairatos valley represent substantial Minoan walls; they may have been revetments for rows of houses or terrace walls for roads. It is probably significant that the whole area of the late neolithic and early bronze age settlement later became a sacred precinct; most of the buildings within that area in the fifteenth century were sanctuaries. For Minoan cemeteries, see Figure 11.

27 Whilst not amounting to proof that the Labyrinth was a temple, it is significant that in Egypt, Mesopotamia and Anatolia there were large, multi-chambered buildings roughly contemporary with the Knossos Labyrinth, and that those buildings were temples.

28 Comparable in size to the Knossos Labyrinth, this Anatolian temple has altars, shrines, and extensive store-rooms.

29 Ivory and gold statuette, 16 centimetres high, in the Boston Museum of Fine Arts. Made about 1600 BC. Provenance unknown, but Evans was probably right in supposing that it was robbed from the East Wing (Great Goddess Sanctuary area) of the Knossos Labyrinth.

30 Generally recognized as the most important collection of faience objects ever recovered from the Aegean. Only a small sample is represented here, but the drawing nevertheless conveys the richness of the finds. The figurine of the Snake Goddess, as reconstructed from incomplete fragments, stands 34 centimetres high. Made in about 1600 BC, it was secreted permanently under the floor in about 1550 BC. The faience plaque represents a goat suckling her kids (about 20 centimetres long). The faience robe is a votive, representing garments that were probably offered to the priestesses or to statues of deities; the crocus motif is associated with worship of the goddess. The cult vessels decorated with vegetation motifs are about 11 centimetres high.

31 This new reconstruction is based on several sources: the ruins themselves, Hood and Taylor's published plan of the present state of the ruins (1981), and Theodore Fyfe's plans of the wall footings as excavated (unpublished manuscript map). The excellent manuscript plans in Mackenzie's Daybooks have also been used. There are significant departures from Evans' map and reconstructions, especially in the area between the southern limb of the Procession Corridor and the East and West Pillar Crypts; this reconstruction attempts a rational compromise between the Mackenzie and Fyfe plans and the present state of what seem to be the original Minoan wall footings. It is by no means clear what the area immediately west of the Destroyed Sanctuary was. Most published plans show the western limb of the Procession Corridor giving way to the cellarage below the South Terrace; in this plan, the building is reconstructed to the common floor level of the Procession Corridor, West Court, and Bull Court, which I believe makes the connections

clearer and more logical. The many different floor levels in the East Wing make the construction of a simple ground-floor plan very difficult. I have attempted a plan which makes the interconnection or (equally important) non-interconnection of chambers as clear as possible. The plan should be used in conjunction with the first-floor plan (Figure 48) and detailed sanctuary plans.

32 This major representation of a cult scene is described in the text. Together with an elaborate painted border of rosettes and running spirals, it covers one of the long sides of a plaster-coated limestone sarcophagus. It was made in 1400 BC, found at Agia Triadha and is now in Heraklion Museum.

33 A large gold ring from a tomb at Isopata north of Knossos. Priestesses dance an ecstatic, maenadic dance in a meadow with lilies. The small figure at the top is thought to be the goddess manifesting. The scene also shows two snakes, an eye, a chrysalis and a shoot. Images like this supply us with invaluable information about the Minoan belief-system.

34 Life-sized, implying a life-sized statue, the feet were found in the central shrine of the Temple at Anemospilia.

35 This reconstruction is based loosely on the one in Rutkowski (1986), but I have tried to make the perspective more naturalistic and the walls more solid-looking. On the right-hand (north) side the original shape of the building is difficult to reconstruct. The three doors and the cellular layout suggest that the façade may have incorporated a tripartite shrine, overlooking the plain where Knossos lay.

36 The reconstruction uses Bogdan Rutkowski's plan and reconstruction as a starting-point (1986, p.77). Rutkowski's reconstruction shows the shrine divided into three equal parts; the plan showing five chambers at ground level implies that there may have been a raised tripartite shrine above the three central chambers, which is how it is reconstructed here. The central compartment is narrow, so it may have carried a single-pillared cella. The flanking compartments are wider, implying that they carried two-pillared cellae. In other words, the Juktas shrine may have been similar in design to the Tripartite Shrine in the temple at Knossos, and it is reasonable to suppose that the latter was deliberately built as a smaller-scale version of the Juktas shrine. The pyre, altar and cave entrance can be seen to the west of the shrine.

37 Design on a pear-shaped libation vase made of chlorite showing reliefs of a peak sanctuary, about 1650–1500 BC. It shows an elaborately decorated shrine, at least three open-air altars on the terraces in front of it, and sacral horns.

38 Black serpentine rhyton made 1500–1450 BC. The (restored) horns were of gilded wood, the eyes of painted rock crystal and the muzzle of white shell. Found in the Bull's Head Sanctuary (Little Palace) along with other cult vessels that had fallen from an upper floor. The vase was filled using a hole in the nape of the neck; the libation poured out of a small hole in the mouth.

39 The drawing is based on part of the design on the gold Vaphio Cup I. The cup was found in a tomb at Vaphio near Sparta, associated with pottery dating to 1500–1450 BC: although found on the mainland, the cup is undoubtedly of Cretan workmanship and reckoned to be one of the masterpieces of Minoan art. The scene shows a bull capture that has gone badly wrong; incidents like these may have fuelled the later stories about the Minotaur and the tribute-children.

40 A heavily restored panel painted in about 1450 BC, one of a series showing bull-leaping scenes found in the cellars below the Great Goddess Sanctuary. The restoration may well not be accurate.

41 Agate seal, now in the Ashmolean Museum, Oxford.

42 Rhyton carved out of black steatite, from Agia Triadha. The lower half of the

vessel is missing, so the decorative frieze is incomplete. A priest in a strange tunic leads the procession of marching, smiling harvesters. Half-way along is a musician playing a sistrum and what appears to be a group of singers. One harvester turns to laugh at another who has tripped and fallen over. The Harvester Vase gives us a vivid picture of the vigour of religious life in the countryside.

43 The bronze age Aegean world. Mainland powers: 1 – Attica, 2 – Argolis, 3 – Messenia, 4 – Hatti, the Hittite empire.

44 The distribution of ashfall is inferred from deposits of ash still preserved on the sea-bed and revealed in boreholes. The limits of the ashfall are shown slightly differently from those shown by Luce, but more consistently with the borehole evidence. It may be highly significant for subsequent historical developments that the ash fell on Crete and its neighbouring islands but not on the Greek mainland (c) or Anatolia (d).

46 Findspots of cult objects and cult wall decoration strongly imply a cult function for the areas immediately round them. Even the limited selection shown on this map implies a cult use for extensive areas of the Labyrinth.

47 The miniature clay pillars support birds, symbolizing the presence of a deity; the intention may have been to represent a tripartite shrine. The clay litter contains the lowest third of a seated, long-skirted figure, presumably a priestess. These and other miniature cult objects were found in the cellarage below the Great Goddess Sanctuary.

48 Evans' scheme for the first floor of the West Wing assumed entrances by way of major staircases in the South Propylaeum area and at the north-west corner. This reconstruction assumes that there was no access at those points. It follows Graham's proposal for large pillared chambers in the north-west quadrant of the West Wing. Elsewhere the plan is guided mainly by the positions of load-bearing walls on the ground floor. Crypt pillars on the ground floor are assumed to be foundations for columns on the floor above. Two light-wells have been inserted, very speculatively, to introduce light to the two ends of the Upper West Wing Corridor. The plan is tentative, but it does suggest an arrangement of relatively separate sanctuaries and sanctuary suites on the first floor.

49 Late bronze age clay goddess with two female worshippers or priestesses. All three were found, though not in this grouping, on a shelf altar in the Late Dove Goddess Sanctuary (Evans' Shrine of the Double-Axes), together with other figurines. They date from Late Minoan IIIA, probably around 1370 or 1360 BC, just after the temple as a whole was abandoned.

50 Professor Chadwick regards these chariot tablets as scribal exercises. Tablet Sc 230, illustrated here, tells us of a chariot, a pair of horses and a tunic belonging to a charioteeer called Opilimnios.

51 Gold signet ring from Knossos. A sacred pillar or baetyl stands in a shrine on the right; a sacred tree grows on top of the shrine and a larger pillar or mast stands in front of it. The god, who may be Velchanos, flies through the air carrying a staff; the small marks round him are apparently intended to suggest movement, rather in the style of a modern cartoon. Note the elaborate dress worn by the priestess, the bared breasts and the prayer gesture.

52 The two similar scenes show a priestess or goddess presiding over a scene of lamentation. A young god tears down the sacred tree growing on the pillar shrine. The gold ring from Arkhanes shows the pillar shrine in tripartite form; it also shows, on the left, a male figure embracing and worshipping a boulder. As so often in Minoan religious art, the figures seem to be overwhelmed by emotion.

53 The reconstruction is necessarily tentative. It is not possible to be sure how many

floors each part of the building originally had: the roof line may well have been more broken up than it is shown here. Even so, the general impression is probably close to the reality.

54 Fragments of the plaster relief were found in or near the eastern limb of the Procession Corridor. Evans had them assembled into a representation of the 'Priest-King', now in Heraklion Museum, and a copy installed some metres north of the original findspot. There is no reason to attribute more importance to this figure than to the many other attendants originally depicted on the corridor walls. Mark Cameron believes that the skin may originally have been painted white, which would imply that the attendant was a eunuch. Although the surviving fragments are pale, some traces of the indian-red paint indicating masculinity can still be seen. The plumed crown probably belonged to a sphinx or griffin which the attendant was leading on a rope.

CHAPTER TITLE ILLUSTRATIONS

Introduction Clay matrix from Knossos. A priestess brings an offering to a priestess or goddess seated on a folding chair in front of an altar surmounted by sacral horns. The mountain setting suggests either a ceremony at a peak sanctuary or a ceremony dedicated to a goddess deemed to dwell at a peak sanctuary.

1 Coin from classical Knossos: the labyrinth motif as badge.
2 Coin from classical Knossos: the Minotaur flexing his muscles.
3 Labyrinth on a sealstone from Agia Triadha, dating from Early Minoan III.
4 Polychrome jar from Knossos, Middle Minoan II, about 1800 BC.
5 Stone anchor, 40 centimetres high, elaborately carved with two octopuses and found in the Labyrinth. It was made in about 1500 BC, possibly as a symbol of Poteidan.
6 Seal showing a giant collared hound with two attendants.
7 Seal from Knossos showing a priestess carrying an elaborate dress and a double-axe: note the snake in the background.
8 Seal showing a goddess with a lion.
9 Potnia on her mountain peak, flanked by lions. A composite image from several incomplete clay impressions (all now in Heraklion Museum), all from the same, lost sealstone, 2 centimetres across and dating from about 1400 BC. Potnia is shown on a rocky peak, brandishing her staff like a wand or sceptre. Below, a male figure assumed to be Velchanos salutes her. The shrine to the left may represent the peak sanctuary or, since it is on lower ground, the temple on the plain. The flanking heraldic lions are shown in the same way as those on the Lion Gate at Mycenae.
10 Labyrinth design on a coin from classical Knossos. This version of the labyrinth became a model for later mazes.
11 Mycenean warriors, from a gold signet ring found in Shaft Grave IV at Mycenae. It is thought by Reynold Higgins to be of Cretan workmanship. The seal-ring is known as 'The Battle in the Glen' and was made in about 1550–1500 BC. It illustrates the warlike nature associated with the Mycenean mainlanders.
12 'Palace Style' jar typical of the grandiose, formal style of the New Temple Period, about 1400 BC.
13 A carved sardonyx sealstone made in the sixteenth or fifteenth centuries BC and found in the New Knossos Labyrinth. It shows the Mistress of Animals with her attendant griffins, a double-axe and what appear to be snakes.

References

GENERAL

Edey, M. (1975) *Lost World of the Aegean*, New York: Time-Life.
Evans, A. (1921-36) *The Palace of Minos at Knossos*, 4 vols, London: Macmillan.
Higgins, R. (1981) *Minoan and Mycenaean Art*, London: Thames & Hudson.
Hood, S. (1971) *The Minoans*, London: Thames & Hudson.
—— (1978) *The Arts in Prehistoric Greece*, Harmondsworth: Penguin Books.
Hood, S. and Smyth, D. (1981) *Archaeological Survey of the Knossos Area*, Athens and London: British School of Archaeology at Athens and Thames & Hudson.
Krzyszkowska, O. and Nixon, L. (eds) (1983) *Minoan Society: Proceedings of the Cambridge Colloquium, 1981*, Bristol: Bristol Classical Press.
Michailidou, A. (1983) *Knossos: a Complete Guide to the Palace of Minos*, Athens: Ekdotike Athenon.
Platon, N. (1968) *Crete*, Paris/Geneva/New York: Nagel.
Rodenwaldt, G. (1927) *Die Kunst der Antike*, Berlin: Propylaen-Verlag.
Sakellarakis, J. A. (1987) *Herakleion Museum: Illustrated Guide to the Museum*, Athens: Ekdotike Athenon.

INTRODUCTION

Faure, P. (1973) *La Vie quotidienne en Crète au temps de Minos*, Paris: Hachette.
Hallager, E. (1977) *The Mycenaean Palace at Knossos*, Stockholm: Medelhavsmuseet, Memoir 1.
Mackenzie, D. (1900–) Daybooks, unpublished, Ashmolean Museum, Oxford.

1 THE LEGENDARY KNOSSOS

Chadwick, J. (1976) *The Mycenaean World*, Cambridge: Cambridge University Press.
Graham, J. W. (1969) *The Palaces of Crete*, 1st edn, Princeton: Princeton University Press.
—— (1987) *The Palaces of Crete*, 2nd edn, Princeton: Princeton University Press.
Luce, J. V. (1969) *The End of Atlantis*, London: Thames & Hudson.

2 THE DISCOVERY OF THE LABYRINTH

BBC Chronicle (1982) *The Man Behind the Mask*, broadcast January 1982.
Deuel, L. (1978) *Memoirs of Heinrich Schliemann*, London: Hutchinson.
Evans, J. (1947) *Time and Chance: the Story of Arthur Evans and his Forebears*, London: Longman.
Falkener, E. (1854) *A Description of Some Important Theatres and Other Remains in Crete*, London: Turner.

Lithgow, W. (1632) *The Totall Discourse.*
Pashley, R. (1835) *Travels in Crete.*
Pococke, R. (1745) *A Description of the East.*
Schliemann, H. (1962) 'Schliemann's Letters to Max Müller in Oxford', *Journal of Hellenic Studies*, 82: 75–105.
Spratt, T. (1865) *Travels in Crete.*

3 ARTHUR EVANS AND THE 1900 DIG AT KNOSSOS

Brown, A. C. (1983) *Arthur Evans and the Palace of Minos*, Oxford: Ashmolean Museum.
Evans, A. (1900–) Photographic Archive, unpublished albums in Ashmolean Museum, Oxford.
—— (1921–36) *The Palace of Minos at Knossos*, 4 vols, London: Macmillan.
Evans, J. (1947) *Time and Chance*, London: Longman.
Mackenzie, D. (1900–) Daybooks, unpublished, Ashmolean Museum, Oxford.
Seager, R. B. (1905) *Excavations at Vasiliki, 1904*, Transactions, Department of Archaeology, University of Pennsylvania.

4 THE NEOLITHIC AND PRE-PALACE PERIODS AT KNOSSOS

Burn, A. R. and Burn, M. (1980) *The Living Past of Greece*, Harmondsworth: Penguin Books.
Edey, M. (1975) *Lost World of the Aegean*, New York: Time-Life.
Evans, A. (1921–36) *The Palace of Minos at Knossos*, 4 vols, London: Macmillan, vol. 3, 301.
Pendlebury, J. D. S. (1939) *The Archaeology of Crete*, London: Methuen.
Renfrew, C. (1972) *The Emergence of Civilization: The Cyclades and the Aegean in the Third Millennium BC*, London: Methuen.
—— (1973) *Before Civilization: the Radiocarbon Revolution and Prehistoric Europe*, London: Jonathan Cape.
Trump, D. (1981) *The Prehistory of the Mediterranean*, Harmondsworth: Penguin Books.
Warren, P. (1975) *The Aegean Civilizations*, London: Elsevier-Phaidon.

5 THE BRONZE AGE PALACE: SIR ARTHUR EVANS' INTERPRETATION

Brown, A. C. (1983) *Arthur Evans and the Palace of Minos*, Oxford: Ashmolean Museum.
Evans, A. (1901) '1899–1900 Knossos', *Annual of the British School at Athens*, 6: 3–70.
—— (1902) '1900–1901 The Palace of Knossos', *Annual of the British School at Athens*, 7: 1–120.
Graham, J. W. (1987) *The Palaces of Crete*, 2nd edn, Princeton: Princeton University Press.
Hallager, E. (1977) *The Mycenean Palace at Knossos*, Stockholm: Medelhavsmuseet, Memoir 1.

Hood, S. (1971) *The Minoans: Crete in the Bronze Age*, London: Thames & Hudson.
Hood, S. and Taylor, W. (1981) *The Bronze Age Palace at Knossos*, Athens and London: British School of Archaeology at Athens and Thames & Hudson.
Mackenzie, D. (1900–) Daybooks, unpublished, Ashmolean Museum, Oxford.
Mosso, A. (1907) *The Palaces of Crete and their Builders*, London: Fisher Unwin.
Palmer, L. R. (1969) *A New Guide to the Palace of Knossos*, London: Faber & Faber.
—— (1969) *The Penultimate Palace of Knossos*, Rome: Edizioni dell' Ateneo.
Platon, N. (1968) *Crete*, Paris/Geneva/New York: Nagel.
—— (1971) *Zakros: the Discovery of a Lost Palace of Ancient Crete*, New York: Scribners.
Raison, J. (1969) *Le Grand Palais de Knossos*, Rome: Edizioni dell' Ateneo.

6 WUNDERLICH'S 'PALACE OF THE DEAD'

Spengler, O. (1926) (English edn) *The Decline of the West*, New York: Knopf.
—— (1935) *Zur Weltgeschichte des Zweiten Vorchristichen Jahrtausends*, Munich.
Wunderlich, H. (1975) *The Secret of Crete*, London: Souvenir Press.

7 THE TEMPLE OF THE GODDESSES

Cadogan, G. (1976) *Palaces of Minoan Crete*, London: Barrie & Jenkins.
Evans, A. (1921–36) *The Palace of Minos at Knossos*, 4 vols, London: Macmillan.
Faure, P. (1973) *La Vie quotidienne en Crète au temps de Minos*, Paris: Hachette.
Gesell, G. (1985) 'Town, palace and house cult in Minoan Crete', *Studies in Mediterranean Archaeology*, 67.
Graham, J. W. (1987) *The Palaces of Crete*, 2nd edn, Princeton: Princeton University Press.
Haskell, H. W. (1983) 'From palace to town administration: evidence of coarse-ware stirrup-jars', in O. Krzyszkowska and L. Nixon (eds), *Minoan Society: Proceedings of the Cambridge Colloquium, 1981*, Bristol: Bristol Classical Press.
Hood, S. (1971) *The Minoans: Crete in the Bronze Age*, London: Thames & Hudson.
—— (1978) *The Arts in Prehistoric Greece*, Harmondsworth: Penguin Books.
Marinatos, N. (1984), *Art and Religion in Thera: Reconstructing a Bronze Age Society*, Athens: D. and I. Mathioulakis.
Marinatos, N. and Hägg, R. (1983) 'Anthropomorphic cult images in Minoan Crete', in O. Krzyszkowska, and L. Nixon (eds), *Minoan Society: Proceedings of the Cambridge Colloquium, 1981*, Bristol: Bristol Classical Press.
Palmer, L. R. (1969) *A New Guide to the Palace of Knossos*, London: Faber & Faber.
Platon, N. (1968) *Crete*, Paris/Geneva/New York: Nagel.
—— (1971) *Zakros: the Discovery of a Lost Palace of Ancient Crete*, New York: Scribners.
Preziosi, D. (1983) *Minoan Architectural Design*, The Hague: Mouton.
Willets, R. F. (1969) *Everyday Life in Ancient Crete*, London: Batsford.

8 BEYOND THE LAYBYRINTH WALLS

Edey, M. (1975) *Lost World of the Aegean*, New York: Time-Life.
Evans, A. (1921–36) *The Palace of Minos at Knossos*, 4 vols, London: Macmillan.
Faure, P. (1973) *La Vie quotidienne en Crète au temps de Minos*, Paris: Hachette.

Gesell, G. (1985) 'Town, palace and house cult in Minoan Crete', *Studies in Mediterranean Archaeology*, 67.

Lehmann, J. (1975) *The Hittites*, London: Collins.

Pendlebury, J. D. S. (1939) *The Archaeology of Crete*, London: Methuen.

—— (1954) *A Handbook to the Palace of Minos, Knossos, with its Dependencies*, London: Max Parrish.

Platon, N. (1971) *Zakros: the Discovery of a Lost Palace of Ancient Crete*, New York: Scribners.

Rutkowski, B. (1986) *The Cult Places of the Aegean*, New Haven, Conn.: Yale University Press.

9 THE LADY OF THE LABYRINTH

Chadwick, J. (1976) *The Mycenaean World*, Cambridge: Cambridge University Press.

Chadwick, J. *et al.* (1986) *Knossos Corpus* vol. 1, Cambridge: Cambridge University Press.

Dodds, E. R. (1951) *The Greeks and the Irrational*, Berkeley and Los Angeles: University of California Press.

Evans, A. (1921–36) *The Palace of Minos at Knossos*, 4 vols, London: Macmillan.

Guthrie, W. K. (1961) *The Religion and Mythology of the Greeks, Cambridge Ancient History*, vol. 2, Cambridge: Cambridge University Press.

Hawkes, J. (1968) *Dawn of the Gods*, London: Chatto & Windus.

Hood, S. (1978) *The Arts in Prehistoric Greece*, Harmondsworth: Penguin Books.

Hooker, J. T. (1983) 'Minoan Religion in the Late Palace Period', in O. Krzyszkowska and L. Nixon (eds), *Minoan Society: Proceedings of the Cambridge Colloquium, 1981*, Bristol: Bristol Classical Press.

Hutchinson, R. (1962) *Prehistoric Crete*, Harmondsworth: Penguin Books.

Kerenyi, K. (1960) *The Gods of the Greeks*, New York: Grove Press.

Malinowski, B. (1954) *Magic, Science and Religion*, New York: Doubleday.

Marinatos, N. (1984) *Art and Religion in Thera: Reconstructing a Bronze Age Society*, D. and I. Mathioulakis.

Nilsson, M. (1950) *The Minoan-Mycenaean Religion*, Lund: G. W. K. Gleerup.

Pendlebury, J. D. S. (1939) *The Archaeology of Crete*, London: Methuen.

Platon, N. (1971) *Zakros: the Discovery of a Lost Palace of Ancient Crete*, New York: Scribners.

Rutkowski, B. (1986) *The Cult Places of the Aegean*, New Haven, Conn.: Yale University Press.

Sakellarakis, Y. and Sakellarakis E. (1981) 'Drama of death in a Minoan temple', *National Geographic*, 159: 205–22.

Trell, B. (1988) 'The Temple of Artemis at Ephesos', in P. A. Clayton and M. J. Price (eds), *The Seven Wonders of the Ancient World*, London: Routledge.

Warren, P. (1975) *The Aegean Civilizations*, London: Elsevier-Phaidon.

—— (1980–1) Knossos: Stratigraphical Museum Excavations, 1978–80, Part 1, *Archaeological Report*, 73–92.

—— (1987) interviewed by Malcolm Billings for 'The Minoans and their gods' in the BBC Radio 4 'Origins' series.

10 THE BULL DANCE

Cooke, D. (1988) personal communication regarding French vâche-fights.
Graham, J. W. (1987) *The Palaces of Crete*, 2nd edn, Princeton: Princeton University Press.
Hooker, J. T. (1983) 'Minoan religion in the Late Palace Period', in O. Krzyszkowska and L. Nixon (eds), *Minoan Society: Proceedings of the Cambridge Colloquium, 1981*, Bristol: Bristol Classical Press.
Pinsent, J. (1983) 'Bull-leaping', in *Minoan Society: Proceedings of the Cambridge Colloquium, 1981*, Bristol: Bristol Classical Press.

11 THE THERA ERUPTION

Chadwick, J. (1976) *The Mycenaean World*, Cambridge: Cambridge University Press.
Frost, K. T. (1909) 'The lost continent', *The Times*, February 1909.
Hood, S. (1978) *The Arts in Prehistoric Greece*, Harmondsworth: Penguin Books.
Luce, J. V. (1969) *The End of Atlantis*, London: Thames & Hudson.
Marinatos, S. (1939) 'The volcanic destruction of Minoan Crete', *Antiquity*, 13: 425–39.
Platon, N. (1968) *Crete*, Paris/Geneva/New York: Nagel.
Popham, M. R. (1984) *The Minoan Unexplored Mansion at Knossos*, Athens and London: British School of Archaeology at Athens and Thames & Hudson.
Wace, A. J. B. and Blegen, C. W. (1939) 'Pottery as evidence for trade and colonization in the Aegean Bronze Age', *Klio*, 14: 131–47.
Warren, P. (1975) *The Aegean Civilizations*, London: Elsevier-Phaidon.

12 THE FALL OF THE LABYRINTH

Baumbach, L. (1983) 'An examination of the personal names in the Knossos tablets', in O. Krzyszkowska, and L. Nixon (eds), *Minoan Society: Proceedings of the Cambridge Colloquium, 1981*, Bristol: Bristol Classical Press.
Blegen, C. (1958) 'A chronological problem', *Minoica* (1958): 61–6.
Boardman, J. (1963) in L. R. Palmer and J. Boardman, *On the Knossos Tablets*, Oxford: Clarendon Press.
Chadwick, J. (1976) *The Mycenaean World*, Cambridge: Cambridge University Press.
Dickinson, O. (1977) *The Origins of Mycenaean Civilisation*, Goteborg.
Hallager, E. (1977) *The Mycenaean Palace at Knossos*, Stockholm: Medelhavsmuseet, Memoir 1.
Hood, S. (1978) *The Arts in Prehistoric Greece*, Harmondsworth: Penguin Books.
Hutchinson, R. (1962) *Prehistoric Crete*, Harmondsworth: Penguin Books.
Mackenzie, D. (1900–) Daybooks, unpublished, Ashmolean Museum, Oxford.
Niemeier, W.-D. (1983) 'The character of the Knossian Palace society in the second half of the fifteenth century BC: Mycenaean or Minoan?', in O. Krzyszkowska and L. Nixon (eds), *Minoan Society: Proceedings of the Cambridge Colloquium, 1981*, Bristol: Bristol Classical Press.
Palmer, L. R. (1969) *A New Guide to the Palace of Knossos*, London: Faber & Faber.
Platon, N. (1968) *Crete*, Paris/Geneva/New York: Nagel.
Powell, D. (1982) *The Villa Ariadne*, Athens: Efstathiadis.
Raison, J. (1969) *Le Grand Palais de Knossos*, Edizioni dell' Ateneo.

Reusch, H. (1961) 'Zum Problem des Thronraumes in Knossos', in V. Georgiev and J. Irmscher, *Minoica und Homer*, Berlin.
Schachermeyr, F. (1964) *Die Minoische Kultur des Alten Kreta*, Stuttgart: Kohlhammer.
Wace, A. J. B. and Blegen, C. W. (1939) 'Pottery as evidence for trade and colonization in the Aegean Bronze Age', *Klio*, 14: 131–47.
Warren, P. (1975) *The Aegean Civilizations*, London: Elsevier-Phaidon.

13 THE JOURNEY OF THE SOUL

Chadwick, J. (1976) *The Mycenaean World*, Cambridge: Cambridge University Press.
Chadwick, J. *et al.* (1986) *Knossos Corpus*, vol. 1, Cambridge: Cambridge University Press.
Dietrich, B. C. (1983) 'Minoan religion in the context of the Aegean', in O. Krzyszkowska and L. Nixon (eds), *Minoan Society: Proceedings of the Cambridge Colloquium, 1981*, Bristol: Bristol Classical Press.
Faure, P. (1973) *La Vie quotidienne en Crète au temps de Minos*, Paris: Hachette.
Goodrich, N. (1960) *The Ancient Myths*, New York: New American Library.
Graham, J. W. (1987) *The Palaces of Crete*, 2nd edn, Princeton: Princeton University Press.
Hawkes, J. (1968) *Dawn of the Gods*, London: Chatto & Windus.
Platon, N. (1968) *Crete*, Paris/Geneva/New York: Nagel.
Popham, M. R. (1984) *The Minoan Unexplored Mansion at Knossos*, Athens and London: British School of Archaeology at Athens and Thames & Hudson.
Rutkowski, B. (1986) *The Cult Places of the Aegean*, New Haven, Conn.: Yale University Press.

Index

Jesus 118
Juktas, Mount 4, 16, 92, 96, 109, 111,
    123–5, 126, 129, 137, 148, 150, 184,
    188, Plate 11

Kairatos River 38, 98, 173
Kairatos Valley 98, 135, 173, 187
Kalokairinos, Minos 1, 21, 22, 23, 24, 29,
    30, 39, 43, 56, 156
Kamares ware 60, 68
Kamikos 14, 16
Kanellopoulos, Kanellos 73
Kannia 110
Karmanor 127
Katsambas 4, 11–12, 145
Kefala hill 12, 20, 21, 22, 23, 24, 30, 35,
    41, 43, 49, 70, 100, 160, 171, 173
Keftiu 62, 154
Kentucky 10
Khaldun, Ibn 152
Khania, see Kydonia
Khersifron 117
kilt 154, 185
Kition 176
Klawiphoros 170
Knossos: bronze age city 15, 18, 20–1,
    36–7, 67, 98, 100, 128, 140, 149, 187;
    classical and archaic city 16, 20–1, 67,
    190; Evans' palace, see Palace of
    Minos; neolithic settlement 39–40, 98,
    100, 187; population 36, 40; site 19–20,
    29; symbolic value 1, 6, 16, 129, 173–6,
    178–9; temple, see Labyrinth
Kourai 107
Kouretes 107
Krakatoa 145
Kydon 11
Kydonia 7, 11, 142, 144, 148
Kydonians 7, 16–7
Kykeon 115, 119, 150
Kytaion 4
Kythera 25

Labyrinth, Knossos
    building (Old Temple) 9, 41–2, 124,
    126, 180
    destructions 16, 65, 122, 129, 140–51,
    152, 180–1
    fall 2, 16, 65, 95, 127, 128, 129, 140–51,
    156–9, 164, 181

layout: 12, 13, 114–5, 185, 187–8, 189;
    adyta 31, 44, 45, 52, 55, 56, 60, 71,
    72, 75, 77–8, 86, 87, 91, 92, 93, 95,
    97, 99, 155, 164, 183, 186; Bull
    Chamber 75, 163; Bull Court 45, 46,
    48, 49, 50, 52, 54, 59, 75, 77, 78, 80,
    82, 83, 85, 100, 101, 114, 117, 135–6,
    137, 138, 140, 163, 170, 177, 184,
    186, 187, Plate 18; Chancel Screen
    Sanctuary 46, 72, 75, 97, 101, 114–
    15, 162, 183, Plate 9; Colonnade of
    the Priestesses 114, 135, 186;
    Columnar Shrines 114, 163;
    Concourse 87–8, 114; Cupbearer
    Sanctuary 47, 75, 83–5, 114, 140,
    177, 184, Plate 13; Destroyed
    Sanctuary 75, 83, 114, 186; Dolphin
    Sanctuary 75, 91–2, 94, 114–15, 162,
    184, 186, Plates 12 and 18; Double-
    Axe Sanctuary 50, 75, 90–1, 93, 97,
    114–15, 177, 179, 184, Plates 10, 12
    and 15; Early Dove Goddess
    Sanctuary 90, 101; East Entrance 12,
    13, 88, 114–15, 169, 184, Plate 16;
    East Pillar Crypt 23, 80, 114, 183,
    187, Plate 1; East Staircase 13, 114;
    Garden Entrance 13, 114; Grand
    Staircase 13, 32–3, 50, 91, 93, 114,
    177, 178, 179, 185, Plate 2; Great
    Goddess Sanctuary 71, 74, 75, 88–90,
    101, 106, 114, 115, 132, 149, 163,
    177, 186, 187, 188, 189; Great
    Sanctuary 58, 163; House or Shrine
    of the Fallen Blocks 114–15; House
    or Shrine of the Sacrificed Oxen
    114–15, 130; Induction Hall 114;
    Initiation Area 71, 75, 86, 87, 114,
    186; Kamares Pottery Store 114;
    Late Dove Goddess Sanctuary 72,
    75, 93–5, 101, 114–15, 121, 149, 157,
    162, 163, 164, 167, 181, 186–7, 189;
    lavatories 92; Lotus Lamp Sanctuary
    75, 85, 114; Lower West Wing
    Corridor 114, 163; Monolithic Pillar
    Crypt 75, 114–15; North-East
    Sanctuary 75, 88, 114–15; North-
    East Store Rooms 114–15; North
    Entrance 12, 13, 56, 57, 87, 114;
    North Entrance Passage 35, 55, 114,
    Plate 3; North Pillar Hall 57, 58, 87;
    North West Adyton 86, 87, 114;